Second Workshop on Natural Language Processing Meets Journalism 2017

Copenhagen, Denmark
7 September 2017

ISBN: 978-1-5108-4759-0

EMNLP 2017

**Second workshop on
Natural Language Processing meets Journalism**

Proceedings of the Workshop

September 7, 2017
Copenhagen, Denmark

Introduction

During the years NLP has matured a suites of technologies able to cope with many problems raised by the contemporary need of global information, and so, it is the high time for the NLP to get engaged in the mass media process as an active partner for both journalists and readers. The EMNLP workshop - at its second edition after the IJCAI-2016 workshop held on July 10th, 2016 in New York - has the potential to attract the interest of researchers both in computational linguistics and journalism, and of professionals in the news production system. The main goal is to have a forum in which it will be possible to share and discuss advancements in natural language processing and real needs in the field of journalism. The workshop received an unexpected number of submissions and the program committee identified 19 papers of high quality. We are happy to notice that papers submitted to this second edition display a large variety of topics that we consider at the core of our initiative. Many interesting aspects of journalism in mass-media age, from discovering bias and incongruent headlines in news to analyzing the content of social media in order to capture hot topics and trends are present. We can confidently say that fundamental topics of natural language processing have been covered this year, a fact that makes all the effort of organizing this workshop worthwhile. There are four excellent papers running for the best paper award and we already know it is a close call. Some of the accepted papers are likely to stir vivid debates, which, as the last year experience proves it, will turn into papers next year. In fact, we can see that some of the ideas that emerged from the papers and the discussions we carried out in the first edition are properly represented in this second edition. While we cannot partition the papers into three or four well defined classes, we can see that the NLP researchers have understood and have developed technologies able to cope with bias detection, sentiment analysis and relevance of specific information.

In an era in which there is no single point of view and the "objectiveness of information" lacks a unilateral standard, playing with language register and clarity in a piece of news are powerful instruments at journalist disposal. NLP may raise some flags on details, and papers such as "Tracking Bias in News Sources Using Social Media: the Russia-Ukraine Maidan Crisis of 2013–2014", "Incongruent Headlines: Yet Another Way to Mislead Your Readers", "Fake news stance detection using stacked ensemble of classifiers", "From Clickbait to Fake News Detection: An Approach based on Detecting the Stance of Headlines to Articles", "An NLP Analysis of Exaggerated Claims in Science News" present interesting and efficient ways to warn the reader against possible abuses in the media.

Sentiment analysis is an important component in understanding the impact of a piece of news and few papers at this workshop focus on this aspect: "Comparing Attitudes to Climate Change in the Media using sentiment analysis based on Latent Dirichlet Allocation", "Improved Abusive Comment Moderation with User Embeddings", "Deception Detection in News Reports in the Russian Language: Lexics and Discourse", "Using New York Times Picks to Identify Constructive Comments", "Using New York Times Picks to Identify Constructive Comments", "Predicting News Values from Headline Text and Emotions".

A group of papers deals with a crucial issue of modern journalism, i.e., how to manage the enormous flow of available information: "What to Write? A topic recommender for journalists", "Data-to-text generation for tailored soccer journalism", "Language-based Construction of Explorable News Graphs for Journalists", "Storyteller: Visual Analytics of Perspectives on Rich Text Interpretations", "Analyzing the Revision Logs of a Japanese Newspaper for Article Quality Assessment", "Unsupervised Event Clustering and Aggregation from Newswire and Web Article", "Semantic Storytelling, Cross-lingual Event Detection and other Semantic Services for a Newsroom Content Curation Dashboard", "A News Chain Evaluation Methodology along with a Lattice-based Approach for News Chain Construction".

In conclusion, we are very happy and proud about the high quality papers dealing with essential topics in modern journalism. We believe that more and more NLP will have an impact on journalism, the force that truly and directly represents all us in the confrontation with the social problems.

Octavian Popescu and Carlo Strapparava

Organizers:

Octavian Popescu, IBM Watson Research Center, USA
Carlo Strapparava, FBK-irst, Italy

Program Committee:

Enrique Alfonseca, Google
Tommaso Caselli, VU Amsterdam University
Dan Cristea, University of Iasi
Liviu P. Dinu, University of Bucharest
Elena Erdmann, TU Dortmund University
Song Feng, IBM Research
Lorenzo Gatti, FBK-irst
Marco Guerini, FBK-irst
James Hamilton, Stanford University
Mark Hansen, Columbia university
Orin Hargraves, University of Colorado
Daisuke Kawahara, Kyoto University
Kristian Kersting, TU Dortmund University
Shervin Malmasi, Harvard Medical School
Rada Mihalcea, University of Michigan
Preslav Nakov, Qatar Computing Research Institute, HBKU
Vivi Nastase, University of Heidelberg
Gözde Özbal, FBK-irst
Martha Palmer, University of Colorado
Siddharth Patwardhan, IBM Research TJ Watson
Preethi Raghavan, IBM Research TJ Watson
Mattia Rigotti IBM Research TJ Watson
Paolo Rosso, Universitat Politecnica de València
Amanda Stent, Bloomberg
Serra Sinem Tekiroglu, FBK-irst
Ngoc Phuoc An Vo, IBM Research
Marcos Zampieri, University of Cologne
Torsten Zesch, University of Duisburg-Essen

Table of Contents

Conference Program

September 7th

Morning

Oral Presentations

Predicting News Values from Headline Text and Emotions
Maria Pia di Buono, Jan Šnajder, Bojana Dalbelo Basic, Goran Glavaš, Martin Tutek
and Natasa Milic-Frayling

Predicting User Views in Online News
Daniel Hardt and Owen Rambow

*Tracking Bias in News Sources Using Social Media: the Russia-Ukraine Maidan
Crisis of 2013–2014*
Peter Potash, Alexey Romanov, Mikhail Gronas, Anna Rumshisky and Mikhail
Gronas

What to Write? A topic recommender for journalists
Alessandro Cucchiarelli, Christian Morbidoni, Giovanni Stilo and Paola Velardi

*Comparing Attitudes to Climate Change in the Media using sentiment analysis
based on Latent Dirichlet Allocation*
Ye Jiang, Xingyi Song, Jackie Harrison, Shaun Quegan and Diana Maynard

Language-based Construction of Explorable News Graphs for Journalists
Rémi Bois, Guillaume Gravier, Eric Jamet, Emmanuel Morin, Pascale Sébillot and
Maxime Robert

Storyteller: Visual Analytics of Perspectives on Rich Text Interpretations
Maarten van Meersbergen, Piek Vossen, Janneke van der Zwaan, Antske Fokkens,
Willem van Hage, Inger Leemans and Isa Maks

*Analyzing the Revision Logs of a Japanese Newspaper for Article Quality Assess-
ment*
Hideaki Tamori, Yuta Hitomi, Naoaki Okazaki and Kentaro Inui

Improved Abusive Comment Moderation with User Embeddings
John Pavlopoulos, Prodromos Malakasiotis, Juli Bakagianni and Ion Androutsopoulos

Lunch

Invited Talk
Cristian Danescu-Niculescu-Mizil - Cornell University

Poster Presentations

Incongruent Headlines: Yet Another Way to Mislead Your Readers
Sophie Chesney, Maria Liakata, Massimo Poesio and Matthew Purver

Unsupervised Event Clustering and Aggregation from Newswire and Web Articles
Swen Ribeiro, Olivier Ferret and Xavier Tannier

Semantic Storytelling. Cross-lingual Event Detection and other Semantic Services for a Newsroom Content Curation Dashboard
Julian Moreno-Schneider, Ankit Srivastava, Peter Bourgonje, David Wabnitz and Georg Rehm

Deception Detection in News Reports in the Russian Language: Lexics and Discourse
Dina Pisarevskaya

Fake news stance detection using stacked ensemble of classifiers
James Thorne, Mingjie Chen, Giorgos Myrianthous, Jiashu Pu, Xiaoxuan Wang and Andreas Vlachos

From Clickbait to Fake News Detection: An Approach based on Detecting the Stance of Headlines to Articles
Peter Bourgonje, Julian Moreno Schneider and Georg Rehm

'Fighting' or 'Conflict'? An Approach to Revealing Concepts of Terms in Political Discourse
Linyuan Tang and Kyo Kageura

A News Chain Evaluation Methodology along with a Lattice-based Approach for News Chain Construction
Mustafa Toprak, Özer Özkahraman and Selma Tekir

Using New York Times Picks to Identify Constructive Comments
Varada Kolhatkar and Maite Taboada

Best paper announcement and Conclusions

Predicting News Values from Headline Text and Emotions

Maria Pia di Buono[1]   **Jan Šnajder**[1]   **Bojana Dalbelo Bašić**[1]
Goran Glavaš[2]   **Martin Tutek**[1]   **Natasa Milic-Frayling**[3]
[1] TakeLab, Faculty of Electrical Engineering and Computing, University of Zagreb
`first.namelastname@fer.hr`
[2] Data and Web Science Group, University of Mannheim, Germany
`goran@informatik.uni-mannheim.de`
[3] School of Computer Science, University of Nottingham, UK
`natasa.milic-frayling@nottingham.ac.uk`

Abstract

We present a preliminary study on predicting *news values* from headline text and emotions. We perform a multivariate analysis on a dataset manually annotated with news values and emotions, discovering interesting correlations among them. We then train two competitive machine learning models – an SVM and a CNN – to predict news values from headline text and emotions as features. We find that, while both models yield a satisfactory performance, some news values are more difficult to detect than others, while some profit more from including emotion information.

1 Introduction

News values may be considered as a system of criteria applied to decide about the inclusion or exclusion of material (Palmer, 2000) and about the aspects of the selected material that should be emphasized by means of headlines. In fact, the informative value of headlines lays its foundations in their capability of optimizing the relevance of their stories for their users (Dor, 2003). To the intent of being optimizers of the news relevance, headlines carry out a set of different functions while meeting two needs: attracting users' attention and summarizing contents (Ifantidou, 2009). In order to attract users' attention, headlines should provide the triggers for the emotional impact of the news, accounting emotional aspects related to the participants of the event or to the actions performed (Ungerer, 1997). As far as the summarization of contents is concerned, headlines may be distinguished on the basis of two main goals: headlines that represent the abstract of the main event and headlines that promote one of the details in the news story (Bell, 1991; Nir, 1993). Furthermore, Iarovici and Amel

(1989) recognize two simultaneous functions: "a semantic function, regarding the referential text, and a pragmatic function, regarding the reader (the receiver) to whom the text is addressed."

In this work we present a preliminary study on predicting news values from headline text and emotions. The study is driven by two research questions: (1) what are the relations among news values conveyed by headlines and the human emotions triggered by them, and (2) to what extent can a machine learning classifier successfully identify the news values conveyed by headlines, using merely text or text and triggered emotions as input? To this end, we manually annotated an existing dataset of headlines and emotions with news values. To answer the first question, we carried out a multivariate analysis, and discovered interesting correlations among news values and emotions. To answer our second research question, we trained two competitive machine learning models – a support vector machine (SVM) and a convolutional neural network (CNN) – to predict news values from headline text and emotions. Results indicate that, while both models yield a satisfactory performance, some news values are more difficult to detect, some profit from including emotion information, and CNN performs better than SVM on this task.

2 Related work

Despite the fact that news values has been widely investigated in Social Science and journalism studies, not much attention has been paid to its automatic classification by the NLP community. In fact, even if news value classification may be applied in several user-oriented applications, e.g., news recommendation systems, and web search engines, few scholars (De Nies et al., 2012; Piotrkowicz et al., 2017) have been focused on this particular topic. Related to our work is the work on predicting

1

Proceedings of the 2017 EMNLP Workshop on Natural Language Processing meets Journalism, pages 1–6
Copenhagen, Denmark, September 7, 2017. ©2017 Association for Computational Linguistics

emotions in news articles and headlines, which has been investigated from different perspectives and by means of different techniques. Strapparava and Mihalcea (2008) describe an experiment devoted to analyze emotion in news headlines, focusing on six basic emotions and proposing knowledge-based and corpus-based approaches. Kozareva et al. (2007) extract part of speech (POS) from headlines in order to create different bag of words pairs with six emotions and compute for each pair the Mutual Information Score. Balahur et al. (2013) test the relative suitability of various sentiment dictionaries in order to separate positive or negative opinion from good or bad news. Ye et al. (2012) deal with the prediction of emotions in news from readers' perspective, based on a multi-label classification. Another strand of research more generally related to our work is short text classification. Short text classification is technically challanging due to the sparsity of features. Most work in this area has focused on classification of microblog messages (Sriram et al., 2010; Dilrukshi et al., 2013; Go et al., 2009; Chen et al., 2011).

3 Dataset

As a starting point, we adopt the dataset proposed for the SemEval-2007 Task 14 (Strapparava and Mihalcea, 2007). The dataset consists of 1250 headlines extracted from major newspapers such as New York Times, CNN, BBC News, and Google News. Each headline has been manually annotated for valence and six emotions (Anger, Disgust, Fear, Joy, Sadness, and Surprise) on a scale from 0 to 100. In this work, we use only the emotion labels, and not the valence labels.

News values. On top of the emotion annotations, we added an additional layer of news value labels. Our starting point for the annotation was the news values classification scheme proposed by Harcup and O'Neill (2016). This study proposes a set of fifteen values, corresponding to a set of requirements that news stories have to satisfy to be selected for publishing. For the annotation, we decided to omit two news values whose annotation necessitates contextual information: "Audio-visuals", which signals the presence of infographics accompanying the news text, and "News organization's agenda", which refers to stories related to the news organization's own agenda. This resulted in a set of 13 news value labels.

News value	IAA		IAA (adj)		Support
	κ	F1	κ	F1	
Bad news	**0.47**	0.526	**0.72**	0.744	85
Celebrity	**0.51**	0.545	**0.74**	0.761	82
Conflict	0.19	0.245	**0.52**	0.564	86
Drama	0.25	0.383	**0.58**	0.663	178
Entertainment	**0.53**	0.684	**0.76**	0.843	351
Follow-up	0.10	0.129	**0.43**	0.451	29
Good news	0.23	0.268	**0.54**	0.563	65
Magnitude	0.08	0.121	0.34	0.371	45
Shareability	0.05	0.101	0.29	0.335	130
Surprise	0.06	0.102	0.38	0.409	43
Power elite	0.36	0.472	**0.66**	0.718	166

Table 1: Original and adjudicated interannotator agreement (Cohen's κ and F1-macro scores) and counts for each news value (agreement scores averaged over three annotator pairs and four annotator groups; moderate/substantial κ agreement shown in bold).

Annotation task. We asked four annotators to independently label the dataset. The annotators were provided short guidelines and a description of the news values. We first ran a calibration round on a set of 120 headlines. After calculating the inter-annotator agreement (IAA), we decided to run a second round of calibration, providing further information about some labels conceived as more ambiguous by the annotators (e.g., "Bad news" vs. "Drama" vs. "Conflict" and "Celebrity" vs. "Power elite"). For the final annotation round, we arranged the annotators into four distinct groups of three, so that each headline would be annotated by three annotators. The annotation was done on 798 headlines using 13 labels. Annotation analysis revealed that two of these labels "Exclusivity" and "Relevance", have been used in a marginal number of cases so we decide to omit these labels from the final dataset.

Table 1 show the Cohen's κ and F1-macro IAA agreement scores for the 11 news value labels. We observe a moderate agreement of $\kappa \geq 0.4$ (Landis and Koch, 1977) only for the "Bad news", "Celebrity", and "Entertainment" news values, suggesting that recognizing news values from headlines is a difficult task even for humans. To obtain the final dataset, we adjudicated the annotations of the three annotators my a majority vote. The adjudicated IAA is moderate/substantial, except for "Magnitude", "Shareability", and "Surprise".

Factor analysis. As a preliminary investigation of the relations among news values and emotions in

Figure 1: A dendrogram of the correlations among factor loadings for news values and emotions. (Emotions are shown in caps.)

headlines, we carry out a multivariate data analysis using factor analysis (FA) (Hair et al., 1998). The main goal of FA is to measure the presence of underlying constructs, i.e., factors, which in our case represent the correlation among emotions and news values, and their factor loading magnitudes. The use of FA is justified here because (1) we deal with cardinal (news values) and ordinal (emotions) variables and (2) the data exhibits a substantial degree of multicollinearity. We applied varimax, an orthogonal factor rotation used to obtain a simplified factor structure that maximizes the variance. We then inspected the eigenvalue scree plot and chose to use seven factors whose values were larger than 1 as to reduce the number of variables without loosing relevant information. To visualize the factor structure and relations among news values and emotions, we performed a hierarchical cluster analysis, using complete linkage with one minus Pearson's correlation coefficient as the distance measure.

Fig. 1 shows the resulting dendrogram. We can identify three groups of news values and emotions. The first group contains the negative emotions related to "Conflict" and "Bad news", and the rather distant "Power elite". The second group contains only news values, namely "Drama", "Celebrity", and "Follow up". The last group is formed by two positive emotions, joy and surprise, which are the kernels of two sub-groups: joy is related to "Good news", "Shareability" and, to a lesser extent, to "Magnitude", while surprise emotions relates to "Entertainment" and "Surprise" news values.

4 Models

We consider two classification algorithms in this study: a support vector machine (SVM) and the CNN. The two algorithms are known for their efficiency in text classification tasks (Joachims, 1998; Kim, 2014; Severyn and Moschitti, 2015). We frame the problem of news values classification as a multilabel task, and train one binary classifier for each news value, using headlines labeled with that news value as positive instances and all other as negative instances.

Features. We use the same feature sets for both SVM and CNN. As textual features, we use the pretrained Google News word embeddings, obtained by training the skip-gram model with negative sampling (Mikolov et al., 2013). For emotion features, we used the six ground-truth emotion labels from the SemEval-2007 dataset, standardized to zero mean and unit variance.

SVM. An SVM (Cortes and Vapnik, 1995) is a powerful discriminate model trained to maximize the separation margin between instances of two classes in feature space. We follow the common practice of assuming additive compositionality of the word embeddings and represent each headline as one 300-dimensional vector by averaging the individual word embeddings of its constituent words, whereby we discard the words not present in the dictionary. Note that this representation is not sensitive to word order. We use the SVM implementation from scikit-learn (Pedregosa et al., 2011), which in turn is based on LIBSVM (Chang and Lin, 2011). To maximize the efficiency of the model, we use the RBF kernel and rely on nested 5×5-cross-validation for hyperparameter optimization, with $C \in \{1, 10, 100\}$ and $\gamma \in \{0.01, 0.1\}$.

CNN. A CNN (LeCun and Bengio, 1998) is a feed-forward neural network consisting of one or more convolutional layers, each consisting of a number of filters (parameter matrices). Convolutions between filters and slices of the input embedding matrix aim to capture informative local sequences (e.g., word 3-grams). Each convolutional layer is followed by a pooling layer, which retains only the largest convolutional scores from each filter. A CNN thus offers one important advantage over SVM, in that it can detect indicative word sequences – a capacity that might be crucial when classifying short texts such as news headlines.

	SVM		CNN	
News value	T	T+E	T	T+E
Bad news	0.652	0.763*	0.778†	**0.848***†
Celebrity	**0.553**	0.534	0.496	0.526
Conflict	0.526	0.487	0.654†	**0.659**†
Drama	0.636	0.637	0.668	**0.681**
Entertainment	0.832	0.783*	0.803	**0.841***
Good news	0.414	0.513	0.509	**0.578**
Magnitude	0.299	**0.515***	0.438	0.507
Power elite	0.596	0.570	0.695†	**0.700**†
Shareability	0.309	0.318	**0.427**†	0.425†

Table 2: F1-scores of SVM and CNN news values classifiers using text ("T") or text and emotions ("T+E") as features. Best result for each news value are shown in bold. "*" denotes a statistically significant difference between feature sets "T" and "T+E" for the same classifier, and "†" a statistically significant difference between SVM and CNN classifiers with the same features ($p < 0.05$, two-tailed permutation test).

In our experiments, we trained CNNs with a single convolutional and pooling layer. We used 64 filters, optimized filter size ($\{3,4,5\}$) using nested cross-validation, and performed top-k pooling with $k = 2$. For training, we used the RMSProp algorithm (Tieleman and Hinton, 2012).

In addition to the vanilla CNN model that uses only the textual representation of a headline, we experimented with a model that additionally uses emotion labels as features. For each headline, the emotion labels are concatenated to the latent CNN features (i.e., output of the top-k pooling layer) and fed to the output layer of the network. Let $\mathbf{x}_T^{(i)}$ be the latent CNN vector of the i-th headline text, and $\mathbf{x}_E^{(i)}$ the corresponding vector of emotion labels. The output vector $\mathbf{y}^{(i)}$, a probability distribution over labels, is then computed as:

$$\mathbf{y}^{(i)} = softmax\left(\mathbf{W} \cdot [\mathbf{x}_T^{(i)}; \mathbf{x}_E^{(i)}] + \mathbf{b}\right)$$

where $\mathbf{W}$ and $\mathbf{b}$ are the weight matrix and the bias vector of the output layer.

5 Evaluation

Table 2 shows the F1-scores of the SVM and CNN news values classifiers, trained with textual features ("T") or both textual and emotion features ("T+E"). We report the results for nine out of 11 news values from Table 1; the two omitted labels are "Follow-up" and "Surprise", for which the number of instances was too low to successfully train

the models. Models for the remaining nine news values were trained successfully and outperform a random baseline (the differences are significant at $p < 0.001$; two-sided permutation test (Yeh, 2000)).

We can make three main observations. First, there is a considerable variance in performance across the news values: "Bad news" and "Entertainment" seems to be the easiest to predict, whereas "Shareability", "Magnitude", and "Celebrity" are more difficult. Secondly, by comparing "T" and "T+E" variants of the models, we observe that adding emotions as features improves leads to further improvements for the "Bad news" and "Entertainment" news values (differences are significant at $p < 0.05$) for CNN, and for SVM also for "Magnitude", but for other news values adding emotions did not improve the performance. This finding is aligned with the analysis from Fig. 1, where "Bad news" and "Entertainment" are the two news values that correlate the most with one of the emotions. Finally, by comparing between the two models, we note that CNN generally outperforms SVM: the difference is statistically significant for "Bad news", "Conflict", "Power elite", "Shareability", regardless of what features were used. This suggest that these news values might be identified by the presence of specific local word sequences.

6 Conclusions and Future Work

We described a preliminary study for predicting news values using headline text and emotions. A multivariate analysis revealed a three-way grouping of news values and emotions. Experiments with predicting news values revealed that both a support vector machine (SVM) and a convolutional neural network (CNN) can outperform a random baseline. The results further indicate that some news values are more easily detectable than others, that adding emotions as features helps for news values that are highly correlated with emotions, and that CNNs ability to detect local word sequences helps in this task, probably because of the brevity of headlines.

This works opens up a number of interesting research directions. One is to study the relation between the linguistic properties of headlines and news values. Another research direction is the comparison between headlines and full-text stories as features for news value prediction. It would also be interesting to analyze how news values correlate with properties of events described in text. We intend to pursue some of this work in the near future.

Acknowledgments

This work has been funded by the Unity Through Knowledge Fund of the Croatian Science Foundation, under the grant 19/15: "EVEnt Retrieval Based on semantically Enriched Structures for Interactive user Tasks (EVERBEST)".

References

Alexandra Balahur, Ralf Steinberger, Mijail Kabadjov, Vanni Zavarella, Erik Van Der Goot, Matina Halkia, Bruno Pouliquen, and Jenya Belyaeva. 2013. Sentiment analysis in the news. *arXiv preprint arXiv:1309.6202*.

Allan Bell. 1991. *The language of news media*. Blackwell Oxford.

Chih-Chung Chang and Chih-Jen Lin. 2011. LIBSVM: A library for support vector machines. *ACM Transactions on Intelligent Systems and Technology*, 2:27:1–27:27.

Mengen Chen, Xiaoming Jin, and Dou Shen. 2011. Short text classification improved by learning multi-granularity topics. In *Twenty-Second International Joint Conference on Artificial Intelligence*.

Corinna Cortes and Vladimir Vapnik. 1995. Support-vector networks. *Machine learning*, 20(3):273–297.

Tom De Nies, Evelien Dheer, Sam Coppens, Davy Van Deursen, Erik Mannens, and Rik Van de Walle. 2012. Bringing newsworthiness into the 21st century. *Web of Linked Entities (WoLE) at ISWC*, 2012:106–117.

Inoshika Dilrukshi, Kasun De Zoysa, and Amitha Caldera. 2013. Twitter news classification using svm. In *Computer Science & Education (ICCSE), 2013 8th International Conference on*, pages 287–291. IEEE.

Daniel Dor. 2003. On newspaper headlines as relevance optimizers. *Journal of Pragmatics*, 35(5):695–721.

Alec Go, Richa Bhayani, and Lei Huang. 2009. Twitter sentiment classification using distant supervision. *CS224N Project Report, Stanford*, 1(12).

Joseph F Hair, William C Black, Barry J Babin, Rolph E Anderson, Ronald L Tatham, et al. 1998. *Multivariate data analysis*, volume 5. Prentice hall Upper Saddle River, NJ.

Tony Harcup and Deirdre O'Neill. 2016. What is news? News values revisited (again). *Journalism Studies*, pages 1–19.

Edith Iarovici and Rodica Amel. 1989. The strategy of the headline. *Semiotica*, 77(4):441–460.

Elly Ifantidou. 2009. Newspaper headlines and relevance: Ad hoc concepts in ad hoc contexts. *Journal of Pragmatics*, 41(4):699–720.

Thorsten Joachims. 1998. Text categorization with support vector machines: Learning with many relevant features. *Machine learning: ECML-98*, pages 137–142.

Yoon Kim. 2014. Convolutional neural networks for sentence classification. In *Proceedings of the Conference on Empirical Methods in Natural Language Processing (EMNLP)*, pages 1746–1751, Doha, Qatar. Association for Computational Linguistics.

Zornitsa Kozareva, Borja Navarro, Sonia Vázquez, and Andrés Montoyo. 2007. Ua-zbsa: a headline emotion classification through web information. In *Proceedings of the 4th international workshop on semantic evaluations*, pages 334–337. Association for Computational Linguistics.

J Richard Landis and Gary G Koch. 1977. The measurement of observer agreement for categorical data. *biometrics*, pages 159–174.

Yann LeCun and Yoshua Bengio. 1998. The handbook of brain theory and neural networks. chapter Convolutional Networks for Images, Speech, and Time Series, pages 255–258. MIT Press, Cambridge, MA, USA.

Tomas Mikolov, Ilya Sutskever, Kai Chen, Greg S Corrado, and Jeff Dean. 2013. Distributed representations of words and phrases and their compositionality. In *Advances in neural information processing systems*, pages 3111–3119.

Raphael Nir. 1993. A discourse analysis of news headlines. *Hebrew Linguistics*, 37:23–31.

Jerry Palmer. 2000. *Spinning into control: News values and source strategies*. A&C Black.

F. Pedregosa, G. Varoquaux, A. Gramfort, V. Michel, B. Thirion, O. Grisel, M. Blondel, P. Prettenhofer, R. Weiss, V. Dubourg, J. Vanderplas, A. Passos, D. Cournapeau, M. Brucher, M. Perrot, and E. Duchesnay. 2011. Scikit-learn: Machine learning in Python. *Journal of Machine Learning Research*, 12:2825–2830.

Alicja Piotrkowicz, Vania Dimitrova, and Katja Markert. 2017. Automatic extraction of news values from headline text. In *Proceedings of EACL*. Association for Computational Linguistics.

Aliaksei Severyn and Alessandro Moschitti. 2015. Twitter sentiment analysis with deep convolutional neural networks. In *Proceedings of the 38th International ACM SIGIR Conference on Research and Development in Information Retrieval*, SIGIR '15, pages 959–962, New York, NY, USA. ACM.

Bharath Sriram, Dave Fuhry, Engin Demir, Hakan Ferhatosmanoglu, and Murat Demirbas. 2010. Short text classification in twitter to improve information filtering. In *Proceedings of the 33rd international ACM SIGIR conference on Research and development in information retrieval*, pages 841–842. ACM.

Carlo Strapparava and Rada Mihalcea. 2007. Semeval-2007 task 14: Affective text. In *Proceedings of the 4th International Workshop on Semantic Evaluations*, pages 70–74. Association for Computational Linguistics.

Carlo Strapparava and Rada Mihalcea. 2008. Learning to identify emotions in text. In *Proceedings of the 2008 ACM symposium on Applied computing*, pages 1556–1560. ACM.

Tijmen Tieleman and Geoffrey Hinton. 2012. Lecture 6.5-rmsprop: Divide the gradient by a running average of its recent magnitude. Technical Report 2.

Friedrich Ungerer. 1997. Emotions and emotional language in english and german news stories. *The language of emotions*, pages 307–328.

Lu Ye, Rui-Feng Xu, and Jun Xu. 2012. Emotion prediction of news articles from reader's perspective based on multi-label classification. In *Machine Learning and Cybernetics (ICMLC), 2012 International Conference on*, volume 5, pages 2019–2024. IEEE.

Alexander Yeh. 2000. More accurate tests for the statistical significance of result differences. In *Proceedings of the 18th conference on Computational linguistics-Volume 2*, pages 947–953. Association for Computational Linguistics.

Predicting User Views in Online News

Daniel Hardt
Copenhagen Business School
dh.itm@cbs.dk

Owen Rambow
Columbia University
rambow@ccls.columbia.edu

Abstract

We analyze user viewing behavior on an online news site. We collect data from 64,000 news articles, and use text features to predict frequency of user views. We compare predictiveness of the headline and "teaser" (viewed before clicking) and the body (viewed after clicking). Both are predictive of clicking behavior, with the full article text being most predictive.

1 Introduction

With so much news being consumed online, there is great interest in the way this news is consumed – what articles do users click on, and why? The data generated in online news consumption constitutes a rich resource for the exploration of news content and its relation to user opinions and behaviors. There are undoubtedly a wide variety of factors that influence reading behavior at online news sights, including the visual presentation of the web site. But certainly the language seen by the user plays a central role.

In this paper we experiment with a dataset from the online news site of Jyllands-Posten, a major Danish newspaper.[1] The data consists both of user logs and news articles. We attempt to predict viewing behavior from the text of articles. We also look at the difference in predictiveness of the text the user sees before clicking, i.e., the headline and the teaser, vs. the body of the article, which the user only sees after clicking, vs. the complete text of the article,

The first question we address is whether a simple lexical representation of articles is predictive of viewer behavior. We investigate bag of words, word vectors, and article length. A second question we investigate is the relative predictiveness of the headline and teaser, which are displayed before clicking, and the body of the article, which is of course only seen after the decision to view.

We explore these questions because we see them as relevant to a fundamental issue in today's media landscape: to what extent are news consumers manipulated by "clickbait", as opposed to making informed decisions about what news to consume? While the term clickbait is difficult to define, we see it as highlighting a potential difference between the promise of a headline or teaser compared to the actual nature of the article being pointed to. The work discussed in this paper is part of an effort (see for example (Blom and Hansen, 2015)) to use large amounts of data and computational methods to understand "clickbait".

2 Data

Our dataset consists of news articles and user logs from the online portal of the Danish daily, Jyllands-Posten. User logs have been maintained since July 2015. An entry in the user logs is created each time a user clicks on a new article on the site. An entry includes the time of the click and the page ID of the article, as well as a user ID if the user is registered on the site. It also includes additional information, including the referring page – the page the user was viewing when they clicked on the article. We collected all online articles published since July 2015, a total of 64,401 articles. The log file includes a total of 213,972,804 article views.

Articles are linked from two types of pages on the Jyllands-Posten website: the start page, and specialized pages for different subject matters (domestic, international, culture, sports, local, etc.).

Jyllands-Posten is a mainstream Danish daily paper, covering all major news topics, with a somewhat right-of center slant. While we have not an-

---

[1] http://jyllands-posten.dk

7

Proceedings of the 2017 EMNLP Workshop on Natural Language Processing meets Journalism, pages 7–12
Copenhagen, Denmark, September 7, 2017. ©2017 Association for Computational Linguistics

alyzed the distribution of topics covered, table 1 gives the most frequent unigrams in the training data, with stopwords manually removed. This listing reveals a focus on immigrants and other perceived external threats to Denmark.

1136	Denmark
652	Danish
633	refugees
618	EU
580	Aarhus (home town of paper)
552	USA
535	Danish
472	Løkke (prime minister)
444	killed
422	Danish
419	DF (Danish anti-immigrant party)
367	police
361	Syria
339	victory
339	death
331	satire
330	Trump
325	children
323	dead
316	Danish
315	Turkey
306	Europe
301	Russia
300	Islamic
286	attack

Table 1: Most frequent words (translated from Danish, note that inflectional variants in Danish of the word *Dansk* 'Danish' result in *Danish* appearing multiple times)

The articles consist of three distinct parts:

- The **headline** of the article, which is the text always displayed as the clickable link to the article on the referring page. It is also repeated on the article page.

- On the article page, there is typically a phrase or short sentence displayed below the headline, called the **teaser**. On the referring page, the teaser is sometimes omitted. We do not have information on whether the teaser was present or not on the referring page.

- The **body** is the text of the actual article, which is only visible after the user has clicked on the headline text.

The text data (headline, teaser, and body) is divided into training and development data, as described in Table 2. (We have a held out test set which we will use in future publications.)

Dataset	Articles	Words
Train	55,061	25,745,832
Development	9,351	4,134,432

Table 2: Text Data: Articles

The average number of views is 3,337, and the median number of views is 795. See Table 3 for the two most viewed headline/teaser combinations, and Table 4 for a headline/teaser with a median number of views (translations from Danish by the authors). There are evident differences between the high and median examples: the highly viewed example deals with material of immediate relevance to many readers. The top example concerns a garden snail that has preoccupied Danish gardeners for years, and promises a new solution. The second concerns a beloved Danish TV Christmas program, in which some off-color language was clearly visible during the children's program. The language used is also more conversational, informal and extreme. By contrast, the median example is purely informative.

H	Watch the unfortunate mistake in TV 2's family Christmas calendar
T	An attentive viewer caught the writing on the board, which the children probably should not see.
H	See the surprising solution in the fight against the killer snail
T	Nature guide in Herning has made a groundbreaking discovery that benefits all garden owners.

Table 3: Headline (H)/Teaser(T) for the articles with the most views (671,480 and 334,820, respectively)

3 The Task: Predicting Clicks Based on Text

Our task is to predict which articles get the most user views. We bin the articles by numbers of clicks into 2, 3, and 4 bins. This defines three different classification tasks: is the article in the

H	International agreement: Elections in East Ukraine this summer
T	The goal is to hold local elections in Donetsk and Lugansk before August. Germany and Ukraine are skeptical.

Table 4: Headline (H)/Teaser(T) for an article with median views (795 views)

top 50% of clicks, in the top 33.3% of clicks, in the top 25% of clicks? We use different parts of the article text to make the prediction. Specifically, we ask how much each of the text elements (headline, teaser, body) contributes to our ability to predict the highly clicked articles. Our working hypothesis is that the headline on its own, or the headline with the teaser, should have higher predictive power than the article alone. This is because the user sees only the headline (and perhaps the teaser) before making the decision to click and read the article. We investigate the following combinations of text elements, to see which provides the most predictive power:

- Headline only: the reader definitely sees this before clicking.

- Headline and teaser: in most cases, the user also sees a teaser before clicking.

- Body only: the reader does not see the body before clicking.

- Full article (headline, teaser, body): the reader sees all this information together only after clicking.

We experiment with the following classifiers, all using the sklearn package: Support Vector Machines with a linear kernel, Logistic Regression (logreg), Random Forests. For all classifiers, we use the same set of features. For the initial experiments we report in this workshop paper, we use the following set of lexical features:

- Bag of Words (BoW): We construct a bag of words from each article represented as a vector whose size is that of the vocabulary. We experiment with three values: a count of occurrences, a weighted count (term frequency), and tf-idf values.

- Word Vectors (vec): We also use word vector features for each word in each article

(Mikolov et al., 2013a,b). These vectors were created using the Python gensim package, using all of the training data. We then form the mean of the word vectors for all words in the text component we are interested in (headline, teaser, or body).

- Text length (wc): the length in words.

4 Results

We found consistently that logistic regression outperforms the other classifiers; we therefore only present results using logreg. Furthermore, we found that term frequency and tf-idf consistently perform about equally, and both outperform simple counts; thus, we report only results using term frequency. These results are shown in Tables 5, 6, and 7 for the top 50%, top 33.3% and top 25% classification tasks, respectively. We provide accuracy results and f-measure results, but we take the f-measure results as the relevant result. The baselines are always choosing the top-clicked category.

We observe that the models consistently beat the baselines (both on accuracy and f-measure). The text features thus are, in general, predictive of users' viewing behavior. Furthermore, we observe across the three tasks that the performance increases from using only the headline to using headline and teaser to using only the body to using the whole article. Put differently, more text is better for this prediction task, contrary to our hypothesis that the body would not contribute predictive power as it is unseen at click time.

In terms of our features, we were surprised to see that the wc (text length) and vec (word vectors) features do not appear to have much effect. While the results for different feature combinations vary somewhat, we do not see variations greater than 0.7% (and usually much less) in the 12 separate experiments (3 tasks and 4 data sources). The one exception is using the body for finding the top 33.3% of clicked articles (Table 6), where the combination of bag of words and word count leads to a drop of 3% over the other feature combinations. We take this to be noise rather than an interesting result.

5 Discussion

Our initial hypothesis was that article body would not be as predictive as headline and particularly

Data Source	Feats	Accuracy		F-measure			Always-H Bl	
		Acc	Bl	Recall	Precision	F-m	Prec	F-m
Headline	bow	0.612	0.513	0.856	0.583	0.694	0.513	0.678
Headline	bow, wc	0.611	0.513	0.856	0.582	0.693	0.513	0.678
Headline	bow, vec, wc	0.612	0.513	0.855	0.583	0.693	0.513	0.678
HeadlineTeaser	bow, wc	0.630	0.513	0.847	0.599	0.701	0.513	0.678
HeadlineTeaser	bow, vec, wc	0.629	0.513	0.847	0.598	0.701	0.513	0.678
HeadlineTeaser	bow	0.627	0.513	0.850	0.596	0.700	0.513	0.678
Body	bow, wc, vec	0.652	0.513	0.907	0.607	0.727	0.513	0.678
Body	bow, wc	0.640	0.513	0.92	0.597	0.724	0.513	0.678
Body	bow	0.650	0.513	0.889	0.609	0.722	0.513	0.678
HeadlineTeaserBody	bow, wc, vec	0.664	0.513	0.891	0.620	0.731	0.513	0.678
HeadlineTeaserBody	bow	0.670	0.513	0.875	0.627	0.731	0.513	0.678
HeadlineTeaserBody	bow, wc	0.662	0.513	0.895	0.618	0.731	0.513	0.678

Table 5: Results for finding the top-clicked 50% of articles using logistic regression

Data Source	Feats	Accuracy		F-measure			Always-H Bl	
		Acc	Bl	Recall	Precision	F-m	Prec	F-m
Headline	bow, wc	0.470	0.355	0.743	0.450	0.560	0.337	0.504
Headline	bow, vec, wc	0.469	0.355	0.740	0.451	0.560	0.337	0.504
Headline	bow	0.467	0.355	0.739	0.448	0.558	0.337	0.504
HeadlineTeaser	bow, vec, wc	0.480	0.355	0.751	0.471	0.579	0.337	0.504
HeadlineTeaser	bow, wc	0.479	0.355	0.752	0.470	0.578	0.337	0.504
HeadlineTeaser	bow	0.474	0.355	0.755	0.464	0.575	0.337	0.504
Body	bow	0.498	0.355	0.793	0.484	0.601	0.337	0.504
Body	bow, wc, vec	0.499	0.355	0.860	0.458	0.597	0.337	0.504
Body	bow, wc	0.446	0.355	0.939	0.407	0.568	0.337	0.504
HeadlineTeaserBody	bow	0.517	0.355	0.813	0.504	0.622	0.337	0.504
HeadlineTeaserBody	bow, vec, wc							
HeadlineTeaserBody	bow, wc							

Table 6: Results for finding the top-clicked 33.3% of articles using logistic regression (some numbers missing for uninteresting reasons)

Data Source	Feats	Accuracy		F-measure			Always-H Bl	
		Acc	Bl	Recall	Precision	F-m	Prec	F-m
Headline	bow, wc	0.363	0.271	0.673	0.357	0.466	0.242	0.390
Headline	bow, vec, wc	0.363	0.271	0.672	0.355	0.465	0.242	0.390
Headline	bow	0.361	0.271	0.665	0.351	0.46	0.242	0.390
HeadlineTeaser	bow, wc	0.370	0.271	0.659	0.368	0.473	0.242	0.390
HeadlineTeaser	bow, vec, wc	0.371	0.271	0.659	0.368	0.472	0.242	0.390
HeadlineTeaser	bow	0.369	0.271	0.662	0.363	0.469	0.242	0.390
Body	bow, wc, vec	0.424	0.271	0.757	0.401	0.525	0.242	0.390
Body	bow, wc	0.419	0.271	0.755	0.399	0.522	0.242	0.390
Body	bow	0.401	0.271	0.763	0.392	0.518	0.242	0.390
HeadlineTeaserBody	bow, wc	0.421	0.271	0.760	0.406	0.529	0.242	0.390
HeadlineTeaserBody	bow, wc, vec	0.421	0.271	0.761	0.406	0.529	0.242	0.390
HeadlineTeaserBody	bow	0.42	0.271	0.765	0.404	0.529	0.242	0.390

Table 7: Results for finding the top-clicked 25% of articles using logistic regression

teaser, since teaser is presumably constructed to induce clicking behaviors, while the article text itself is not visible to the user at the time a clicking decision is made. Thus we find it quite surprising that body is more predictive than headline and teaser, and the model combining headline, teaser and body is the best.

How can it be that the body is more predictive than the text the user actually sees when deciding to click? Here we offer some hypotheses. First, we note that some clicks are the result of social media referrals (this information is present in our log data). In these cases, it makes sense that body data is predictive, since presumably the referrer read the article before making the referral. Second, it is possible that the headline on its own gives readers a lot of semantic information which we are not capturing with our features, but which the whole article does provide. So human readers can "imagine" the article before they read it and implicitly base their behavior on their expectation.

In general, although the bow features are consistently predictive, there is little or no improvement from the vec and wc features. We expected that wc (text length) might be relevant in some ways: for example, that short, punchy teasers might tend to be more effective. No such effect has been observed however. The vec (word embeddings) feature was used to compute an average vector for the entire text. Computing an average of word vectors has been shown effective in other document classification tasks (Alkhreyf and Rambow,

2017). However, clearly such a vector loses a lot of information about a text, and more fine-grained modeling is needed.

6 Plans for Future Work

This work lays the foundation for multi-faceted investigations of news data, language, and user behavior and preferences. We have extracted aggregate totals of article views from the user logs. This dataset, which includes logs of all user behavior since 2015, has rich potential for further data mining. For example, the logs include the referring page for each user view. We intend to produce separate models for views resulting from social media referrals. Our hypothesis is that the body of the article is (even) more predictive in these cases, since the decision to view is, indirectly, based on a reading of the body of the article. We also intend to mine the logs to divide users into different classes based on their reading behavior. In addition, we plan to examine further our use of word embeddings, to explore ways in which they could be better exploited for prediction of views. We will also experiment with topic modeling.

Ultimately, we seek to shed some light on basic questions about online news. In particular, we would like to characterize the nature of different text types in headlines, teasers and article bodies, and in the process to use NLP techniques to help explore the difference between clickbait and genuine journalistic quality.

Acknowledgments

We thank A. Michele Colombo and Ha Le Hgoc
for help with the data and experiments. We also
thank Jyllands-Posten for giving us access to the
data.

References

Sakhar Alkhreyf and Owen Rambow. 2017. Work
hard, play hard: Email classification on the Avocado
and Enron corpora. In *Proceedings of Textgraphs-
11, ACL Workshop*.

Jonas Nygaard Blom and Kenneth Reinecke Hansen.
2015. Click bait: Forward-reference as lure in online news headlines. *Journal of Pragmatics* 76:87 –
100.

Tomas Mikolov, Ilya Sutskever, Kai Chen, Greg S Corrado, and Jeff Dean. 2013a. Distributed representations of words and phrases and their compositionality. In *Advances in neural information processing
systems*. pages 3111–3119.

Tomas Mikolov, Wen-tau Yih, and Geoffrey Zweig.
2013b. Linguistic regularities in continuous space
word representations. In *Hlt-naacl*. volume 13,
pages 746–751.

Tracking Bias in News Sources Using Social Media:
the Russia-Ukraine Maidan Crisis of 2013–2014

Peter Potash, Alexey Romanov, Anna Rumshisky
Department of Computer Science
University of Massachusetts Lowell
{ppotash,aromanov,arum}@cs.uml.edu

Mikhail Gronas
Department of Russian
Dartmouth College
mikhail.gronas@dartmouth.edu

Abstract

This paper addresses the task of identifying the bias in news articles published during a political or social conflict. We create a silver-standard corpus based on the actions of users in social media. Specifically, we reconceptualize bias in terms of how likely a given article is to be shared or liked by each of the opposing sides. We apply our methodology to a dataset of links collected in relation to the Russia-Ukraine Maidan crisis from 2013-2014. We show that on the task of predicting which side is likely to prefer a given article, a Naive Bayes classifier can record 90.3% accuracy looking only at domain names of the news sources. The best accuracy of 93.5% is achieved by a feed forward neural network. We also apply our methodology to gold-labeled set of articles annotated for bias, where the aforementioned Naive Bayes classifier records 82.6% accuracy and a feed-forward neural networks records 85.6% accuracy.

1 Introduction

The proliferation of online information sources and the dissolution of the centralized news delivery system creates a situation where news no longer comes from a restricted set of reputable (or not-so-reputable) news organizations, but rather from a collection of multiple distributed sources such as blogs, political columns, and social media posts. In times of social or political conflict, or when contentious issues are involved, such sources may present biased opinions or outright propaganda, which an unprepared reader is often not equipped to detect. News aggregators (such as Google News) present the news organized by top-

ics and popularity. But an adequate understanding of a news story or a blog post requires weeding out the "spin" or "framing", which reflects the source's position on the spectrum of conflicting opinions. In short, we need to know not only the *content* of the story, but also the *intent* behind it.

Many supervised approaches to bias detection rely on text analysis (Recasens et al., 2013; Iyyer et al., 2014), effectively detecting words, phrases, and memes characteristic of an ideology or a political position. All such methods can be characterized as *language-based methods* of bias detection. In contrast, the methods that we term *reaction-based* use human response to a news source in order to identify its bias. Such response is registered, for example, in social media when users post links to news sources, or like the posts that contain such links. We observe that with respect to divisive issues, users tend to split into cohesive groups based on their *like* streams: people from conflicting groups will like and pass around sources and links that express the opinions and the sentiment common only within their group. Put simply, reaction-based methods determine the bias of a source by how the communities of politically like-minded users react to it, based on the amount of liking, reposting, retweeting, etc., the text gets from the opposing groups. Such methods have recently been used with success in the context of liberal/conservative biases in US politics (Conover et al., 2011; Zhou et al., 2011; Gamon et al., 2008).

We believe the language-based and reaction-based methods are complementary and should be combined to supplement each other. Much work in bias detection relies on pre-existing annotated corpora of texts with known conservative and liberal biases. Such corpora obviously do not exist for most ideologies and biases found outside of American or Western discourse. In this work, we propose to use a reaction-based analysis of biases

Proceedings of the 2017 EMNLP Workshop on Natural Language Processing meets Journalism, pages 13–18
Copenhagen, Denmark, September 7, 2017. ©2017 Association for Computational Linguistics

in news sources in order to create a large silver standard of bias-marked text that will be used to train language-based bias detection models. This is done by collecting the articles reacted upon (liked/linked/posted) by the members of opposing political groups in social networks. We thus conceptualize the bias of a news article in terms of how likely it is to be referenced by one of the opposing groups, following the idea that any publicity is good publicity, and any reference to a source can in a some sense be considered a positive reference. The resulting "silver" corpus is slightly noisier than a manually annotated gold standard such as the one used in (Iyyer et al., 2014), but makes up for this deficiency by not being limited in size.

In this work, we use the Russia-Ukraine Maidan conflict of 2013–2014 as a case study for predicting bias in a polarized environment. We collect a large silver corpus of news articles using the posts in the user groups dedicated to the discussion of this conflict in a Russian social media network VKontakte, and evaluate several methods of using this data to predict which side is likely to like and share a given article. We use features derived both from a source's URL as well as the text of the article. We also analyze the news sharing patterns in order to characterize the specific conflict represented in our case study. Lastly, we annotate a small corpus of news articles for bias in relation to the Maidan crisis. We are then able to test the effectiveness of classifiers on gold-standard data when trained solely with silver-labeled data.

Our results show that predicting bias based on the frequency of sharing patterns of users representing opposing communities for our case study is quite effective. Specifically, a Naive Bayes classifier using only the domain name of a link as a feature (a one-hot input representation) achieves 90% accuracy on a bias prediction task. We compare an SVM-based classification method with a Feed Forward Neural Network (FFNN), and find that the best accuracy of 93.5% is achieved by the FFNN.

2   Dataset

In this study, we use data from Russian-speaking online media, posted during the Ukrainian events of 2013-2014. We use the largest Russian social network "VKontakte" (VK)[1]. According to

[1] http://vk.com

Domain Name	Google News	Antimaidan groups	Evromaidan groups
segodnya.ua	102	95	232
unian.net	78	160	2311
zn.ua	72	38	395
lenta.ru	70	869	146
news.liga.net	61	63	777
ru.tsn.ua	54	65	809
korrespondent.net	52	333	571
rbc.ua	34	91	115
ria.ru	21	8968	109
vestifinance.ru	19	104	6
glavred.info	19	12	117
forbes.ua	18	11	66
rian.com.ua	17	58	11
pravda.com.ua	17	197	6307
vz.ru	16	2092	8
vesti.ru	15	831	54
lb.ua	15	18	222
biz.liga.net	15	6	56
slon.ru	14	29	77
gordonua.com	14	34	762
gazeta.ru	12	454	94
interfax.com.ua	12	45	131
obozrevatel.com	11	57	670
podrobnosti.ua	10	60	275
top.rbc.ru	10	406	118
interfax.ru	9	1166	39
ntv.ru	8	408	36
mk.ru	8	150	44
pravda.ru	7	282	4
gigamir.net	7	5	16
focus.ua	6	8	101
forbes.ru	6	54	6
nbnews.com.ua`	6	27	117
ng.ru	6	33	5
rosbalt.ru	6	90	61

Table 1: Statistics of the occurrences of domains extracted from Google News.

liveinternet.ru, VKontakte has 320 million registered users and is the most popular social network in both Russia and Ukraine. During the conflict, both pro-Russian (also known as "Antimaidan") and pro-Ukrainian side (also known as "Pro-" or "Evromaidan") were represented online by large numbers of Russian-speaking users.

We have built a scalable open stack system for data collection from VKontakte using the VK API. The system is implemented in Python using a PostgreSQL database and Redis-based message queue. VK API has a less restrictive policy than Facebook's API, making it an especially suitable social network for research. Our system supports the API methods for retrieving the group members, retrieving all posts from a wall, retrieving comments and likes for a given post, and so on.

In order to seed the data collection, we selected the most popular user groups from the two opposing camps, the Evromaidan group (154,589 members) and the Antimaidan group (580,672 members). We then manually annotated other groups to which the administrators of these two groups belonged, selecting groups with political content. This process produced 47 Evromaidan-related groups with 2,445,661 unique members and 51 Antimaidan-related groups with 1,942,918 unique members.

To create a dataset for our experiments, we randomly selected 10,000 links, 5,000 each from Antimaidan and Evromaidan-related group walls. Links are disregarded if they appear on walls from both sides, which is to ensure an unambiguous assignment of labels. We made a 90%/10% train/test split of the data. The labels for the links correspond to whether they came from an Antimaidan or Evromaidan related wall. We refer to these datasets as our silver-labeled training and test sets.

3 News Sharing Patterns in Polarized Communities

In this section we investigate whether the bias of a news article can be detected by examining the users who shared or liked this article. If the link to this article is predominantly shared by Evromaidan users, then it is more likely to cover the events in a way favorable to the Evromaidan side, and vice versa. Examining the links shared by "Antimaidan" and "Evromaidan" groups, we see that they have a very small number of shared links in common. The "Antimaidan" groups have posted 239,182 links and the "Evromaidan" groups have posted 222,229 links, but the number of links that have been posted by both sides is only 1,888, which are 0.79% and 0.85% of links posted to Antimaidan and Evromaidan groups, respectively, an alarmingly small number. This general mutual exclusion of link sharing makes our label assignment strategy realistic for our case study, since links are rarely shared by both communities.

In order to check how many links from a news aggregator are actually posted on the groups walls, we have collected links from the first 5 pages of Google News Russia by using "maidan" and "Ukraine" query words. This resulted in a total of 1,039 links. Out of these, 106 were posted on the "Antimaidan" group walls and 113 on the "Evromaidan" group walls.

In order to investigate the possibility of charac-terizing a news source, rather than a specific news article in terms of its bias, we also extracted domain names from the links collected from Google News, as well as the links from the group walls. This produced 126 unique domain names from Google News, out of which only 7 domains were not presented on the groups wall, for a total of 14 links, or 1.3%. Examining the number of occur-rences of each domain name on each side's group walls is quite instructive, since for most sources a clear preference from one of the sides can be ob-served.

4 Bias Annotation

In order to evaluate our methodology on gold-labeled data, as opposed to the silver-labeled dataset from Section 2, we have annotated the news articles from Section 3. Of the 1,039 links from the Google News query, only 678 were ac-tive at the time of the annotation. Two different annotators labeled the articles on a scale from -2 to 2, where -2 is strongly Antimaidan, -1 is weakly Antimaidan, 0 is neutral, 1 is weakly Pro-maidan, and 2 is strongly Promaidan. The annota-tors could also label NA if the article isn't related to the Maidan crisis. We then merged the non-zero labels to be either Pro or Anti Maidan, like our sil-ver data. In terms of labels where both annotators agreed, there are 40 Anti, 95 Pro, and 215 neutral articles. We test our methodology on the articles with a Pro or Anti bias (we were unable to scrape 3 of the Pro articles, so there are 92 Pro articles for testing).

5 Predicting Bias

In this section, we describe our experiments for predicting issue-based bias of links shared online, using the Maidan crisis as a case study.

5.1 Feature Representation

We define a feature representation for each article that will use the following types of features:

Domain Name This features is simply the domain name of the link. There are a total of 1,043 domain names in the training set. The use of this feature is inspired by the uneven distribution of domain name sharing present in Table 1. Most importantly, this feature provides a single non-zero value for its representation, which allows us to evaluate how effective domain names are for predicting bias.

Text-Based Features We initially scrape the full HTML page from links and strip the HTML content using BeautifulSoup[2], followed by tokenization of the text. We use a bag-of-words representation of the text with count-based features[3]. We filter the vocabulary to contain words that occur in at least 10 documents and at most in 90% of documents. This representation has 53,274 dimensions.

URL-Based Features Each article appears in our system as a link. We conjecture that we can better determine bias using features of this link. There are three features taken from the link: 1) domain name, 2) domain extension, and 3) path elements. For example, The URL `http://nlpj2017.fbk.eu/business-website-services` will have the following features: 'nlpj2017' and 'fbk' will be domain features, 'eu' will be an extension feature, and 'business-website-services' will be a path feature. We use the same vocabulary filtering strategy as with the text features – minimum frequency of ten documents and a maximum frequency of 90% of documents[4]. This representation has 277 dimensions.

5.2 Models

Our experiments are a binary classification task. We experimented with three types of classifiers. The first is a Naive Bayes classifier. The second classifier is an SVM. Both the Naive Bayes and SVM classifiers are implemented in scikit-learn (Pedregosa et al., 2011) using default settings. The second classifier is a FFNN, implemented in Keras (Chollet et al., 2015). The FFNN has two layers[5], each with size 64, and ReLu activation (Nair and Hinton, 2010) for the hidden layer.

6 Results and Discussion

The results of our experiments on the silver-labeled test set are shown in Table 2. Since the

---

[2]`http://www.crummy.com/software/BeautifulSoup/`

[3]We also experimented with tfidf and binary features, but found count features to perform the best.

[4]Filtering of URL features greatly reduces the feature size, as it is 11,516 dimension in total. Also, the SVM classifier gains 11% accuracy with filtering.

[5]We also experimented with adding more layers, but did not find a gain in performance.

Model	Features	Accuracy
Naive Bayes	Domain Name	90.3
SVM	URL	87.0
SVM	Text	90.2
SVM	URL+Text	90.2
FFNN	URL	91.3
FFNN	Text	**93.5**
FFNN	URL+Text	93.1

Table 2: Results of our supervised experiments for predicting bias on the silver-labeled test set.

Model	Features	Accuracy
Naive Bayes	Domain Name	82.6
SVM	URL	80.3
SVM	Text	73.5
SVM	URL+Text	72.7
FFNN	URL	78.0
FFNN	Text	71.2
FFNN	URL+Text	**85.6**

Table 3: Results of our supervised experiments for predicting bias on gold-labeled data.

dataset is balanced, random guessing would produce 50% accuracy. We can see from the results that all systems perform very well when compared to random guessing, with the best accuracy posted by the FFNN at 93.5%. The main result that should be noted is the performance of the Naive Bayes classifier using only domain names, which is effectively determining bias purely based on which side has shared a given domain name the most. This method is highly competitive, outperforming all SVM models, and trailing the FFNN with URL features by only 1%. This result confirms the unbalanced sharing habits shown in Table 1. Furthermore, the high accuracy of the domain name/URL features could potentially be an indicator of just how polarizing the Maidan issue is, as the two sides are highly separable in terms of the sources and links they share in their respective communities.

One interesting result is that, regardless of the classifier, combining URL and text features does not increase the accuracy of text features alone, and even sees a drop in performance for the FFNN. This could potentially be explained by Karamshuk et al.'s (2016) assertion that the text on web pages contains markers of its URL features. However, when combining URL and text features, URL features are represented in different dimensions than the text features, so the classifier could potentially treat them differently than if they were just appearing in the text.

# Training Ex.	Accuracy
9,000	90.2
4,500	89.2
2,250	88.4
1,124	86.0
562	83.3
280	81.2
140	78.5
70	77.1
34	71.7
16	49.9

Table 4: Accuracy of the SVM model with text features based on differing amounts of training data. Evaluation is done on silver-labeled test set.

Table 3 shows the results of our models on the gold-labeled test set described in Section 4. First, we establish a trend of domain names being a highly informative feature. Secondly, we see a model that makes a dramatic improvement combining URL and text features; the FFNN. However, when using either URL or text features individually, the SVM performs better on this test set.

Effects of Training Set Size

Table 4 Shows the accuracy of the SVM model with text features based on differing amounts of training data evaluated on the silver-labeled test set. There are several interesting insights from these results. First, reducing the initial training set size by 75% reduces accuracy less than 2%. Second, even with just 280 training examples, the model still achieves above 80%; similarly, the model still achieves above 70% accuracy with only 34 training examples. Lastly, the model sees its accuracy drop to that of random guessing only once it is given 16 training examples.

7 Related Work

Most state-of-the-art work on bias detection deals with known pre-defined biases and relies either strictly on text or strictly on user reactions in order to determine the bias of a statement. For example, Recasens et al. (2013) developed a system for identifying the bias-carrying term in the sentence, using a dataset of Wikipedia edits that were meant to remove bias. The model uses a logistic regression classifier with several types of linguistic features including word token, word lemma, part-of-speech tags, and several lexicons. The classifier also looks at the edits that have previously been made on the article. Using the same dataset, Kuang and Davison (2016) build upon previous approaches by using distributed representations of words and documents (Pennington et al., 2014; Le and Mikolov, 2014) to create features for predicting biased language.

Iyyer et al. (2014) created a system that detects the political bias of a sentence using a recursive neural network to create multi-word embeddings. The model starts with the individual embeddings of the sentence's words and systematically combines them to create the sentence embeddings. These sentence embeddings are then used as input to a supervised classifier that predicts the author's political affiliation for the sentence. The model is trained on a set of sentences annotated down to phrase-level for political bias. The authors argue that, unlike bag-of-words models, the sentence embeddings capture the full semantic composition of the sentence.

The work most similar to ours is that of Karamshuk et al. (2016). While both their work and ours seek to predict the bias of a news source, the key difference is in how we construct our datasets. Karamshuk et al. manually annotate specific news sources to identify partisan slant, and label an article's bias based on its source. Our labeling is based on the sharing patterns of users in a polarized setting (see Section 2 for a further description of our dataset). Lastly, Karamshik et al. use a bag of (word vector) means to construct features for their classification experiments, which has been shown to be a poor representation for text classification (Zhang et al., 2015). The authors' best accuracy is 77% in their binary classification tasks.

A different approach to bias detection consists in analyzing not the texts themselves, but the way the texts circulate or are reacted upon within a social network. Examples of such an approach are found in the work of Gamon et al (2008) who analyze the links between conservative and liberal blogs and the news articles they cite, as well as the expressed sentiment toward each article. Zhou et al (2011) detected and classified the political bias of news stories using the users' votes at such collaborative news curation sites as diggs.com. Relatedly, Conover et al (2011) used Twitter political tags to show that retweet patterns induce homogeneous, clearly defined user communities with extremely sparse retweets between the communities.

8 Conclusion

In this paper we address the issue of predicting the partisan slant of information sources and articles. We use the the Russia-Ukraine Maidan crisis of 2013-2014 as a case study, wherein we attempt to predict which side of the issue is likely to share a given link, as well as its corresponding article. Our best classifier, a FFNN, achieves 93.5% accuracy on the binary classification task using a BOW representation of the link content, and 91.3% accuracy using only information from the URL itself. Moreover, a Naive Bayes classifier using only the domain name of a link can record 90.3% accuracy, outperforming an SVM with more complex features. This remarkably high accuracy dictates that this case study exhibits high polarization in terms of its news sources, as well as its semantic content. We also evaluate our methodology – training a classifier with silver-labeled data based on user actions – on a gold-labeled test annotated for bias in relation to the Maidan crisis. The classifier using only domain names continues its impressive performance, recording an 82.6% accuracy. Conversely, a FFNN records 85.6% accuracy. For our case study, we find that the situation when two opposing sides share the same links is extremely rare.

Acknowledgments

This work was supported in part by the U.S. Army Research Office under Grant No. W911NF-16-1-0174.

References

François Chollet et al. 2015. Keras. `https://github.com/fchollet/keras`.

Michael Conover, Jacob Ratkiewicz, Matthew Francisco, Bruno Gonçalves, Filippo Menczer, and Alessandro Flammini. 2011. Political polarization on twitter. In *ICWSM*.

Michael Gamon, Sumit Basu, Dmitriy Belenko, Danyel Fisher, Matthew Hurst, and Arnd Christian König. 2008. Blews: Using blogs to provide context for news articles. In *ICWSM*.

Mohit Iyyer, Peter Enns, Jordan Boyd-Graber, and Philip Resnik. 2014. Political ideology detection using recursive neural networks. In *Proceedings of the Association for Computational Linguistics*. pages 1113–1122.

Dmytro Karamshuk, Tetyana Lokot, Oleksandr Pryymak, and Nishanth Sastry. 2016. Identifying partisan slant in news articles and twitter during political crises. In *International Conference on Social Informatics*. Springer, pages 257–272.

Sicong Kuang and Brian D Davison. 2016. Semantic and context-aware linguistic model for bias detection.

Quoc Le and Tomas Mikolov. 2014. Distributed representations of sentences and documents. In *Proceedings of the 31st International Conference on Machine Learning (ICML-14)*. pages 1188–1196.

Vinod Nair and Geoffrey E Hinton. 2010. Rectified linear units improve restricted boltzmann machines. In *Proceedings of the 27th international conference on machine learning (ICML-10)*. pages 807–814.

Fabian Pedregosa, Gaël Varoquaux, Alexandre Gramfort, Vincent Michel, Bertrand Thirion, Olivier Grisel, Mathieu Blondel, Peter Prettenhofer, Ron Weiss, Vincent Dubourg, et al. 2011. Scikit-learn: Machine learning in python. *Journal of Machine Learning Research* 12(Oct):2825–2830.

Jeffrey Pennington, Richard Socher, and Christopher D Manning. 2014. Glove: Global vectors for word representation. In *EMNLP*. volume 14, pages 1532–1543.

Marta Recasens, Cristian Danescu-Niculescu-Mizil, and Dan Jurafsky. 2013. Linguistic models for analyzing and detecting biased language. In *ACL (1)*. pages 1650–1659.

Xiang Zhang, Junbo Zhao, and Yann LeCun. 2015. Character-level convolutional networks for text classification. In *Advances in neural information processing systems*. pages 649–657.

Daniel Xiaodan Zhou, Paul Resnick, and Qiaozhu Mei. 2011. Classifying the political leaning of news articles and users from user votes. In *ICWSM*.

What to Write? A topic recommender for journalists

Giovanni Stilo and **Paola Velardi**
Sapienza University of Rome, Italy
{stilo, velardi}@di.uniroma1.it

Alessandro Cucchiarelli and **Giacomo Marangoni** and **Christian Morbidoni**
Università Politecnica delle Marche, Italy
{a.cucchiarelli, g.marangoni, c.morbidoni}@univpm.it

Abstract

In this paper we present a recommender system, What To Write and Why (W^3), capable of suggesting to a journalist, for a given event, the aspects still uncovered in news articles on which the readers focus their interest. The basic idea is to characterize an event according to the echo it receives in online news sources and associate it with the corresponding readers' communicative and informative patterns, detected through the analysis of Twitter and Wikipedia, respectively. Our methodology temporally aligns the results of this analysis and recommends the concepts that emerge as topics of interest from Twitter and Wikipedia, either not covered or poorly covered in the published news articles.

1 Introduction

In a recent study on the use of social media sources by journalists (Knight, 2012) the author concludes that "social media are changing the way news are gathered and researched". In fact, a growing number of readers, viewers and listeners access online media for their news (Gloviczki, 2015). When readers feel involved by news stories they may react by trying to deepen their knowledge on the subject, and/or confronting their opinions with peers. Stories may then solicit a reader's *information* and *communication* needs. The intensity and nature of both needs can be measured on the web, by tracking the impact of news on users' search behavior on on-line knowledge bases as well as their discussions on popular social platforms. What is more, on-line public's reaction to news is almost immediate (Leskovec et al., 2009) and even anticipated, as for the case of planned

media events and performances, or for disasters (Lehmann et al., 2012). Assessing the focus, duration and outcomes of news stories on public attention is paramount for both public bodies and media in order to determine the issues around which the public opinion forms, and in framing the issues (i.e., how they are being considered) (Brooker and Schaefer, 2005). Futhermore, real-time analysis of public reaction to news items may provide useful feedback to journalists, such as highlighting aspects of a story that needs to be further addressed, issues that appear to be of interest for the public but have been ignored, or even to help local newspapers echo international press releases.

The aim of this paper is to present a news media recommender, What to Write and Why (W^3), for analyzing the impact of news stories on the readers, and finding aspects – still uncovered in news articles – on which the public has focused their interest. The purpose of W^3 is to support journalists in the task of reshaping and extending their coverage of breaking news, by suggesting topics to address when following up on such news items. For example, we have found that a common pattern for news readers is to search events of the same type occurred in the past on Wikipedia, which is not surprising per se: however, among the many possible similar events, our system is able to identify those that the majority of readers consider (sometimes surprisingly) highly associated with breaking news, e.g., searching for the 2013 CeaseFire program in Baltimore during Egypt's ceasefire proposal in Gaza on July 2014.

2 Methodology

Our methodology is in five steps, as shown in the workflow of Figure 1:

Step 1. Event detection: We use SAX*, an unsupervised temporal mining algorithm that we

19

Proceedings of the 2017 EMNLP Workshop on Natural Language Processing meets Journalism, pages 19–24
Copenhagen, Denmark, September 7, 2017. ©2017 Association for Computational Linguistics

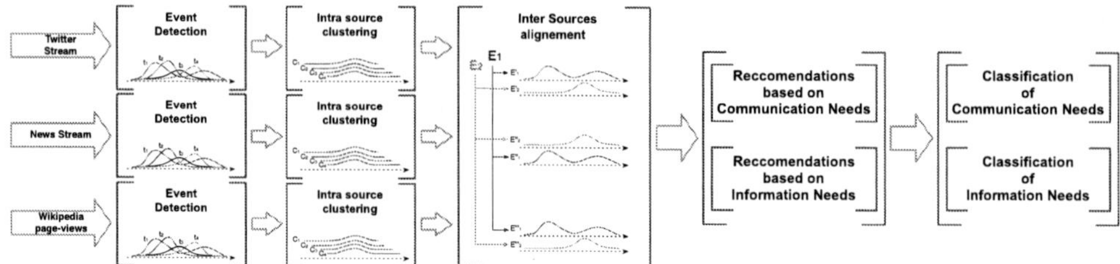

Figure 1: Workflow of W^3

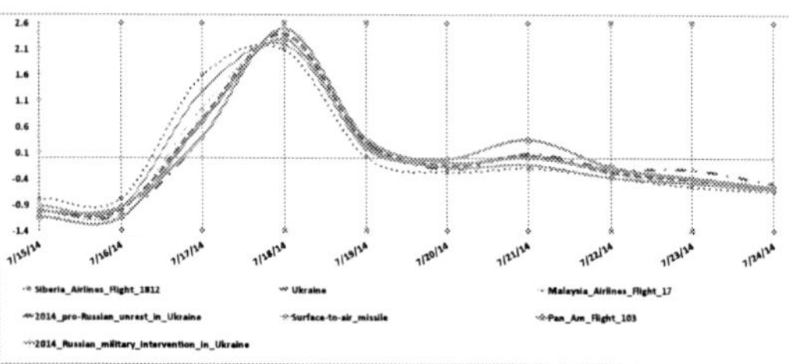

Figure 2: Cluster of normalized time series of Wikipedia page views for Malaysia Airline crash on July 2014.

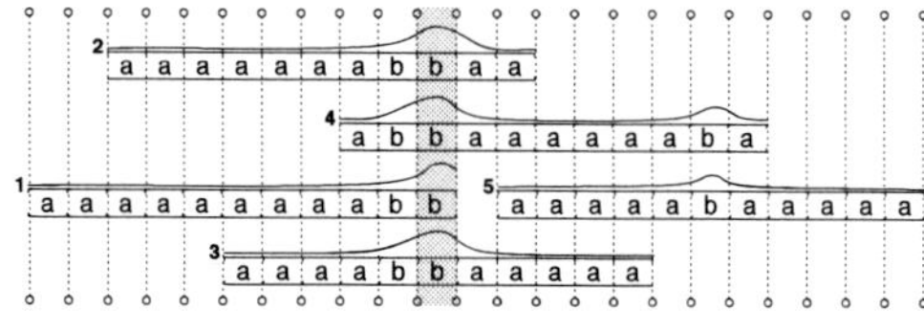

Figure 3: SAX* strings associated to a temporal series $s(t)$ in 5 adjacent or overlapping windows.

introduced in (Stilo and Velardi, 2016), to cluster tokens – words, entities, hashtags, page views – based on the *shape similarity* of their associated signals $s(t)$. In SAX*, signals observed in temporal windows L_k are first transformed into strings of symbols of an alphabet Σ; next, strings associated to *active* tokens (those corresponding to patterns of public attention) are clustered based on their similarity. Each cluster is interpreted as related to an event e_i. Clusters are extracted independently from on-line news (N), Twitter messages (T) and Wikipedia page views (W).

For example, the cluster in Figure 2 shows Wikipedia page views related to the Malaysia Airline crash on July 2014. We remark that SAX* blindly clusters signals without prior knowledge of the event and its occurrence date, and furthermore, it avoids time-consuming processing of text strings, since it only considers active tokens.

Step 2. Intra-source clustering: Since clusters are generated in *sliding windows L_k* of equal length L and temporal increment Δ, clusters referring to the same event but extracted in partly overlapping windows may slightly differ, especially for long-lasting events, when news updates motivate the emergence of new sub-topics and the decay of others. An example is in Figure 3, showing for simplicity a cluster with a unique signal $s(t)$ which we can also interpret as the cluster centroid. The Figure also shows the string of symbols

associated with the signal in each window (with $\Sigma = \{a, b\}$).

For a better characterization of an event, we merge clusters referring to the same event and extracted in adjacent windows, based on their similarity. Merged clusters form *meta-clusters*, denoted with m_i^S, where the index i refers to the event and $S \in \{N, T, W\}$ to the data source. With reference to Figure 3, the signals in windows 1, 2, 3 and 4 would be merged, but not the signal in window 5.

An example from the T dataset is shown in Table 1: note that the first two clusters show that initially Twitter users where concerned mainly about the tragedy (clusters C9 and C5), and only later did their interest focus on political aspects (e.g., Barack Obama, Vladimir Putin in C17 and C18).

Step 3. Inter-source alignment: Next, an alignment algorithm explores possible matches across the three data sources N, T and W. For any event e_i, we eventually obtain three "aligned" meta-clusters m_i^N, m_i^T and m_i^W mirroring respectively the media coverage of the considered event and its impact on readers' communication and information needs.

Step 4. Generating a recommendation: The input to our recommender is the news meta-clusters m_i^N related to an event e_i first reported on day d_0 and extracted during an interval I : $d_0 \le d \le d_{0+x}$, where d_{0+x} is the day in which the query is performed by the journalist. The system compares the three aligned meta-clusters

Table 1: The Twitter meta-cluster capturing the Malaysia Airlines flight crash event and its composing clusters

Clusters

C9 [tragic, crash, tragedi, Ukraine 1.0, Malaysia_Airlines 0.6, Airline 0.66, Malaysia_Airlines_Flight_17 0.65, Malaysia 0.60, Russia 0.51, Aviation_accidents_and_incidents 0.36, Airliner 0.35, Malaysia_Airlines_Flight_37 0.28, United_States 0.21, Tragedy 0.20, Boeing_777 ...]

C5 [tragic, tragedi, Airline 1.0, Malaysia_Airlines_Flight_17 0.97, Malaysia_Airlines 0.70, Malaysia 0.58, Ukraine 0.40, Twitter 0.39, Gaza_Strip 0.32, CNN 0.26, Tragedy 0.25, God 0.24, Airliner 0.22, Israel 0.22, Malaysia_Airlines_Flight_370 0.22, Netherlands 0.21,..]

C17 [tragedi, tragic, Malaysia_Airlines_Flight_17 1.0, Airline 0.89, Malaysia_Airlines 0.62, Malaysia 0.54, Gaza_Strip 0.42, Twitter 0.38, Ukraine 0.38, Hamas 0.33, Barack_Obama 0.32, Israel 0.29, Vladimir_Putin 0.27, God 0.26, CNN 0.25, Hell 0.25, Airliner 0.23, Malaysia_Airlines_Flight_37 0.20,...]

T_C18 [tragedi, tragic, Malaysia_Airlines_Flight_17 1.0, Airline 0.98, Malaysia_Airlines 0.80, Tragedy , Malaysia 0.54, Gaza_Strip 0.50, Ukraine 0.48, Hamas 0.408, Israel 0.38, Barack_Obama 0.7, Twitter 0.37, Vladimir_Putin 0.36, CNN 0.32, Airliner 0.28, Malaysia_Airlines_Flight_370 0.26, Hell 0.252, ...]

Meta-cluster

[tragedi 0.22, tragic 0.22, airline 0.20, malaysia_airlines_flight_17 0.20, ukraine 0.19, malaysia_airlines 0.19, malaysia 0.17, russia 0.129, tragedy 0.12, vladimir_putin 0.12, airliner 0.12, crash 0.12, gaza_strip 0.11, barack_obama 0.11, aviation_accidents_and_incidents 0.11, cnn 0.106, malaysia_airlines_flight_370 0.10, god 0.10, ...]

to identify in m_i^T and m_i^W the set of most relevant entities [1], respectively E_i^T and E_i^W. A set of entities E_i in either T or W is further partitioned in $R_i^{in\_news}$ and R_i^{novel}, representing, respectively, the event-related topics already discussed, and those not yet considered in news items. The first set is interesting for journalists in order to understand which topics mostly attracted the attention of the public, while the second set includes event-related, but still uncovered, topics that W^3 recommends to discuss. For example, the following is a recommendation generated from the analysis of Wikipedia page views, related to Scottish Independence elections on September 17th, 2014: *[scotland, wales, alex_salmond, united_kingdom, scottish_national_party, flag_of_scotland, william_wallace, countries_of_the_united_kingdom, mary_queen_of_scots, tony_blair, braveheart, flag_of_the_united_kingdom, republic_of_ireland].* When comparing these entities with the aligned news meta-clusters, the set of *novel* entities R_i^{novel} is: *[flag_of_scotland, william_wallace, countries_of_the_united_kingdom, mary_queen_of_scots, tony_blair, braveheart]* and all the others are also found in news.

Step 5. Classification of information and communication needs: In addition to recommendations, we automatically assign a category both to event clusters m_i^N in news, and to related entities in Twitter and Wikipedia aligned meta-clusters m_i^T and m_i^W, in order to detect recurrent discussion topics and search patterns in relation to specific event *types*. To do so, we exploit both BabelNet (Navigli and Ponzetto, 2010),

dataset	# clusters	# m.clusters	av. size m.clusters
News	9396	829	122.46
Twitter	4737	413	136.76
Wikipedia	5450	535	6.44

Table 2: Statistics on data and results

a large-scale multilingual semantic network[2], and the Wikipedia Category graph.

3 Discussion

To conduct our study, we created three datasets: Wikipedia PageViews (W), On-line News (N) and Twitter messages (T). Data was collected during 4 months from June 1st, 2014 to September 30th. Table 2 shows some statistics. Note that Wikipedia clusters are smaller, since cluster members are only named entities (page views).

We defined the following evaluation framework: i) Given an event e_i and related news $n_i \in N_i$, we generate recommendations as explained in Step 4, in a selected interval prior to the day of the query. ii) *Automated evaluation*: we we select the top K scored recommendations and measure the *saliency* of $R_i^{in\_news}$ and *serendipity* of R_i^{novel} in an automated fashion, and we compare the performance against a primitive recommender, in analogy with (Murakami et al., 2008) and (Ge et al., 2010); ii) *Manual evaluation*: we select the top K scored recommendations in R_i^{novel} for a restricted number of 21 high-impact world-wide events, and we perform manual evaluation using the *Crowdflower.com* platform, providing detailed evaluation guidelines for human annotators. Using this ground truth, we measure the global *serendipity* of W^3 recommendations.

<hr>

[1] We used TextRazor `https://www.textrazor.com` and DataTXT `https://dandelion.eu/semantic-text/entity-extraction-demo/` to extract entities respectively from Twitter and news items

[2] `http://babelnet.org/about`

3.1 Automated Evaluation

We first build two *primitive recommenders* (PRs) for Wikipedia and Twitter, which we use as a baseline. The input to a PR is the same as for W^3 (see Step 4).

Wikipedia PR: The Wikipedia PR is based on finding connected components of the Wikipedia hyperlink page graph (like in (Hu et al., 2009)), when considering only the topmost visited pages in a temporal slot. More precisely, for each day d in the interval $I' : d_{0-x} \leq d \leq d_{0+x}$ [3], we select the top $H \geq K$ visited named entities of the day E_d^W. Entities are ranked by frequency of page views[4]. Next, we create clusters c_j^d obtained by extracting the connected components of E_d^W in the Wikipedia hyperlink graph. Let $C^{I'}$ be the set of all clusters $c_j^{I'}$ in I'. From this set, we select the top r clusters based on the Jaccard similarity with news meta-clusters m_i^N. A "primitive" recommendation for event e_i on day d_{0+x} is the set PR_i^W of topmost K ranked entities in the r previously selected clusters. Like in W^3 recommendations, PR_i^W is a ranked list of entities some of which are also found in m_i^N, and some others are novel.

Twitter PR: For each entity $e \in m_i^N$ we retrieve and recommend the top K co-occurring entities in tweets in the considered interval.

Note that both primitive recommenders are far from being naive. A hyperlink graph to characterize users' intent in Wikipedia search is used in (Hu et al., 2009) (although the authors use Random Walks rather than connected components analysis to identify related pages). Co-occurrences with top ranked news terms has been used in (Weiler et al., 2014) to track on Twitter the evolution and the context around events. We generate recommendations using four systems: $W^3(T)$, $W^3(W)$, $PR(T)$ and $PR(W)$. The first two originate from What To Write and Why when applied to Twitter and Wikipedia, respectively. The second two are generated by the two primitive recommenders described above. For all systems, we consider the first K top ranked entities, as we said.

To assess the quality of "not novel" recommended entities in W^3 (and similarly for the other systems), for any $r_j \in R_i^{in\_news}$ we retrieve all the

news N_i related to m_i^N meta-clusters, and compute the *saliency* of r_j as follows:

$$saliency\,(r_j, n_i) = \beta \times occ^{title}\,(r_j, n_i) + (1 - \beta) \times occ^{snip}\,(r_j, n_i)$$

(1)

where $n_i \in N_i$, $occ^{title}(r_j, n_i)$ is the number of occurrences of r_j in the title of n_i, while $occ^{snip}(r_j, n_i)$ is the number of occurrences of r_j in the text snippet of n_i and β has been experimentally set to 0.7. The intuition is that recommended entities in $R_i^{in\_news}$ *are salient if they frequently occur in the title and text of news snippets*, where occurrences in the title have a higher weight. The total saliency of r_j is then:

$$saliency\,(r_j) = \frac{\sum_{n_i \in N_i} saliency(r_j, n_i)}{|N_i|} \times IDF\,(r_j)$$

(2)

where $IDF(r_j)$ is the inverse document frequency of r_j in all news of the considered temporal slot, and is used to smooth the relevance of terms with high probability of occurrence in all documents. The average saliency of $R_i^{in\_news}$ is:

$$saliency\,\left(R_i^{in\_news}\right) = \frac{\sum_{r_j \in R_i^{in\_news}} saliency(r_j)}{|R_i^{in\_news}|}$$

(3)

To provide an estimate of the *serendipity* of novel recommendations, we compute the NASARI similarity (Camacho-Collados et al., 2016) of entities $r_k \in R_i^{novel}$ with in-news entities $r_j \in E_i^N$ and we weight these values with the saliency of r_j. The intuition is that *serendipitous recommendations are those concerning topics which have not been discussed so far in on-line news, but are highly semantically related with highly salient topics in news*:

$$serend.\,(r_k \in R_i^{novel}) = \frac{\sum_{r_k \in R_i^{novel}, r_j \in E_i^N} (NASARI(r_k, r_j) \times saliency(r_j))}{|R_i^S|}$$

(4)

Note that this formulation is not conceptually different from other measures used in literature (e.g, (Tran et al., 2015),(Murakami et al., 2008)), that commonly assign a value to novel recommendations proportionally to their relevance and informativeness, however given the absence of prior knowledge on users' choices, we assume that semantic similarity with salient entities in news items is a clue for relevance.

In Table 3 we summarize the results of our experiments, that we run over the full dataset (see

---

[3] Since rumors on an event can be anticipated wrt the day d_0 in which the first news item is published

[4] Note that E_d^W could be straightly used for recommendation, however it would be an excessively rough strategy.

Table 3: Percentage difference in performances between W^3 and PRs on Twitter and Wikipedia

Source	Saliency	Serendipity	F-Value
Twitter d0	-28%	+91%	+15%
Wikipedia d0	+172%	+656%	+371%
Twitter d2	-34%	+81%	+8%
Wikipedia d2	+106%	+547%	+286%

Table 4: Excerpt of selected events

Date	Event
11/06/2014	Al-Qaeda Faction Seizes Key Iraqi City
14/06/2014	England vs. Italy at the 2014 World Cup
30/06/2014	Limiting Rights: Imposing Religion on Workers
05/07/2014	Wimbledon: Novak Djokovic and Roger Federer Reach Men's Final
...	
22/09/2014	Nasa's Newest Mars Mission Spacecraft Enters Orbit Around Mars

Table 2). We set the maximum number of provided recommendations $K = 10$ for Wikipedia (where clusters are smaller) and $K = 50$ for Twitter. All recommendations are gathered either the same day (d_0) of the first news item on the event e_i, or two days after $(d_2 = d_0 + 2)$. In analogy with (Murakami et al., 2008) and (Ge et al., 2010), we show the percentage difference in performance between W^3 and Primitive Recommenders (PRs). Besides *saliencey* and *serendipity*, we also compute the harmonic mean between the two (the F value). The Table shows that for Wikipedia, W^3 outperforms the PR both in saliency and serendipity (it is up to 656% more serendipitous than the baseline) while in Twitter, W^3 shows better serendipity (+91%) but lower salience (-28%). Comparatively, the performance of W^3 is much better on Wikipedia than on Twitter, probably due to the limited evidence provided by the 1% available traffic. We also noted that two days after the main event (x=2), both serendipity and saliency only slightly decrease showing that newswires have covered only a small portion of users' communication and information needs.

3.2 Manual Evaluation

In manual evaluation, in order to start from a clean representation of each event for all systems, we selected 21 relevant (with topmost number of news, tweets and wikipedia views) events in the considered 4-months period, and we manually identified the relevant news items N_i for each event e_i in a $\pm$ 1-day interval around the event peak day d_0. An excerpt of 5 events is shown in Table 4. We then automatically extracted named entities from these news items.

For each of the four systems $W^3(T)$, $W^3(W)$, $PR(T)$ and $PR(W)$ and each event e_i, we generate the first $K = 5$ *novel* recommendations, and we use the *CrowdFlower.com* platform to assess the relevance of these recommendations[5]. For each item of news, annotators are asked to decide if an entity IS or IS NOT relevant with reference to the reported news ("not sure" is also allowed). "Relevant" means that either the entity is semantically related to the domain of the news, or that it is factually related. The task was run on April 23rd, 2017, and we collected 1344 total judgements. To compute the performance of each system, we use the Mean Average Precision (MAP)[6], which takes into account the rank of recommendations. The results are shown in Table 5, which shows, in agreement with the automated evaluation of Table 3, a superiority of W^3 and also confirms that the difference between W^3 and the primitive recommender is much higher in Wikipedia than in Twitter. We also note that the absolute performance of the recommender is higher in Twitter, which is not in contradiction with Table 3, since here we are focusing on world-wide high impact news, those for which our 1% Twitter stream provides sufficient evidence to obtain clean clusters, such as those in Table 1.

3.3 Analysis of Information Needs

To analyze readers' behavior more systematically, we classified events meta-clusters automatically, extending the work in (Košmerlj et al., 2015), were the authors have manually classified 13,883 Wikipedia event-related articles in 9 categories. Furthermore, we classified recommendations, i.e., tokens in m_i^T and m_i^W meta-clusters associated to each event e_i, using BabelNet hypernymy (*IS_A*) relations[7], and their mapping onto Wikipedia Categories. In Figure 4 we plot the category distribution of Wikipedia articles (more specifically, we plot only novel recommendations extracted by W^3) that readers have accessed in correspondence of different event types. The Bubble plot shows several interesting patterns: for example,

---

[5]The saliency of $R_i^{in\text{-}news}$ is well assessed by formula (2)

[6]https://www.kaggle.com/wiki/MeanAveragePrecision
[7]http://babelnet.org/about

Source	W³	BR
Twitter	0.934	0.851
Wikipedia	0.789	0.363

Table 5: MAP (mean average precision) of compared systems in Crowdflower.com evaluation (on a sample of 21 breakings news)

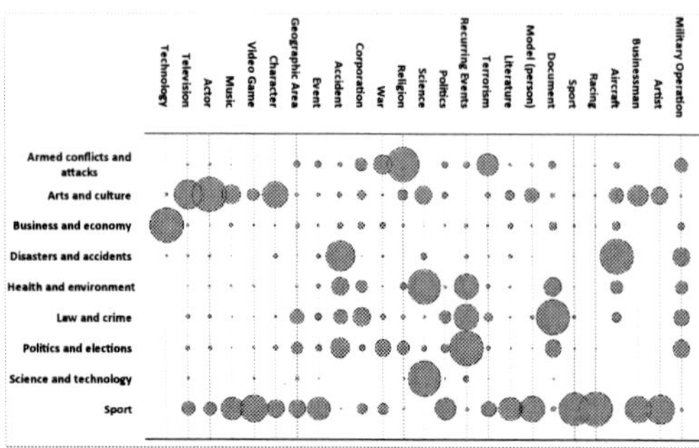

Figure 4: Bubble plot of event categories and associated information needs (during Summer 2014)

Religion is the main searched category for events classified as Armed Conflicts and Attacks, mirroring the fact that religion is perceived as being highly related with latest world-wide conflicts. Accordingly, users try to deepen their knowledge on these aspects. Disasters and accidents mostly include members in the same Wikipedia category (Disasters) and also Aircraft, since the Malaysia crash was the dominating event in the considered period. Business and Economy draw the attention of readers mostly when related to Technology, e.g., new devices being launched. Law and Crime events induce in readers the need to find out more about specific laws and treaties (the category Documents). Finally, we note that Sport is the event category showing the highest dispersion of information needs. While many of the bubbles in Figure 4 indeed show real information needs (e.g, VideoGames refers to the many sport games launched on the market, Model (person) refers to gossip about football players, and in general all people and media related categories refer to the participation of celebrities in sporting events), a number of bubbles can be considered as noise, e.g., Literature, Politics. In fact, Sport was the dominating event type during the considered period (2014 World Football Cup), therefore it is reasonable that sport-related clusters are those cumulating the highest number of system errors.

References

R. Brooker and T. Schaefer. 2005. *Public Opinion in the 21st Century: Let the People Speak?.* New directions in political behavior series. Houghton Mifflin Company.

J. Camacho-Collados, M. Taher Pilehvar, and R. Navigli. 2016. Nasari: Integrating explicit knowledge and corpus statistics for a multilingual representation of concepts and entities. *Artificial Intelligence* 240:36–64.

M. Ge, C. Delgado-Battenfeld, and D. Jannach. 2010. Beyond accuracy: Evaluating recommender systems by coverage and serendipity. In *Proc. of RecSys'10.* pages 257–260.

P. J. Gloviczki. 2015. *Journalism in the Age of Social Media*, Palgrave Macmillan US, pages 1–23.

J. Hu, G. Wang, F. Lochovsky, J. Sun, and Z. Chen. 2009. Understanding user's query intent with wikipedia. In *Proc. of WWW'09.* pages 471–480.

M. Knight. 2012. Journalism as usual: The use of social media as a newsgathering tool in the coverage of the iranian elections in 2009. *Journal of Media Practice* 13(1):61–74.

A. Košmerlj, E. Belyaeva, G. Leban, M. Grobelnik, and B. Fortuna. 2015. Towards a complete event type taxonomy. In *Proc. of WWW'15.* pages 899–902.

J. Lehmann, B. Gonçalves, J. J. Ramasco, and C. Cattuto. 2012. Dynamical classes of collective attention in twitter. In *Proc. of WWW'12.* pages 251–260.

J. Leskovec, L. Backstrom, and J. Kleinberg. 2009. Meme-tracking and the dynamics of the news cycle. In *Proc. of KDD '09.* pages 497–506.

T. Murakami, K. Mori, and R. Orihara. 2008. Metrics for evaluating the serendipity of recommendation lists. In *Proc. of the 2007 Conf. on New Frontiers in AI.* Springer, pages 40–46.

R. Navigli and S. P. Ponzetto. 2010. BabelNet: Building a very large multilingual semantic network. In *Proc. of the 48th Annual Meeting of the ACL.* pages 216–225.

G. Stilo and P. Velardi. 2016. Efficient temporal mining of micro-blog texts and its application to event discovery. *Data Min. Knowl. Discov.* 30(2):372–402.

T. Tran, C. Niedere, N. Kanhabua, U. Gadiraju, and A. Anand. 2015. Balancing novelty and salience: Adaptive learning to rank entities for timeline summarization of high-impact events. In *Proc. of CICM'15.* Springer, volume 19, pages 1201–1210.

A. Weiler, M. Grossniklaus, and M.H. Scholl. 2014. Event identification and tracking in social media streaming data. In *Proc. of the Work. of the EDBT/ICDT'14.* CEUR-WS, pages 282–287.

Comparing Attitudes to Climate Change in the Media using sentiment analysis based on Latent Dirichlet Allocation

Ye Jiang[1], Xingyi Song[1], Jackie Harrison[2], Shaun Quegan[3], and Diana Maynard[1]

[1]Department of Computer Science
[2] Department of Journalism Studies
[3]School of Mathematics and Statistics
University of Sheffield, Western Bank, Sheffield, S10 2TN, UK
{*yjiang18,x.song,j.harrison,s.quegan,d.maynard*}@*sheffield.ac.uk*

Abstract

News media typically present biased accounts of news stories, and different publications present different angles on the same event. In this research, we investigate how different publications differ in their approach to stories about climate change, by examining the sentiment and topics presented. To understand these attitudes, we find sentiment targets by combining Latent Dirichlet Allocation (LDA) with SentiWordNet, a general sentiment lexicon. Using LDA, we generate topics containing keywords which represent the sentiment targets, and then annotate the data using SentiWordNet before regrouping the articles based on topic similarity. Preliminary analysis identifies clearly different attitudes on the same issue presented in different news sources. Ongoing work is investigating how systematic these attitudes are between different publications, and how these may change over time.

1 Introduction

Editorial decisions in newspaper articles are influenced by diverse forces and ideologies. News publications do not always present unbiased accounts, but typically present frames reflecting opinions and attitudes which can heavily influence the readers' perspectives (Spence and Pidgeon, 2010). Climate change is a controversial issue in which this kind of framing is very apparent. Although bias among different news sources has been discussed previously (Fortuna et al., 2009; Evgenia and van Der Goot, 2008), sentiment analysis has not been commonly applied to newspaper articles for this purpose.

Sentiment analysis is typically implemented on short documents such as Twitter (Pak and Paroubek, 2010; Agarwal et al., 2011) and customer reviews (Pang et al., 2008; Shelke et al., 2017). However, newspaper articles have diverse context length, so their content is much more complicated than other types of sources, especially as these articles are normally cross-domain. A variety of topics might be discussed in the context of a particular climate change issue. Thus, we need to understand what the target of the opinion is in each case, i.e. which aspect of climate change the opinion is about. For instance, using the methods described in this work, we found in reports about the IPCC 2008 (Intergovernmental Panel on Climate Change) that The Independent talked about carbon dioxide emission, but The Guardian concentrated on issues of rising sea levels.

Furthermore, unlike with short documents where one can just find a single sentiment for that document, in order to understand the overall opinion in articles about climate change, we need to look at each opinion and its target separately, as multiple targets may be addressed in a single article. Additionally, even when reporting on the same event and topic, different newspaper sources will have diverse focuses. However, unlike with tweets or customer reviews, newspaper articles must give at least some semblance of objectivity, and often refrain from using explicit positive or negative vocabulary.

In this paper, we examine a set of articles about climate change in four UK broadsheets during the last decade. It is impractical to manually identify topics and analyse all the opinions about them in this large set. We therefore propose a topic modelling method to generate topics using Latent Dirichlet Allocation (LDA), and then cluster the articles into groups with similar topics. Then we perform sentiment analysis on each cluster, in or-

Proceedings of the 2017 EMNLP Workshop on Natural Language Processing meets Journalism, pages 25–30
Copenhagen, Denmark, September 7, 2017. ©2017 Association for Computational Linguistics

der to investigate the opinions, how they differ in the 4 sources, and how they may have changed over time.

2 Related Work

Research on sentiment analysis for news articles is not entirely new (Yi et al., 2003; Wilson et al., 2005). Henley et al. (2002) analysed violence-related reports in different newspapers and found that there is a significant difference between the manner of reporting the same violence-related issues. They also found newspaper sentiments reflecting the corresponding ideologies of the editors. However, they applied their content analysis on a limited number of articles, so that the vocabulary for the analysis was also small and strict. Wiebe et al. (2004) applied a classification task for detecting subjectivity and objectivity in newspaper articles. Their work depended on several newspaper datasets which were manually labelled.

Sentiment analysis has been more commonly implemented on newspaper titles. Strapparava and Mihalcea (2007) automatically classified titles with a valence indication, while Burget et al. (2011) proposed a method that classified 6 emotions in Czech newspapers based on their headlines. Burscher et al. (2016) proposed selection and baseline approaches to analyse sentiments in headlines and entire articles respectively, with clustering performed by combining K-means cluster analysis and sentiment analysis. Others have analysed the quotations in newspaper articles. Balahur et al. (2009) extracted annotated quotations from Europe Media Monitor (EMM), and classified them into positive and negative classes using several sentiment lexicons and a Support Vector Machine (SVM) classifier. Both quotations and headlines are short pieces of text, which means that the sentiment analysis is less noisy, and also that the source and target of the sentiment could easily be identified. However, those short pieces of text could not always reveal the insights of news, missing much useful information.

LDA is a generative probabilistic model which has been used to extract abstract topics from documents. It investigates the hidden semantic structure from large amounts of text without requiring manual coding, thus reducing time and cost (Blei et al., 2003). Feuerriegel et al. (2016) applied LDA to extract 40 topics from German financial newspaper articles and found that some topics have an important effect on the stock price market. Xu and Raschid (2016) also developed two probabilistic financial community models to extract topics from financial contracts. However, the implementation of LDA on newspaper articles is less known.

3 Method

3.1 Data

The data for our experiment consists of 11,720 newspaper articles collected from 4 UK broadsheets – *The Guardian, The Times, The Telegraph* and *The Independent* – between 2007 and 2016. These articles were extracted from LexisNexis by searching all four sources for those containing the keywords "Climate Change" at least 3 times in total.

3.2 Pre-processing

In order to identify the topics that can best represent events and issues with respect to climate change, we use a part of speech tagger to annotate all the words, and only keep the nouns for the LDA model. For the sentiment analysis, all words are included.

3.3 LDA model

Typically, the number of topics in the LDA model is determined by computing the log-likelihood or perplexity. However, Bigelow (2002) has shown that predictive likelihood (or equivalently, perplexity) and human judgment are often not correlated, and even sometimes slightly anti-correlated. In this paper, we therefore treat the topics as clusters, and apply the Silhouette Coefficient instead. This method has been previously used for finding the optimal number of topics (Panichella et al., 2013; Ma et al., 2016), and is suitable for our LDA approach, since LDA is fully unsupervised. Nevertheless, in future work, it may be worth evaluating some probability measures such as log-likelihood and perplexity, and comparing the performance using these methods.

$$Sil = \frac{b - a}{max(a, b)} \tag{1}$$

where a is the mean distance between a point and other points in the same cluster, and b is the mean distance between a point and other points in the next nearest cluster. In the silhouette analysis (Ma et al., 2016), silhouette coefficients close to +1 indicate that the samples in the cluster are far away

Sources	Topics
The Guardian	copenhagen,world,deal,agreement,summit,president,obama,china,action,treaty
The Times	copenhagen, world, cent, deal, president, summit, agreement, conference, china, year
The Telegraph	world, carbon, copenhagen, summit, deal, cent, agreement, energy, time, president
The Independent	world, carbon, copenhagen, deal, cent, agreement, year, conference, cancun, government

Table 1: Topics in 2009

Topic_ID	Keywords
Topic 1	0.31*food 0.84*land 0.79*world ...
Topic 2	0.53*year 0.98*science 0.03*time ...
Topic 3	0.29*world 0.21*car 0.18*weather...

Table 2: Example of Topic list in The Guardian 2007

Articles	Topic_ID	Distributions
Article 1	1	0.519842
Article 2	12	0.348175
Article 3	7, 12	0.412394, 0.1492813
Article 4	2	0.249132

Table 3: Example of topic-document matrix

from the neighbouring clusters. In contrast, a negative silhouette coefficient means that the samples might have been assigned to the wrong cluster.

In our case, we repeatedly ran the analysis on the entire dataset with a different number of topics (0-30) and added the silhouette value for each number of topics to the plot in Figure 1. We can see that when the number of topics reaches 20, it has the highest silhouette coefficient score which indicates the best clustering result.

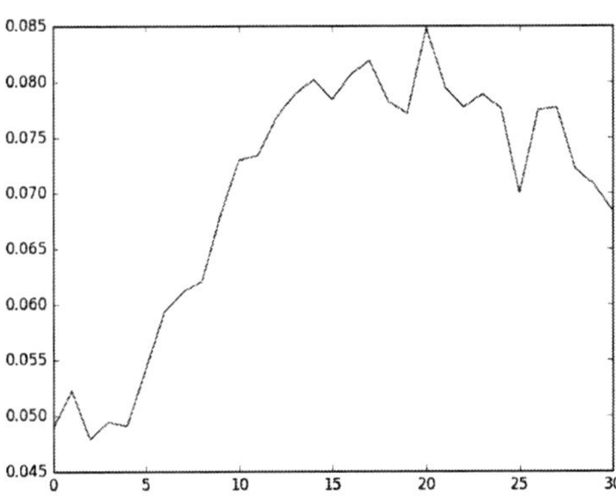

Figure 1: Silhouette analysis for LDA model

Once the number of topics has been determined at 20, the LDA assigns keywords to one of the topics of the news article, based on the probability of the keywords occurring in the topics. This assignment also gives topic representations of all the articles. We repeatedly updated the assignment for 50 iterations to generate both topic distribution in the articles and word distribution in the topics. For each topic in the LDA model, we select the top 10 keywords with their distribution to represent the corresponding topic (see Table 2).

Each article is assigned to a set of topics, and each topic generates a set of keywords based on the vocabulary of the articles. After acquiring the topics from the LDA model, we convert the bag-of-words model into a topic-document matrix, which can be seen as a lower dimensionality matrix (Table 3).

We then select the highest distribution topic among 20 topics from each news article in different news sources.

3.4 Applying SentiWordNet

To automatically annotate the articles with sentiment labels, we use SentiWordNet[1], which contains roughly 155,000 words associated with positive and negative sentiment scores. The keywords in each topic indicate the sentiment targets to be annotated with the corresponding score from SentiWordNet. For each article, the scores for all targets are combined and normalised (to a score between -1 and +1) to deal with the fact that some clusters have more articles than others. The different attitudes of each news source on the same climate change issue can then be analysed once we have a score for each article. For this, we manually check the keywords in the topic lists in each news source in each year, and group those topics containing at least two of the same keywords. Specifically, we analysed every keyword in each topic ID from 2007 to 2016 in each news source, and extract the keywords which occur in each topic. Then we also extract the topic IDs based on those keywords, and group the IDs based on the topics that contain at least two identical keywords. We assume that those news articles have similar or the same topics, as well as sentiment targets, though this also requires verification. We note that

---

[1] http://sentiwordnet.isti.cnr.it/

Detected Sentences
Positive
China itself defended its crucial role in saving the Copenhagen conference from failure. (The Guardian, 28 Dec, 2009)
Don't panic. Copenhagen really wasn't such a disaster. (The Independent,15 Dec, 2009)
Negative
The move emerged from the chaotic Copenhagen conference on climate change. (The Telegraph, 21 Dec, 2009)
Copenhagen puts nuclear options at risk. (The Times, 23 Dec, 2009)

Table 4: Example sentences with sentiment polarity detected in the four news source in 2009.

the current method of grouping similar topics between news sources manually could introduce human bias. Future work will look at ways to avoid this.

4 Results and Discussion

We compared the 4 news sources by analysing the clusters we identified. For some years, there was no single topic that appeared in the clusters (probably because different newspapers attached different levels of importance to most topics). One example that stands out, however, is the reporting by all 4 broadsheets of the Copenhagen Summit in 2009 (see Table 1). The clusters all contain the keywords "copenhagen" and "agreement", which refer to the Copenhagen Summit explicitly. This feature identified the main topics that also can be seen as the sentiment targets. We utilised this feature to compare the different attitudes toward the same issue (Copenhagen Summit) between four news sources. However, the keywords are mostly different between the sources in other years. For instance, some topics in *The Guardian* and *The Times* have large numbers of keywords such as "gas" and "energy" in 2012, but topics in the *The Telegraph* in that year are associated with the keyword "wind", while *The Independent* has keywords like "government" and "investment".

In Figure 2, we show how sentiment differs between the reports about the Copenhagen Summit in 2009 in the 4 newspapers. Table 4 gives also some examples of positive and negative sentences found. A manual check of a random selection of the relevant articles confirms the general tendency. Most of the articles used some negative words, such as "failures", "collapse", "drastic". However, Figure 2 indicates that the overall sentiment is relatively impartial to positive (the average sentiment score across all sources is +0.15). *The Guardian* is the most positive, while *The Times* is the most negative. We suspect that some of the keywords may be a bit misleading (e.g agreement is typically positive), which might influence the sentiment analysis.

However, there are some clear indications that match the automatic analysis results. While *The Guardian* does have some quite negative reports about the summit, mentioning things like "catastrophic warming", it also tries to focus on the hope aspect ("The talks live. There is climate hope. A bit. Just."). *The Independent* tends also towards the positive, talking about leaders achieving "greater and warmer agreement". The Telegraph, on the other hand, plays more on the fear and alarmist aspect, talking about "drastic action" and "imminent dangerous climate change", although also about positive steps towards the future. The Times, on the other hand, emphasises the role of honesty; although its overall tone is not overwhelmingly negative, it does mention repeatedly the fear and alarmist aspect of climate change and some of the negative points about the summit (for example that Obama will not be there).

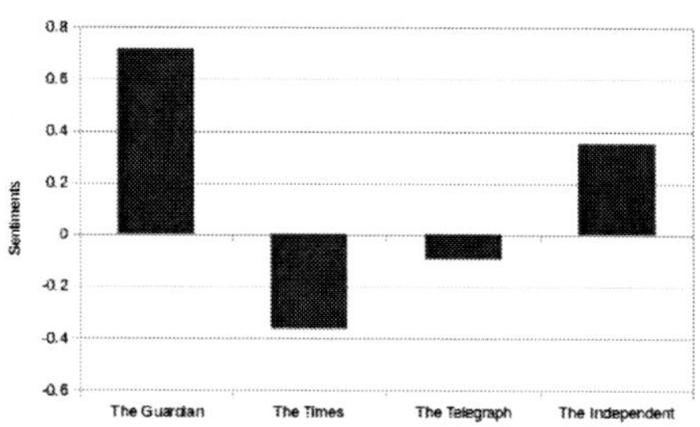

Figure 2: Attitudes of four news sources to the Copenhagen Summit in 2009

In future work, we plan a number of improvements. SentiWordNet is not ideal because it does not cover all the terminology in the specific domain of climate change, nor does it deal with context (see (Maynard and Bontcheva, 2016) for a discussion on these points). We will therefore develop a semi-supervised learning approach, based on a small corpus of manually annotated news articles that we will create, combining lexicon-based and corpus-based methods with co-training, in order to take the best of each. The lexicon-based method will combine LDA with word-embeddings to build a domain-specific lexicon, while the corpus-based method will use a stacked denoising auto-encoder to extract features from news articles. The preliminary results demonstrate the comparison of attitudes between different publications in a single year. However, the attitude towards such climate change topic may change over time. Ongoing work is investigating how the attitudes may change over time between different publications.

5 Conclusion

In this paper, we have described a methodology and a first experiment aimed at understanding the attitudes expressed by different newspapers when reporting about climate change. Traditionally, these kind of analyses have only been carried out manually, and are therefore limited to small case studies. Our aim, however, is to apply such techniques on a large scale, looking at thousands of documents and studying the differences over time, geographic area and newspaper type. While this is only one example about different attitudes to an event, it nevertheless shows a nice case study about how we might use the approach to analyse the different attitudes expressed in the news about the same topic.

Due to the difficulty of annotating news articles manually, and the fact that existing labelled data is rare, an unsupervised approach is more suitable in this case. In contrast to most of the existing sentiment classification approaches, our method is fully unsupervised, which provides more flexibility than other supervised approaches. The preliminary results demonstrate that our method is able to extract similar topics from different publications and to explicitly compare the attitudes expressed by different publications while reporting similar topics.

The methodology is domain-independent and could also be applied to different languages given appropriate lexical resources. Besides the co-training approach mentioned above, there are a number of other ways to extend this work: in particular, we aim to extend the sentiment analysis to consider not just positive and negative attitudes, but also the emotions expressed, and to analyse the effect this might have on readers. The current method also ignored word ordering, so that issues like negation are not considered. We therefore will extend our method to include higher order information in our future experiments.

References

Apoorv Agarwal, Boyi Xie, Ilia Vovsha, Owen Rambow, and Rebecca Passonneau. 2011. Sentiment analysis of twitter data. In *Proceedings of the workshop on languages in social media*. Association for Computational Linguistics, pages 30–38.

Alexandra Balahur, Ralf Steinberger, Erik Van Der Goot, Bruno Pouliquen, and Mijail Kabadjov. 2009. Opinion mining on newspaper quotations. In *Web Intelligence and Intelligent Agent Technologies, 2009. WI-IAT'09. IEEE/WIC/ACM International Joint Conferences on*. IEEE, volume 3, pages 523–526.

Cindi Bigelow. 2002. Reading the tea leaves. *New England Journal of Entrepreneurship* 5(1):1.

David M Blei, Andrew Y Ng, and Michael I Jordan. 2003. Latent dirichlet allocation. *Journal of machine Learning research* 3(Jan):993–1022.

Radim Burget, Jan Karasek, and Zdeněk Smekal. 2011. Recognition of emotions in czech newspaper headlines. *Radioengineering* 20(1):39–47.

Bjorn Burscher, Rens Vliegenthart, and Claes H de Vreese. 2016. Frames beyond words: applying cluster and sentiment analysis to news coverage of the nuclear power issue. *Social Science Computer Review* 34(5):530–545.

Belyaeva Evgenia and Erik van Der Goot. 2008. News bias of online headlines across languages. *The study of conflict between Russia and Georgia* 73:74.

Stefan Feuerriegel, Antal Ratku, and Dirk Neumann. 2016. Analysis of how underlying topics in financial news affect stock prices using latent dirichlet allocation. In *System Sciences (HICSS), 2016 49th Hawaii International Conference on*. IEEE, pages 1072–1081.

Blaz Fortuna, Carolina Galleguillos, and Nello Cristianini. 2009. Detection of bias in media outlets with statistical learning methods. *Text Mining* page 27.

Nancy M Henley, Michelle D Miller, Jo Anne Beazley, Diane N Nguyen, Dana Kaminsky, and Robert Sanders. 2002. Frequency and specificity of referents to violence in news reports of anti-gay attacks. *Discourse & Society* 13(1):75–104.

Shutian Ma, Chengzhi Zhang, and Daqing He. 2016. Document representation methods for clustering bilingual documents. *Proceedings of the Association for Information Science and Technology* 53(1):1–10.

Diana Maynard and K. Bontcheva. 2016. Challenges of Evaluating Sentiment Analysis Tools on Social Media. In *Proceedings of LREC 2016*. Portoroz, Slovenia.

Alexander Pak and Patrick Paroubek. 2010. Twitter as a corpus for sentiment analysis and opinion mining. In *LREc*. volume 10.

Bo Pang, Lillian Lee, et al. 2008. Opinion mining and sentiment analysis. *Foundations and Trends® in Information Retrieval* 2(1–2):1–135.

Annibale Panichella, Bogdan Dit, Rocco Oliveto, Massimiliano Di Penta, Denys Poshyvanyk, and Andrea De Lucia. 2013. How to effectively use topic models for software engineering tasks? an approach based on genetic algorithms. In *Proceedings of the 2013 International Conference on Software Engineering*. IEEE Press, pages 522–531.

Nilesh Shelke, Shriniwas Deshpande, and Vilas Thakare. 2017. Domain independent approach for aspect oriented sentiment analysis for product reviews. In *Proceedings of the 5th International Conference on Frontiers in Intelligent Computing: Theory and Applications*. Springer, pages 651–659.

Alexa Spence and Nick Pidgeon. 2010. Framing and communicating climate change: The effects of distance and outcome frame manipulations. *Global Environmental Change* 20(4):656–667.

Carlo Strapparava and Rada Mihalcea. 2007. Semeval-2007 task 14: Affective text. In *Proceedings of the 4th International Workshop on Semantic Evaluations*. Association for Computational Linguistics, pages 70–74.

Janyce Wiebe, Theresa Wilson, Rebecca Bruce, Matthew Bell, and Melanie Martin. 2004. Learning subjective language. *Computational linguistics* 30(3):277–308.

Theresa Wilson, Janyce Wiebe, and Paul Hoffmann. 2005. Recognizing contextual polarity in phrase-level sentiment analysis. In *Proceedings of the conference on human language technology and empirical methods in natural language processing*. Association for Computational Linguistics, pages 347–354.

Zheng Xu and Louiqa Raschid. 2016. Probabilistic financial community models with latent dirichlet allocation for financial supply chains. In *Proceedings of the Second International Workshop on Data Science for Macro-Modeling*. ACM, page 8.

Jeonghee Yi, Tetsuya Nasukawa, Razvan Bunescu, and Wayne Niblack. 2003. Sentiment analyzer: Extracting sentiments about a given topic using natural language processing techniques. In *Data Mining, 2003. ICDM 2003. Third IEEE International Conference on*. IEEE, pages 427–434.

Language-based Construction of Explorable News Graphs for Journalists

Rémi Bois and **Guillaume Gravier**
CNRS, IRISA & INRIA Rennes
263 Avenue Général Leclerc
35042 Rennes, France

Eric Jamet and **Maxime Robert**
CRPCC, Université de Rennes 2
Place du recteur Henri Le Moal
35043 Rennes, France

Emmanuel Morin
LS2N, Université de Nantes
2 Chemin de la Houssinière
44300 Nantes, France

Pascale Sébillot
INSA Rennes, IRISA & INRIA Rennes
263 Avenue Général Leclerc
35042 Rennes, France

Abstract

Faced with ever-growing news archives, media professionals are in need of advanced tools to explore the information surrounding specific events. This problem is most commonly answered by browsing news datasets, going from article to article and viewing unaltered original content. In this article, we introduce an efficient way to generate links between news items, allowing such browsing through an easily explorable graph, and enrich this graph by automatically typing links in order to inform the user on the nature of the relation between two news pieces. User evaluations are conducted on real world data with journalists in order to assess for the interest of both the graph representation and link typing in a press reviewing task, showing the system to be of significant help for their work.

1 Introduction

With content being massively made accessible grows the need for analytics and efficient organization of news collections so as to help users search and explore large amounts of content to gain knowledge and insight. Entity extraction and linking, along with topic and event detection, are now widely available to journalists in order to describe content and help search pieces of information. While these techniques are instrumental to content description and search, they are not sufficient to user-friendly exploration and navigation of a collection to gain insight, e.g., to summarize or to synthesize information. In the absence of a precise search intent, exploration is much more adapted than search.

News data have been extensively studied due to the relatively large accessibility and interest to both media professionals and general public, however mostly from the search angle. Typical search-based approaches consist in organizing datasets around clusters, in which similar or topically close news articles are grouped. The created clusters can be further processed to be displayed as threads (Ide et al., 2004), or according to temporal relations (Muller and Tannier, 2004). However, pitfalls appear when dealing with large timeframes, as the number of clusters to display becomes overwhelming. In this work, we rather focus on an exploration scenario without precise information need, where one has to get a comprehensive view on a topic in a limited amount of time, and for which the methods mentioned above are not suited. For this scenario, the usual approach consists in creating links between pairs of documents within the collection, allowing users to directly go from one news piece to another. By following links, the user is able to navigate the collection, choosing his next step among a limited set of links that are related to the news item he is currently viewing. Structures created by connecting pairs of news pieces can be seen as graphs, in which nodes correspond to documents, and edges are links between document pairs. Such collection structuring can lead to interesting applications, such as the ability to find a path connecting two arbitrary nodes, connecting the dots between two information pieces (Shahaf and Guestrin, 2010). In this context, we put forward the notion of *explorable* graphs linking news pieces in such a way that media professionals can easily find all relevant information on a topic by browsing the graph. Departing from standard approaches, e.g., $\mathcal{E}$-NN graphs, we propose a novel nearest neighbor graph construction algorithm based on lexical similarity that creates links in a reasonable number to avoid user overload and disorientation, yet ensur-

Proceedings of the 2017 EMNLP Workshop on Natural Language Processing meets Journalism, pages 31–36
Copenhagen, Denmark, September 7, 2017. ©2017 Association for Computational Linguistics

ing relevance and serendipitous drift. We further propose a typology of links between news pieces along with rules for automatic link categorization. These two elements, graph construction and link categorization, result in an explorable organization of large collections of news. We prove the interest of this organization to media professionals, and in particular that of link categorization, by means of user tests, where journalists were asked to write a synthesis on a particular topic in a limited amount of time.

2 Explorable news graph

Related studies on music recommendation have proven that explorability, or browsing capabilities, have a big impact on user experience (Seyerlehner et al., 2009) but, to the best of our knowledge, no attempts have been made at formalizing a list of necessary properties for explorable recommendations. We thus propose a set of intuitive properties that a graph should exhibit to be explorable:
Property 1: A link between two nodes indicates that those nodes are related in some way. The user should not be faced with senseless links that would lead to disorientation;
Property 2: There exists a path between any two given nodes. This ensures that the user can drift away from his original topic of interest and discover new information;
Property 3: The shortest path between any two given nodes should be reasonably small. The user can go from one topic to another in a relatively small number of steps;
Property 4: There is a reasonable amount of outgoing links for any given node. This ensures that the user is not overloaded by the number of proposed links;
Property 5: The amount of incoming links is proportional to the popularity of the node. The user should easily get access to the main topics of the collection.

The two main approaches to create graphs are the $\mathcal{E}$ nearest neighbors ($\mathcal{E}$-NN) and the K nearest neighbors (K-NN). They consist in linking each node to its closest neighbors–closeness being calculated by means of similarity measures–and rely on a fixed threshold that is either a number of neighbors K for K-NN or a similarity score $\mathcal{E}$ for $\mathcal{E}$-NN. In practice, finding their respective optimal thresholds, K or $\mathcal{E}$, is difficult and requires some annotation to estimate the ratio of irrelevant links,

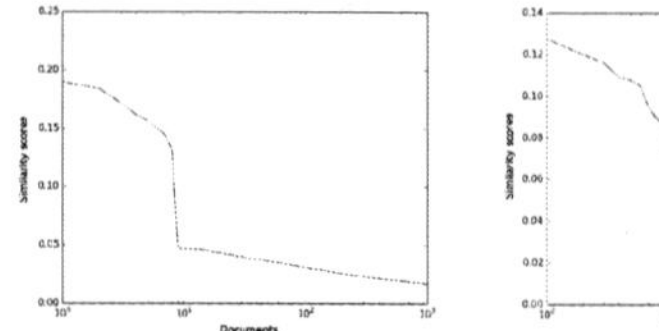

Figure 1: Illustration of similarity drops between close neighbors and far ones on two real-world examples.

a process that is often complex and subjective (Ge et al., 2010). Moreover, graphs created with those methods exhibit some strong limitations in terms of explorability. K-NN graphs do not discriminate between news that are heavily discussed, and that could thus rightfully be linked to many other news pieces, and news that are reported by only a few medias, with few connections to other items. Using the same threshold K for the whole collection thus leads to links that are too few for some news items, and too numerous for others. The use of a distance threshold in $\mathcal{E}$-NN graphs skirts this issue by reducing the number of unrelevant links. However, $\mathcal{E}$-NN graphs tend to create very large hubs (Radovanović et al., 2010) , with a few nodes being connected to hundreds of others, causing navigation in such structures to be cumbersome.

Since the existence of a unique threshold for the entire collection leads to poorly crafted graphs, we propose a new method allowing to adapt the threshold on a per node basis, automatically deciding on the appropriate number of near neighbors by detecting a large gap in the representation space between close neighbors and far ones. Such gaps are known to happen naturally in large collections such as social graphs (Danisch et al., 2013) and are linked to the variations of the density of points in the representation space (Kriegel et al., 2011). For an item i corresponding to node v_i, the gap corresponds to a drop in the similarity between item i and other items sorted in descending order of similarity. Only items appearing before the gap are linked to item i. In our experiments, standard NLP approaches are used for lexical similarity scoring and drop detection. First, a tf-idf weighting and a cosine similarity measure allow us to obtain efficient similarity scores for document pairs. Then, after sorting in descending order all documents according to their similarity with a node/document of interest, we detect the largest drop in similar-

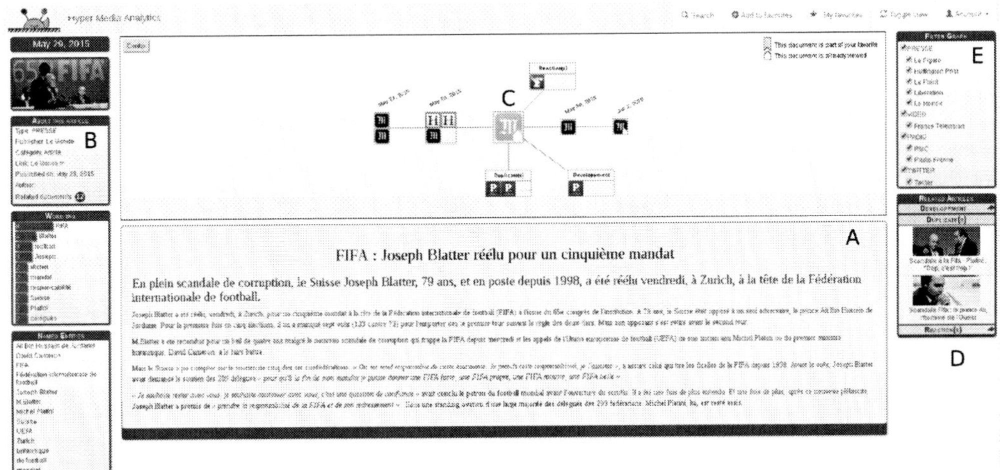

Figure 2: The LIMAH news exploration and analytics interface

ity among consecutive documents. The shallow lexical representation described above allows us to detect such drops, as illustrated in Figure 1, which do not appear when using semantic vectorial representations such as averaged word2vec or doc2vec (Mikolov et al., 2013).

Even with explorable graphs, the connection existing between two nodes can sometimes be puzzling to the user. We thus propose to characterize links between nodes according to a typology specifically crafted for news collections. News data depend a lot on chronology, which resulted in many approaches organizing collections as timelines so as to be able to follow the evolution of specific stories. The temporal relation is clearly the most important type of relations according to media professionals (Gravier et al., 2016). But it is insufficient alone, in particular when exploring large news datasets that include articles with very similar content from different newswires that tends to clutter timelines. Extending temporal relations, we used a typology consisting of 7 types of oriented links (Bois et al., 2015) defined as follows:

Near duplicate identifies a link between two nodes discussing the same event, where the target node provides little to no additional information compared to the source node;

Anterior/Posterior indicates a target node reporting on an event related to the source that occurred before (resp. after) the event of the source node;

Summary/Development corresponds to a link providing a subset (resp. superset) of information with respect to the source;

Reacts/In reaction to designates a reference (resp. followup) to another news piece in the collection.

In order to automatically categorize each link according to the above typology, we apply a set of handcrafted rules. Near duplicates are detected first based on a cosine similarity over tf-idf weighted terms. Summaries and developments are then detected by comparing documents' lengths. We then assign the reaction type by detecting cue phrases such as "reacted to", "answered to", or "declared that". Remaining links are considered as temporal relations and given the anterior/posterior type depending on publication dates.

3 Explorability evaluation and user validation

In order to assess for the explorability of graphs created with our novel method, we performed experiments on dataset (Gasparetti, 2016) composed of a five month monitoring of Google News over 4 categories (health, science, business, and entertainment), each of them containing around 15,000 articles. While this dataset provides a groundtruth based on clusters rather than pairing of documents, it can be used as a estimation of the correctness of our approach: elements that we link and belong to the same cluster can be considered as correct, and elements that we link but do not belong to the same cluster can be considered as incorrect. Since a perfect precision in these conditions would lead to a poorly explorable graph only composed of separate clusters, the goal here is rather to obtain explorable graphs while maintaining a high precision. Results revealed that not only our parameter-free method obtained good precision scores around the 70% mark, but also managed to regroup most nodes (over 93% of them) in a single component allowing users to drift away from topic to topic in a single walk. Results not reported within the scope of this paper show that our method builds graphs that offer much better trade-offs between precision and connectivity than K-NN and $\mathcal{E}$-NN graphs.

Interest to media professionals was evaluated by means of user testing involving journalism students. We ran experiments on a French news dataset gathered online. Documents were extracted over a 3 week period from a number of French newswires websites and include press articles, videos, and radio podcasts. Podcasts and videos underwent speech transcription so as to obtain textual representations. To deal with possibly long audio or video recordings, topic segmentation based on automatic transcripts (Guinaudeau et al., 2012) was used, each segment being treated as a document per se. In total, the resulting collection contains 4,966 news articles, 1,556 radio segments and 290 video segments. We ran our nearest neighbors algorithm on the collection as well as link categorization, creating 17,468 links in total: 10,980 temporal, 3,878 quasi-duplicates, 725 reactions, and 575 summaries/developments.

The starting point of the end-user interface[1] , called LIMAH for Linking Media in Acceptable Hypergraphs, is a full-fledged search bar using keywords. Search classically returns a list of documents ranked by relevance, from which the user can choose an entry point for navigation. Selecting an entry point brings the user to the content visualization and navigation part of the interface, composed of 5 parts, illustrated in Fig. 2. In this view, the user can initially see the entry point document itself (A) and the links that departs from it. In addition to the original content, metadata and keywords are displayed (B), as both were judged crucial in the preliminary usefulness studies (Gravier et al., 2016). Links appear in one of two ways. The graph view (C) quickly shows how related documents appear on a navigable section, facilitating the comprehension of the development of

---

[1]Demo available on `http://limahweb.irisa.fr/texmix/`

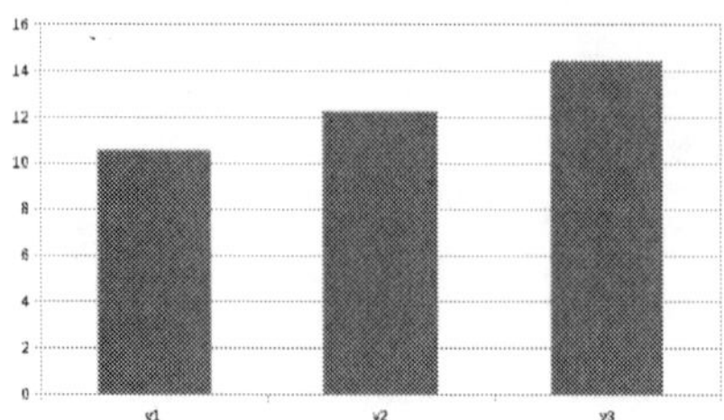

Figure 3: Knowledge extracted from the dataset depending on the version of the LIMAH interface.

a story. Users can navigate the graph: a mouseover on a node highlights the keywords in common with the entry point document; a click on a node enables viewing the content in zones A and C. To enable further exploration, a double click on a node defines the node as the new entry point and changes the graph and metadata displayed. For convenience, on the right side (D), links are also provided as a list of recommendations organized by link types, omitting chronological links that only appear on the graph section. At any time, filters listed in the top right section (E) allow selecting specific sources and a new entry point can be found from the search bar.

In order to evaluate the interest of the graph structure and link typing to professionals, we compare three versions of the interface. Version 1 only provides the search engine, allowing for comparison with today's usage and with a technology that users are very familiar with. In this case, areas C, D, and E are hidden. Version 2 adds the recommendation and graph structure but converts all link types to temporal, organizing data in a linear fashion. Recommendations in zone D are thus uncategorized and every link in zone C is shown on a timeline. Version 3 corresponds to the whole interface, as presented above.

The study involved 25 journalism students in their last years of studies, split in three test pools of 8 to 9 people. The user test involved a pre questionnaire, an information gathering task, a post questionnaire, and a final open discussion in which users could provide feedback on their use of the tool. Users were shown a short video explaining how to use the interface, and received no additional support during tests. The information gathering task consisted in writing a synthesis about a particular subject in a limited amount of time, using the interface to find as much relevant information on the topic as possible. The chosen topic was Solar Impulse 2, a solar-powered aircraft that circumnavigated the globe from March 2015 to July 2016. Bad weather conditions necessitating the plane to land and consequences of this unexpected halt are reported in 17 articles in the dataset, representing a total of 68 distinct information pieces over a long timespan. As the dataset comes from a large set of newswires, some pieces of information are repeated, while others are mentioned by only one or two sources. Users had to complete this task in 20 minutes, a time long enough to fully read a few articles, but short enough to forbid reading totally most of them.

A preliminary manual annotation was performed on each document related to the Solar Impulse topic in order to list all individual facts and the documents in which they appeared. This annotation was used to assess for the exhaustiveness of the syntheses created by users. Exhaustiveness was measured by coding each synthesis according to the proportion of the 68 information pieces it contains. Figure 3 shows the average number of information pieces gathered by users for each version of the system under test. On average, versions 2 and 3 allowed to retrieve more information more efficiently. Results show that 10.57 (resp. 12.10 and 14.44) pieces of information were found for version 1 (resp. version 2 and version 3). Moreover, version 3 allowed to retrieve rarer pieces of information that appear in only a few documents in the collection. Surprisingly enough, the superiority of version 3 is not due to a higher amount of documents viewed by users. Rather, as shown in Figure 4, users of version 3 saw on average less documents than users of version 2, indicating that the better explorability lead to a better choice of which articles to read rather than an ability to read more of them.

During the open discussion following the tests, users from version 3 were mostly positive about their experience with the tool, calling it "useful", with a "good accessibility", and an "interesting take on recommendation". A few users mentioned a difficulty to handle the back and forth between the graph representation and the search interface.

4 Conclusion

Appropriate graph representations of news articles can help professionals gather information more efficiently, as evidenced by the study presented

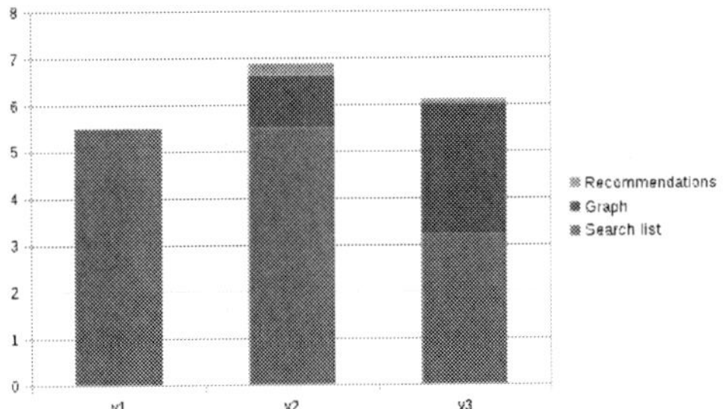

Figure 4: Number and origin of the articles viewed for the 3 versions of the LIMAH interface.

in this paper. In particular, we experimentally demonstrated that categorizing automatically hyperlinks established between articles further improves the amount and quality of the information retrieved while exploring to gain insight on a particular topic. We also proposed a parameter-free nearest neighbors algorithm that was shown to offer a better trade-off between relevance of the links and their number than standard nearest neighbors graph construction algorithms. Overall, organizing news collections in this way was proved to be helpful to journalists for their everyday work.

5 Acknowledgments

This work was funded by the CominLabs excellence laboratory, and financed by the National Research Agency under reference ANR-10-LABX-07-01. We are immensely grateful to Arnaud Touboulic for his key contribution in the design and implementation of the LIMAH interface.

References

Rémi Bois, Guillaume Gravier, Pascale Sébillot, and Emmanuel Morin. 2015. Vers une typologie de liens entre contenus journalistiques. In *22e Conférence Traitement Automatique des Langues Naturelles*. pages 515–521.

Maximilien Danisch, Jean-Loup Guillaume, and Bénédicte Le Grand. 2013. Towards multi-egocentred communities: A node similarity approach. *International Journal of Web Based Communities* 9(3):299–322.

Fabio Gasparetti. 2016. Modeling user interests from web browsing activities. *Data Mining and Knowledge Discovery* pages 1–46.

Mouzhi Ge, Carla Delgado-Battenfeld, and Dietmar Jannach. 2010. Beyond accuracy: evaluating recommender systems by coverage and serendipity. In *4th*

Conference on Recommender Systems. pages 257–260.

Guillaume Gravier, Martin Ragot, Laurent Amsaleg, Rémi Bois, Grégoire Jadi, Éric Jamet, Laura Monceaux, and Pascale Sébillot. 2016. Shaping-up multimedia analytics: Needs and expectations of media professionals. In *22nd MMM Conference, Perspectives on Multimedia Analytics*. pages 303–314.

Camille Guinaudeau, Guillaume Gravier, and Pascale Sébillot. 2012. Enhancing lexical cohesion measure with confidence measures, semantic relations and language model interpolation for multimedia spoken content topic segmentation. *Computer Speech and Language* 26(2):90–104.

Ichiro Ide, Hiroshi Mo, Norio Katayama, and Shinichi Satoh. 2004. Topic threading for structuring a large-scale news video archive. In *International Conference on Image and Video Retrieval*. pages 123–131.

Hans-Peter Kriegel, Peer Kröger, Jörg Sander, and Arthur Zimek. 2011. Density-based clustering. *Wiley Interdisciplinary Reviews: Data Mining and Knowledge Discovery* 1(3):231–240.

Tomas Mikolov, Ilya Sutskever, Kai Chen, Greg S. Corrado, and Jeff Dean. 2013. Distributed representations of words and phrases and their compositionality. In *Advances in Neural Information Processing Systems*. pages 3111–3119.

Philippe Muller and Xavier Tannier. 2004. Annotating and measuring temporal relations in texts. In *20th International Conference on Computational Linguistics*. pages 50–56.

Miloš Radovanović, Alexandros Nanopoulos, and Mirjana Ivanović. 2010. Hubs in space: Popular nearest neighbors in high-dimensional data. *Journal of Machine Learning Research* 11(Sep):2487–2531.

Klaus Seyerlehner, Peter Knees, Dominik Schnitzer, and Gerhard Widmer. 2009. Browsing music recommendation networks. In *10th International Society for Music Information Retrieval Conference*. pages 129–134.

Dafna Shahaf and Carlos Guestrin. 2010. Connecting the dots between news articles. In *16th ACM SIGKDD International Conference on Knowledge Discovery and Data Mining*. pages 623–632.

Storyteller: Visual Analytics of Perspectives on Rich Text Interpretations

Maarten van Meersbergen
Janneke van der Zwaan
Willem van Hage
Netherlands eScience Center
Science Park 140
Amsterdam, The Netherlands
Email: m.vanmeersbergen@esciencecenter.nl
j.vanderzwaan@esciencecenter.nl
w.vanhage@esciencecenter.nl

Piek Vossen
Antske Fokkens
Inger Leemans
Isa Maks
VU University Amsterdam
De Boelelaan 1081
Amsterdam, The Netherlands
Email: piek.vossen@vu.nl
antske.fokkens@vu.nl
inger.leemans@vu.nl
isa.maks@vu.nl

Abstract

Complexity of event data in texts makes it difficult to assess its content, especially when considering larger collections in which different sources report on the same or similar situations. We present a system that makes it possible to visually analyze complex event and emotion data extracted from texts. We show that we can abstract from different data models for events and emotions to a single data model that can show the complex relations in four dimensions. The visualization has been applied to analyze 1) dynamic developments in how people both conceive and express emotions in theater plays and 2) how stories are told from the perspective of their sources based on rich event data extracted from news or biographies.

1 Introduction

People frequently write about the changes in the world and about the emotions that these events arouse. Events and emotions typically have complex structures and are difficult to detect and represent. According to our estimation, standard news articles contain about 200 event mentions on average (Vossen et al., 2016). These events stand in complex temporal and causal relations to each other, while the text can also present different perspectives on their impact. Especially when considering event data from many different sources that may report on the same events, the extracted data quickly becomes very complex.

Most systems that handle large collections of text use some kind of topic clustering. Documents are grouped together on the basis of a similarity measure and clustering technique. In the case of streaming text, such as news and tweets, topic modeling and clustering is also done dynamically over time, indicating when a cluster appears and dies out. Dynamic clustering can be seen as a rough approximation of the temporal bounding of a real world event. Although topic modeling works well as an indicator of trending real world events, it does not tell the story in detail as a sequence of events with participants and causal/temporal relations across these events.

In this paper we present Storyteller, a visual analytics tool for complex multidimensional textual data. Storyteller groups events with multiple participants into storylines. As such, it can give insight into complex relations by providing multiple perspectives on time-based textual data. We explain the capabilities of Storyteller by applying it to semantically linked news data from the NewsReader project,[1] using different perspectives on the data to visualize complex relations between the events found by its Natural Language Processing (NLP) pipeline. These visualizations give more insight into the performance of the system and how well complex event relations approximate the storylines people construct when reading news. We further show the usability of the Storyteller visualization for general purpose event-based textual data by applying it to other use cases, namely the *Embodied Emotions* and *BiographyNet* projects provided by other humanities experts.

The paper is structured as follows. In Section 3, we present the semantic model for events used in NewsReader. Section 4 explains the Storyteller visualization tool that loads the NewsReader data and provides different views and interactions. We show the capacity of data generalization by the tool by applying it to other projects with biograph-

---

[1] http://www.newsreader-project.eu/

37

Proceedings of the 2017 EMNLP Workshop on Natural Language Processing meets Journalism, pages 37–45
Copenhagen, Denmark, September 7, 2017. ©2017 Association for Computational Linguistics

ical data and emotions in Dutch 17th century theater plays in Section 5. Section 2 explains how
our work differs from others. Section 6 concludes
with future plans.

2   Related work

Interactive graphics have been used for before to
analyze high dimensional data (Buja et al., 1996;
Martin and Ward, 1995; Buja et al., 1991), but
fast, web-based and highly interactive visualizations with filtering are a fairly new development.
With the advent of the open source libraries *D3.js*
(Bostock et al., 2011), *Crossfilter.js* (Square, 2012)
and *DC.js* (dcj, 2016), we now have the tools to
rapidly develop custom visual applications for the
web.

The *egoSlider* (Wu et al., 2016) uses a similar visualization to our co-participation graph for
Egocentric networks. Our visualization can however display co-participation of all participants
rather than just for one. The interactive filtering,
our other views on the multidimensional data, and
the immediate link to the original data are also not
present in egoSlider.

The TIARA system (Liu et al., 2012) visualizes
news stories as theme rivers. It also has a network
visualization of actor-actor relations. This can be
used when the corpus consists of e-mails, to show
who writes about what to whom. In StoryTeller,
the relations are not based on metadata but are relations in the domain of discourse extracted from
text.

3   Multi-dimensional event data from text

The NewsReader system automatically processes
news and extracts *what* happened, *who* is involved,
and *when* and *where* it happened. It uses a cascade
of NLP modules including named entity recognition and linking, semantic role labeling, time expression detection and normalization and nominal and event coreference. Processing a single
news article results in the semantic interpretation
of mentions of events, participants and their time
anchoring in a sequence of text.

In a second step, the mention interpretations
are converted to an instance representation according to the Simple Event Model (Van Hage
et al., 2011) or SEM. SEM is an RDF representation that abstracts from the specific mentions
within a single or across multiple news articles.
It defines individual components of events such

as the action, the participants with their roles and
the time-anchoring. A central notion in News-
Reader is the event-centric representation, where
events are represented as instances and all information on these events is aggregated from all the
mentions in different sources. For this purpose,
NewsReader introduced the Grounded Annotation
Framework (GAF, (Fokkens et al., 2013)) as an extension to SEM through *gaf:denotedBy* relations
between instance representations in SEM and their
mentions represented as offsets to different places
in the texts. Likewise, information that is the same
across mentions in different news articles gets de-
duplicated and information that is different gets
aggregated. For each piece of information, the
system stores the source and the perspective of the
source on the information. The result is a complex multidimensional data set in which events and
their relations are defined according to multiple
properties (Vossen et al., 2015). The Storyteller
application exploits these dimensions to present
events within a context that explains them, approx-
imating a story.

The following dimensions from the News-
Reader data are used for the visualization. **Event**
refers to the SEM-RDF ID: the instance identi-
fier. The **actors** in the news article, which are described using role labels that come from different
event ontologies, such as PropBank (Kingsbury
and Palmer, 2002), FrameNet (Baker et al., 1998),
and ESO (Segers et al., 2015). A **climax** score
indicating the relevance of the event (normalized
between 0 and 100) for a story. The climax score
is a normalized score based on the number of mentions of an event and the prominence of each mention, where early mentions count as more prominent. A **group** label that uniquely identifies the
event-group to which the event belongs. In News-
Reader, groups are formed by connecting events
by topic overlap of the articles in which they are
mentioned and by sharing the same actors. Each
group also has a **groupScore** which indicates the
relevance of the group or storyline for the whole
collection. For NewsReader, this is the highest
climax score within the group of events normalized across all the different groups extracted from
a data set. The group's **groupName** consists of the
most dominant topic within the group in comparison with all other groups based on IDF*TF. Event
groups are the basis for event-centric story visualizations.

The **labels** represent all the different wordings used to mention the event. The **prefLabel** is the most-frequent label for the event. **Time** refers to the date to which the event is anchored. **Mentions** is a list of mentions of the event in source texts. A mention consists of a **snippet**, the offsets of the label in that snippet (**snippet_char**), the **URI** of the source text, and **char**, the character offsets for the raw text inside the source. Next we show an abbreviated example of a NewsReader event in the JSON format used in Storyteller:

```
{ "timeline":
  "events": [{
    "actors": {
    "actor:": [
      "dbp:European_Union",
      "dbp:United_Kingdom",
      "dbp:The_Times",
      "dbp:Government_of_the_United_Kingdom"
    ]
  },
  "prefLabel": ["stop"],
  "time": "20140622",
  "climax": 89,
  "event": "ev194",
  "groupName": "[Community sanction]",
  "groupScore": "099",
  "labels": [
    "stop",
    "difficulty",
    "pressure"
  ],
  "mentions": [{
    "char": [ "5665", "5673" ],
    "perspective": [{
      "source": "author:FT_reporters"
    }],
    "snippet": [" Sunday Times, said
        they were extremely concerned
        about the UK's difficulties in
        stopping the EU from introducing
        measures that continue to
        erode Britain's competitiveness"],
    "snippet_char": [ 81, 89 ],
    "uri": ["http://www.ft.com/thing/
    f2bc1380-fa32-11e3-a328-00144feab7de"]
  }, {
(...)
```

4 Storyteller

The Storyteller application consists of 3 main *coordinated views* (Wang Baldonado et al., 2000): a participant-centric view, an event-centric view and a data-centric view.

User interaction is a key component in the design. The rich text data are too complex to visualize without it, as they contain numerous interconnected events, participants and other properties. Given that the estimated processing capacity for accurate data of human sight is limited to around 500 kbit per second (Gregory and Zangwill, 1987), a large number of connections can make the visual exploration very difficult without filters to slice the data into humanly manageable portions. This section presents the 3 views and describes how filtering can be applied.

The interactivity focuses mostly on analysis through filtering. The user can apply filters by clicking through various components of the charts. These filters are then dynamically applied to the other parts of the application, reducing the amount of data on the screen. This allows a user to *drill-down* into the data, gaining knowledge of its composition in the process.

4.1 Participation-centric view

The participation-centric view (Figure 1), which is our own graph design that we have dubbed a *Co-Participation graph*, is an interactively filterable version of the *XKCD Movie Narrative Charts* (Munroe, 2009). It is placed at the top of the Storyteller page and visualizes the participants of all the events. The major participants are placed on the Y-axis and the events they participate in are placed (as ovals) on a timeline. Each participant's timeline has a different color. If different participants take part in the same event, the lines are bent towards and joint in this event, showing the co-participation through this intersection. Events receive descriptive labels. Hovering the mouse cursor over an event will show further details, such as the mentions of that specific event.

4.1.1 Axis ordering

The X-axis is a timeline stretching between the first of the events shown and the last. The Y-axis is slightly more complicated. The ordering of the participants is of great importance to the legibility of the resulting chart. If this is done improperly, the resulting chart will be cluttered because of many curved lines crossing each other unnecessarily. We solved this legibility problem by ordering the elements in such a way that the participant lines travel straight for as long as possible. We do this by re-ordering the elements on the Y-axis in order of co-appearance on the timeline, from bottom to top. We start by determining the first and bottom-most line. For this, we select the first event on the timeline and determine the participants of this event. We then loop over all events that share these participants in order of appearance on the timeline. Every time a new co-participant is found

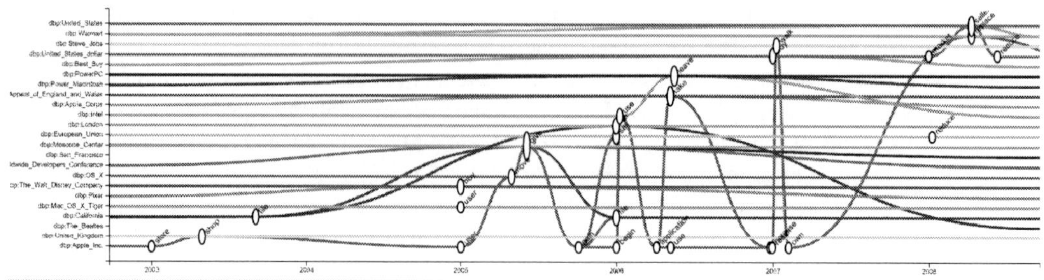

Figure 1: The Co-Participation graph in its unfiltered state, with a NewsReader dataset loaded

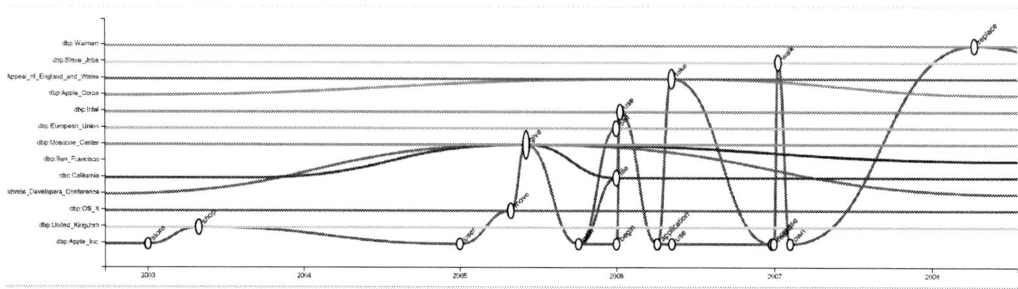

Figure 2: The Co-Participation graph in a filtered state, showing only those events where Apple_Inc. co-participates

in one of these events, it is added to the list. Once all events have been processed in this manner, the algorithm has clustered events that share participants making the resulting graph much easier to read.

4.1.2 Filtering

An alphabetic list of all of the participants present in the dataset is displayed left of the Co-participants graph. The length of the colored bar indicates the number of events in which the participant occurs. This number is shown when hovering the mouse over the bar.

Clicking on one of the items in the participant list applies a filter to the dataset. The Co-participation graph only shows the lines with events that involve the selected participant. This means that the line of the selected participant and those of participants that co-participate with the selected participant are displayed. Selecting more than one participant reduces the graph to those events in which all selected participants co-participate.

4.2 Event-centric view

Figure 3 shows the event-centric view. This second view in the Storyteller demo shows time ordered sequences of events grouped in different rows. The grouping can be determined in different ways and according to different needs.

In NewsReader, each row in the graph approximates the structure of a story, as defined in (Vossen et al., 2015): consisting of one or more climax events, preceded by events that build up towards the climax and following events that are the consequence of the climax defined by prominence (see section 3). Preceding and following events are selected on the basis of co-participation and topic-overlap: so-called bridging relations. The size (and color) of the event bubbles represents the climax score of the event.

A climax event together with all bridged events approximate a story, where we expect events to increase in bubble size when getting closer to the climax event (the biggest bubble in a row) and then gradually decrease after the climax event. The size of the events thus mimics the topical development of for example streaming news, while we still show details on the events within such a topic. The first row presents the story derived from the

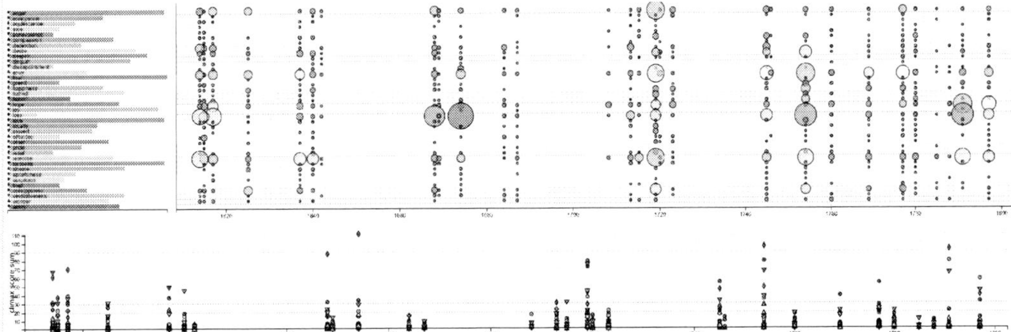

Figure 3: The event-centric view, with data of the Embodied Emotions project (See: Use Cases).

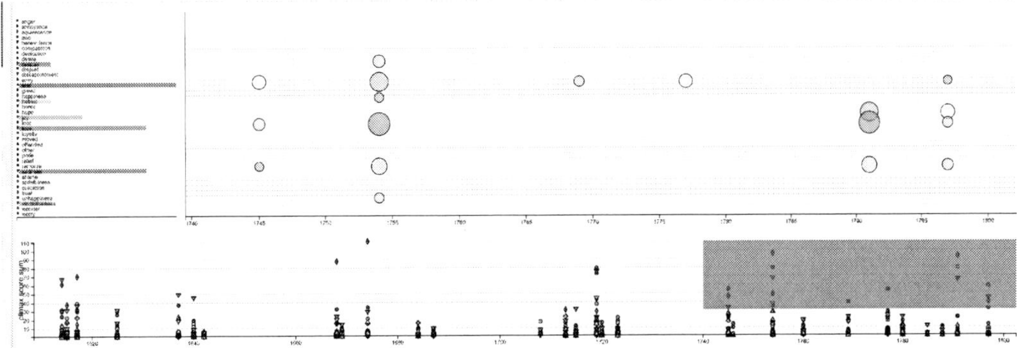

Figure 4: The same event-centric view, with a filter applied to only show high-climax events from the year 1740 and onwards.

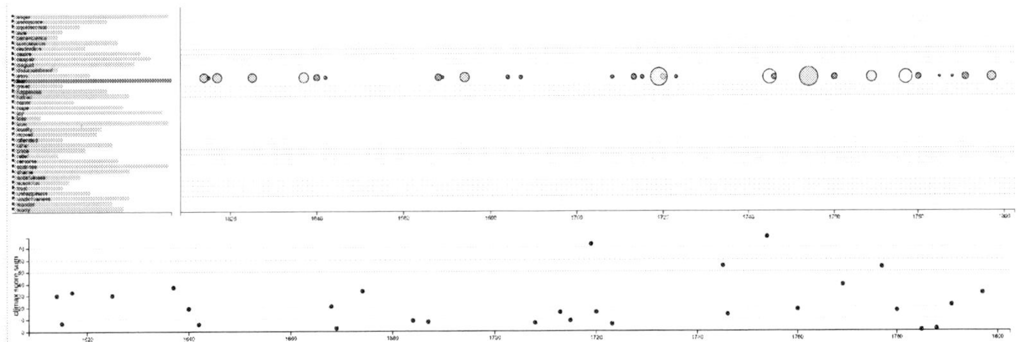

Figure 5: The same event-centric view, with a filter applied to only show events with the fear emotion.

climax event with the highest score (normalized to 100). The next rows show stories based on lower scoring climax events that are not connected to the main story. We thus apply a greedy algorithm in which the most prominent events has the first chance to absorb other events.

Stories are labeled by the climax event's group-Name (consisting of the topic that is dominant for the set of events making up the story and the highest climax score within the event). In addition to the label, each row has a colored bar that indicates the cumulative value of the climax scores of all the events within a story. Note that the story with the highest climax event does not necessarily have the largest cumulative score. If an event is mentioned a lot but poorly connected to other events, the cu-

41

mulative score may still be lower than that of other stories.

The bottom graph of the second view plots individual events for climax score on the Y-axis so that events from the same story may end up in different rows. Group membership is indicated by symbols representing the events. This view shows how events from a story are spread over climax scores and time.

4.2.1 Filtering

The user can select a story by clicking on the index of stories to the left. Unlike the Participation-centric view, selecting more than one group or row adds data to the representation. This is intentionally different from the co-participation graph, where multiple selections intersect (groups can, in this context, by definition not intersect), because stories are separated on the basis of lack of overlap.

In the bottom graph of the event-centric view, the user can make selections by dragging a region in the Y/X space with the mouse. A region thus represents a segment in time and a segment of climax scores. This enables both selecting time intervals (by dragging a full height box between two particular time frames) and selection of the most (or least) influential events, which can be used to exclude outliers in the data but also to select and inspect them.

All filters are applied globally: this means that participant selection in the top view influences the event-centric visualization and vice-versa.

4.3 Data-centric view

At the bottom of the Storyteller page, we see text snippets from the original texts that were used to derive the event data. It lists all events visualized for a given set of filters. Events are presented with the text fragments they are mentioned in and the event word is highlighted. The event labels are given separately as well, where synonyms are grouped together. Furthermore, the table shows the scores, the date and the group name or story label. No selections can be made through this view.

4.4 The full system

The seven tasks of the Visual Information Seeking Mantra

Overview Gain an overview of the entire collection.

Zoom Zoom in on items of interest.

Filter Filter out uninteresting items.

Details-on-demand Select an item or group and get details when needed.

Relate View relationships among items.

History Keep a history of actions to support undo, replay, and progressive refinement.

Extract Allow extraction of sub-collections and of the query parameters.

(Shneiderman, 1996)

We designed Storyteller following the (authoritative) Taxonomy for data visualizations (Shneiderman, 1996), phrased as the 7 tasks of the Visual Information Seeking Mantra:

We initiate the visualization with the **Overview** task presenting the initial (unfiltered) view. The **Filter** and **Zoom** tasks allow the selection of subsets of items in multiple ways through the different views. The **Details-on-demand** task provides detailed mouse-over information boxes as well as a view into the raw data that is maintained while filtering. The co-participation graph supports the main **Relate** task, the filter state displays the **History**, and finally, the data-view allows users to **Extract**.

Storyteller is built to be as generic, reusable and maintainable as possible. We have used only Free and Open Source (FOSS) software web visualization tools and libraries and made Storyteller itself fully FOSS as well. The code is available on github[2] and a demo is also available.[3]

5 Expert Panel Use Cases

The Storyteller demo has been used in two use cases other than NewsReader. We briefly describe both use cases in this section.

5.1 Embodied Emotions

Embodied Emotions (Zwaan et al., 2015) is a digital history project that investigates the relation

---

[2] `https://github.com/NLeSC/ UncertaintyVisualization/`
[3] `http://nlesc.github.io/ UncertaintyVisualization/`

Figure 6: The data-centric view, showing the raw data and offsets for the text snippets, as well as the (colored) labels as found in the text. The data displayed here is from 17th century dutch theatre plays

between body parts and emotions in Dutch stage plays over time (i.e. in what body parts do people experience emotions, and through which bodily acts do they express emotions). In our Storyteller visualization, emotions are events and body parts are participants. The visualization can be applied at two levels. First, the X-axis of the Co-participation graph can be used to represent the acts of a single play. Second, the X-axis can be used as a timeline where we plot which emotions and body parts are linked to each other in plays published in a specific year.

Intersections indicate when different body parts are associated with the same emotion. The current online demo shows the second type of visualization: emotion/body-part pairs occurrence per year.[4] The climax score in this visualization reflects the prominence of the emotion (the occurrence of the emotion related to the number of sentences).

5.2 BiographyNet

The BiographyNet (Ockeloen et al., 2013) use case involves the visual exploration of biographies of prominent people in Dutch history. The biographies have been processed by a pipeline similar to the one used for NewsReader. However, the data is radically different: biographies mainly contain events related to the subject of the biography and we do not find many instances of cross-document event co-reference.

The BiographyNet demo[5] therefore does not focus on event instances but on event types: we extract all events related to a person that can be linked to a specific year from the biographical text and meta data. The biography subjects are the participants in our visualization, the event types are the events. If two people are born in the same year, study during the same year or die in the same year, etc., their lines intersect. The BiographyNet visualization thus allows historians to perform generation analyses: what other events have people born in a specific year have in common? The climax score reflects the number of participants involved in an event. The event-centric visualization thus shows which events are prominent in a given year.

6   Conclusion

The fast and efficient web-based visualizations of the output of NLP pipelines allows us to visually analyze complex storylines spanning years. This means that we can now analyze news articles with much more context, be it by looking at co-participants, co-occurrence or other such criteria. This changes literature study from first having to read all the text to build an overview to first having a rough overview that allows you to decide which text to read later.

Storyteller's event-based input format makes it easy to port to new data sources. We described two other projects with different graph-like data (biographies and emotions) that can be served with the same application thanks to this generic input format.

There are many directions in which this research could be advanced in the future. First, the interaction model should be completed. Although Storyteller allows the user to select and filter the data in almost all graphs, other interactivity could

---

[4] http://nlesc.github.io/
EmbodiedEmotions/
[5] http://nlesc.github.io/BiographyNet/

be added. For example, currently, the data table (view 3) only shows the results of filters and selections applied in other views. This table could be made interactive by adding search functionality. This means that the data can be filtered based on user queries. Another possibility for improved interaction is to allow the user to re-order events, participants and groups according to different criteria (e.g., based on frequency, or alphabetically).

While we now have a visualization capable of displaying a decently sized data, it cannot handle the sheer volume of *all* available news data. We are currently implementing an interface that generates manageable data structures on the basis of user queries from a triple store that contains massive event data from the processed news in RDF (i.e. possibly millions of news articles and billions of triples). The user queries are translated into SPARQL requests and the resulting RDF is converted to the JSON input format. This solution requires that some structures, e.g. the climax score and the storylines, need to be computed beforehand. The user should make a visually supported selection *overview, zoom and filter* before querying the database to obtain all required data and displaying the current views.

The NewsReader data exhibits various degrees of uncertainty and source perspectives on the event data (e.g. whether the source believes the event has actually happened, or whether it is a positive or negative speculation or expectation of the source). These are modeled through the RDF representation as well but have not yet been considered in the tool. In the next version of the Storyteller application, we aim to visualize this data layer as well.

Feedback from domain experts who explored data from the three different use cases indicates that a proper understanding of the tool and the data is required in order to get meaningful results. In addition to developing tutorials that help researchers to get the most out of Storyteller, we propose two types of user studies. First, we need to evaluate Storyteller's usability. Second, we need to evaluate to what extent Storyteller generates results (data and views) that are useful for the different domains.

Acknowledgment

The authors would like to thank the Netherlands Organisation for Scientific Research (NWO) and the Netherlands eScience Center for sponsoring this research.

References

2016. DC.js dimensional charting javascript library.

C. F. Baker, C. J. Fillmore, and J. B. Lowe. 1998. The Berkeley FrameNet project. In *Proc. of ACL*, pages 86–90.

M. Bostock, V. Ogievetsky, and J. Heer. 2011. D^3 data-driven documents. *Visualization and Computer Graphics*, 17(12):2301–2309.

A. Buja, D. Cook, and D. F. Swayne. 1996. Interactive high-dimensional data visualization. *Journal of computational and graphical statistics*, 5(1):78–99.

A. Buja, J. A. McDonald, J. Michalak, and W. Stuetzle. 1991. Interactive data visualization using focusing and linking. In *Proc. of Visualization'91*, pages 156–163. IEEE.

Antske Fokkens, Marieke van Erp, Piek Vossen, Sara Tonelli, Willem Robert van Hage, Luciano Serafini, Rachele Sprugnoli, and Jesper Hoeksema. 2013. GAF: A grounded annotation framework for events. In *The 1st Workshop on Events*, Atlanta, USA.

R. L. Gregory and O. L. Zangwill. 1987. *The Oxford companion to the mind.* Oxford University Press.

P. Kingsbury and M. Palmer. 2002. From treebank to propbank. In *LREC*. Citeseer.

S. Liu, M. X. Zhou, S. Pan, Y. Song, W. Qian, W. Cai, and X. Lian. 2012. Tiara: Interactive, topic-based visual text summarization and analysis. *Transactions on Intelligent Systems and Technology*, 3(2):25.

A. R. Martin and Matthew O. Ward. 1995. High dimensional brushing for interactive exploration of multivariate data. In *Proc. of Visualization'95*, page 271.

R. Munroe. 2009. Xkcd# 657: Movie narrative charts.

N. Ockeloen, A. Fokkens, S. ter Braake, P. Vossen, V. De Boer, G. Schreiber, and S. Legêne. 2013. Biographynet: Managing provenance at multiple levels and from different perspectives. In *Proc. of LISC2013*, pages 59–71. CEUR-WS. org.

R. Segers, P. Vossen, M. Rospocher, L. Serafini, E. Laparra, and G. Rigau. 2015. ESO: A frame based ontology for events and implied situations. In *Proceedings of MAPLEX 2015*, Yamagata, Japan.

Ben Shneiderman. 1996. The eyes have it: A task by data type taxonomy for information visualizations. In *IEEE Symposium on Visual Languages*, pages 336–343.

Square. 2012. Crossfilter.js fast multidimensional filtering for coordinated views.

W. R. Van Hage, V. Malaisé, R. Segers, L. Hollink, and G. Schreiber. 2011. Design and use of the simple event model (sem). *Web Semantics: Science, Services and Agents on the World Wide Web*, 9(2):128–136.

P. Vossen, T. Caselli, and Y. Kontzopoulou. 2015. Storylines for structuring massive streams of news. In *Proc. of CNewS 2015*, Bejing, China.

Piek Vossen, Rodrigo Agerri, Itziar Aldabe, Agata Cybulska, Marieke van Erp, Antske Fokkens, Egoitz Laparra, Anne-Lyse Minard, Alessio Palmero Aprosio, German Rigau, Marco Rospocher, and Roxane Segers. 2016. Newsreader: Using knowledge resources in a cross-lingual reading machine to generate more knowledge from massive streams of news. *Knowledge-Based Systems*, 110:60 – 85.

M. Q. Wang Baldonado, A. Woodruff, and A. Kuchinsky. 2000. Guidelines for using multiple views in information visualization. In *Proc. of AVI*, pages 110–119. ACM.

Y. Wu, N. Pitipornvivat, J. Zhao, S. Yang, G. Huang, and H. Qu. 2016. egoslider: Visual analysis of egocentric network evolution. *Visualization and Computer Graphics*, 22(1):260–269.

J. M. van der Zwaan, I. Leemans, E. Kuijpers, and I. Maks. 2015. Heem, a complex model for mining emotions in historical text. In *Proc. of IEEE eScience*, pages 22–30.

Analyzing the Revision Logs of a Japanese Newspaper
for Article Quality Assessment

Hideaki Tamori[1]   **Yuta Hitomi**[1]   **Naoaki Okazaki**[2]   **Kentaro Inui**[3]

[1] Media Lab, The Asahi Shimbun Company
[2] Tokyo Institute of Technology
[3] Tohoku University

`{tamori-h, hitomi-y1}@asahi.com, okazaki@chokkan.org`
`inui@ecei.tohoku.ac.jp`

Abstract

We address the issue of the quality of journalism and analyze daily article revision logs from a Japanese newspaper company. The revision logs contain data that can help reveal the requirements of quality journalism such as the types and number of edit operations and aspects commonly focused in revision. This study also discusses potential applications such as quality assessment and automatic article revision as our future research directions.

1 Introduction

Quality journalism deserves serious consideration, particularly given the disruptions of existing publishing companies and the emergence of new publishing companies, citizen journalism, and automated journalism. Although no consensus exists for the definition of quality journalism, Meyer (2009) describes several aspects that constitute quality journalism; for example, credibility, influence, accuracy, and readability. To the best of our knowledge, this is the first attempt to analyze the large-scale revision logs of professionals in the field of journalism. In this study, we explore aspects of quality journalism through analyses of the newspaper article revision logs. More specifically, we analyze the revision processes as editors refine the drafts written by reporters so that they are of publication quality.

While our attempt is still in the early stages, this paper reports the statistics of the actual revisions made by professionals and shows the usefulness of the revision logs. We also discuss the future directions of this research, for example, the potential to present feedback to reporters, extract guidelines for 'good' articles, and develop systems for automatic revision and sentence merging and spitting.

2 Analysis of revision logs

This section describes the daily activities of a newspaper company needed to publish articles and the analysis of the revision logs.

2.1 Flow of editing and publishing articles

A reporter drafts an article and sends it to an editor, who has over ten years' experience as a journalist. The editor proofreads the article and forwards it to a reviewers section. The reviewers in this section fact-check the article. Finally, designers adjust the article so that they fit in the newspaper and website. In this way, a newspaper article is revised many times from the original submission.

Figure 1 compares the text from an article written by a reporter and the same text after it has been revised by an editor. The editor revises the text using insertion, deletion, and replacement. This example also shows the operations of sentence reordering and splitting.

2.2 Aligning original sentences with revised sentences

Revision logs present two versions of an article: the one written by a reporter (the original version) and the final version revised by an editor (the revised version). However, these logs do not provide details about the editing process used to transform the original version into the final version (e.g., individual operations of word insertion/deletion, sentence reordering). Hence, we estimate sentence alignments between the original and revised versions using the *maximum alignment* method (Kajiwara and Komachi, 2016).

The accuracy, precision, recall, and F1 score were 0.995, 0.996, 0.951, and 0.957, respectively, on a dataset consisting of 50 articles in which the correct alignments were assigned by a human.[1]

---

[1]We chose 0.06 for word similarity threshold and 0.70 for

Proceedings of the 2017 EMNLP Workshop on Natural Language Processing meets Journalism, pages 46–50
Copenhagen, Denmark, September 7, 2017. ©2017 Association for Computational Linguistics

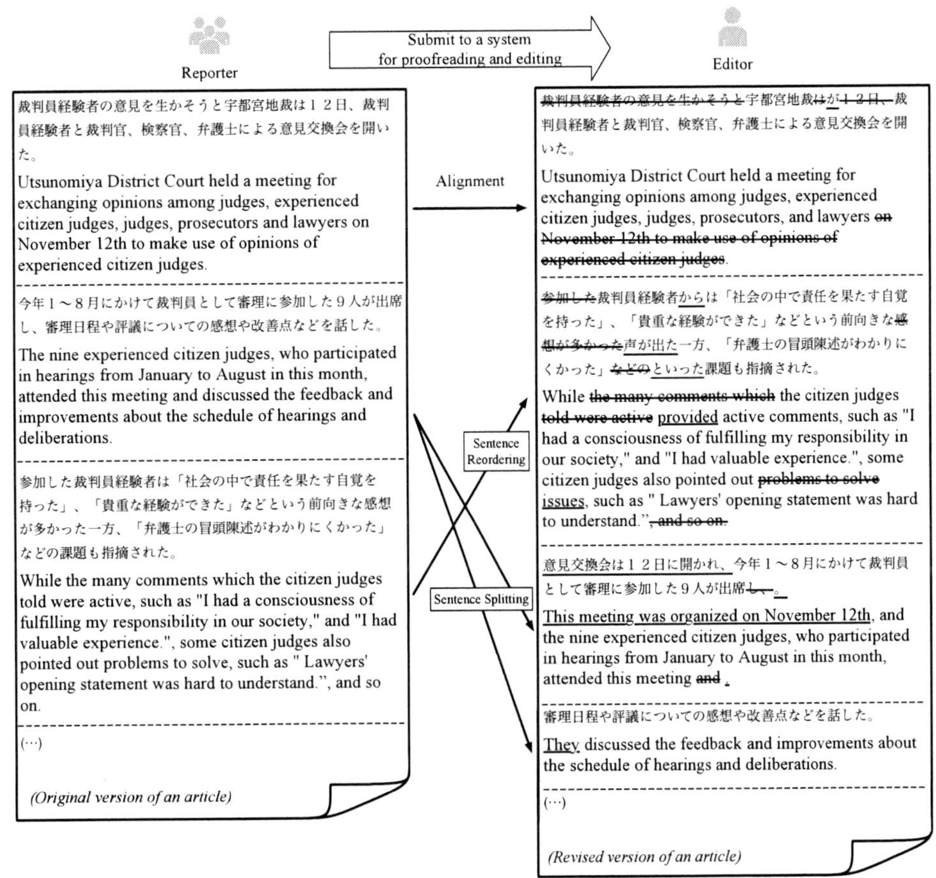

Figure 1: Comparison of the original and revised versions of some text. In the revised version, the strikethrough and underlined parts indicate deletions and insertions, respectively.

The precision, recall, and F1 score calculated from only the sentence pairs that are changed during revision were 0.926, 0.895, and 0.910, respectively. There may be some room for improving the performance of the alignments but it is sufficient for this analysis.

2.3 Data analysis of the revision logs

To analyze the details of the revision processes, we inspected articles published from October 1, 2015 to September 30, 2016. We applied MeCab (Kudo et al., 2004), a Japanese morphological analyzer, with the enhanced dictionary NEologd[2], to split the sentences into words (morphemes) and recognize their parts-of-speech.

The dataset analyzed in this study contains 120,331 articles with 1,903,645 original sentences and 1,884,987 revised sentences. The dataset consists of a Japanese newspaper's articles[3], which have a mixed domain (genre) of the news, and most of the articles have the same writing style. We obtained 2,197,739 sentence pairs using the alignment method described in Section 2.2. The number of aligned pairs is larger than that of the sentences because an original sentence can be aligned to multiple sentences in the revised version. About half of the sentence pairs (1,108,750) were unchanged during the revision process, and the remaining pairs (1,088,989) were changed. In this section, we report the statistics of the edit operations in the changed pairs. We found that newspaper companies produce a huge number of sentences, about half of which are revised, for analy-

---

sentence similarity threshold, optimizing the F1 score on a development set consisting of 150 articles. We used word embeddings that are pre-trained by the original articles and revised articles to compute sentence similarity.

[2] https://github.com/neologd/mecab-ipadic-neologd

[3] The Asahi Shimbun Company provided this dataset.

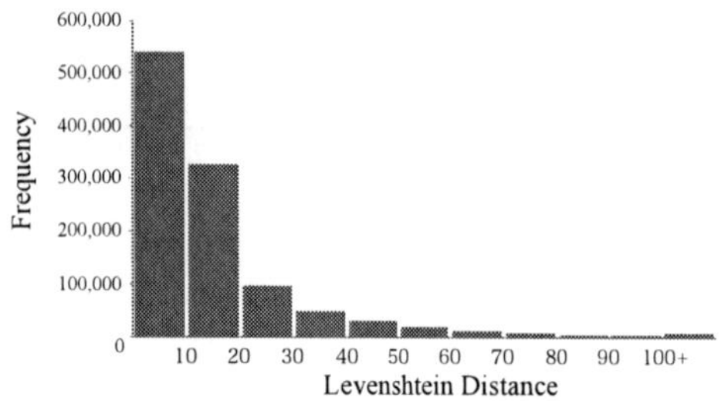

Figure 2: Distribution of the Levenshtein distance of changed sentence pairs.

Original sentence:
市場に同じ魚が出回りすぎると、魚の単価が下がってしまう。

If the same kind of fish is distributed in large quantities
in the market, the unit price of the fish manages to decrease.

Revised sentence:
市場に同じ魚が出回りすぎるの水揚げが重なると、魚の単価が
下がってしまうる。

If the same kind of fish is distributed landed in large quantities
in the market, the unit price of the fish manages to decrease
is decreasing.

Figure 3: An example of the original and revised sentence pair whose Levenshtein distance is 15.

# of words	Insertion	Deletion	Replacement
1	139,790	160,975	1,424,118
2	118,261	151,641	303,293
3	57,397	53,789	115,525
4	35,272	31,719	75,909
5	21,339	20,435	33,805
6	13,295	14,756	21,419
7	14,599	13,030	24,400
8	8,631	9,301	10,707
9	10,196	10,760	8,475
Over 10	48,754	60,523	61,387
Total	467,534	526,929	2,079,038

Table 1: Number of edit operations with respect to the number of words involved.

Tag	Count
Noun	1,255,113
Noun + Noun	174,306
Particle	157,840
Symbol	128,584
Noun + Particle	106,548
Verb	85,709
Symbol + Noun	47,635
Particle + Noun	42,714
Particle + Verb	41,342
Prefix	41,194
Noun + Symbol	37,580
Verb + Auxiliary	20,836
Auxiliary	18,145
Noun + Verb	14,153
Adverb	9,009
Others	101,714

Table 2: Distribution of parts-of-speech as targets for the edit operations involving one or two words.

sis just within a year.

Figure 2 presents the distribution of the Levenshtein distance between the original and revised sentences. The mean of the Levenshtein distances of the revised pairs (15.04) indicates that the dataset includes many examples in which drafts are deeply edited by the editors. Figure 3 is an example of the sentence pair which has the mean of the Levenshtein distance of the dataset (15).

Table 1 lists the number of insertions, deletions, and replacements, according to the number of words involved in the edit operations. We found that 56.20% of the total edit operations were replacements for one or two words, and this fact indicates that editors revised these articles with impressive attention to detail.

Table 2 shows the number of edit operations separated by different part-of-speech. The most frequent target for revisions is nouns, followed by particles (postpositions). This result indicates that revisions in terms of both content and readability are important for improving the quality of articles.

3 Future directions for quality assessment and automatic article revision

There are several possible future directions for the utilization of the revision logs.

3.1 Feedbacks to reporters

We can use the revision logs for improving the writing skills of reporters. An interesting finding in the revision logs is that the articles of young reporters (1–3 years' experience) tend to be revised more than those of experienced reporters (31–33 years' experience): the mean Levenshtein distances of these young and experienced reporters are 15.82 and 12.95, respectively. As exemplified by this finding, the revision logs can indicate the main types of revisions that a particular group of reporters or an individual reporter receives. We will explore the potential of the revision logs for assessing the writing quality of a reporter and presenting them with feedback.

3.2 Establishing guidelines for writing articles

Most textbooks on Japanese writing (including the internal handbook for reporters produced by the newspaper company) recommend that a Japanese sentence should be 40 to 50 characters long (Ishioka and Kameda, 2006). We could confirm that the newspaper articles satisfy this criterion: the revised sentences are 41.10 characters long on average. In this way, we can analyze the revision logs to extract various criteria for establishing the guidelines for 'good' articles.

3.3 Automatic article revision within sentences

Another future direction is to build a corpus for improving the quality of articles. The revision logs collected for a year (excluding duplicates) provide 517,545 instances of replace operations, 79,639 instances of insertions, and 54,111 instances of deletions that involve one or two words. Table 3 shows some instances of the replace operations. It may not be straightforward to use the revision logs for error correction because some edit operations add new information and remove useless information. Nevertheless, the logs record the daily activities of how drafts are improved by the editors. In future, we plan to build an editing system that detects errors and suggests wording while the reporters write drafts. We can use natural language processing techniques for these tasks because local error correction has been previously researched (Cucerzan and Brill, 2004).

3.4 Automatic sentence merging and splitting

The alignment method found 69,891 instances of sentence splitting (wherein an original sentence is split into multiple sentences) and 68,550 instances of sentence merging (wherein multiple original sentences are merged into one sentence). Table 4 shows examples of sentence splitting and merging. We observe some sentences are also compressed during sentence merging and splitting. We can use these instances as a training data for building a model for sentence splitting and merging (with compression), and this may be an interesting task in the field of natural language processing.

4 Conclusion

In this paper, we explored the potential of the revision logs of a newspaper company for assessing

Original	Revised
同政府関係者 this Government officials	韓国政府関係者 Korean Government officials: specification
放射線汚染 contamination by radial ray	放射能汚染 radiologically contamination
破顔し broke into a smile	笑顔で話し spoke with a smile: simplification
バラティ Varety	バラエティー Variety: typo
タンパク質 Protain: written in Katakana and Kanji	たんぱく質 Protain: written in Hiragana and Kanji
買えた could buy	買える can buy

Table 3: Examples of commonly replaced words/phrases.

Splitting
(S1) 新たな窓口を設けるなど内部通報制度も強化し、通報は問題が発覚する前の 88 件 (14 年度) から 263 件 (15 年度) と 3 倍に増えた。 They enhance whistle-blowing systems by providing such as new counseling offices, and the number of whistle-blowing was increased three times from 88 in 2014, in which this issue was found out, to 263 in 2015.
(S2) 新たな窓口を設けるなど内部通報制度も強化。通報は 2015 年度に 263 件と、不正会計問題の発覚前の 14 年度の 88 件から約 3 倍に増えたという。 They enhance whistle-blowing systems by providing such as new counseling offices. As a result, the number of whistle-blowing was increased three times from 88 in 2014, in which this issue was found out, to 263 in 2015.

Merging
(M1) 同署によると、事務所南側 1 階の窓が割られ、室内にある防犯カメラのモニター 4 台がすべて壊されていた。食器棚も倒され、食器が散乱していたという。 Police said that the window on the first floor of the office south is broken, and all four displays for the security camera was destroyed. Police also said that the cupboard was knocked down, and the dished are scattered in the room.
(M2) 署によると、室内の防犯カメラのモニター全 4 台が壊され、食器棚が倒れて食器が散乱していた。 Police said the all four displays for the security camera was destroyed, the cupboard was knocked down, and the dished are scattered in the room.

Table 4: Examples of sentence splitting and merging. Sentences S1 and M1 are the original sentences, and S2 and M2 are the revised sentences. In the merging example, we can also observe the sentence compressing; the part "the window on the first floor of the office south is broken" was eliminated in M2.

the quality of articles. In addition to presenting the revision logs statistics, we discussed the future

directions of this work, which include feedback to
reporters, guidelines for 'good' articles, automatic
article revision, and automatic sentence merging
and splitting.

References

Silviu Cucerzan and Eric Brill. 2004. Spelling correction as an iterative process that exploits the collective knowledge of web users. In *Proc of EMNLP*. pages 293–300.

Tsunenori Ishioka and Masayuki Kameda. 2006. Automated Japanese essay scoring system based on articles written by experts. In *Proc of ACL*. pages 233–240.

Tomoyuki Kajiwara and Mamoru Komachi. 2016. Building a monolingual parallel corpus for text simplification using sentence similarity based on alignment between word embeddings. In *Proc of COLING*. pages 1147–1158.

Taku Kudo, Kaoru Yamamoto, and Yuji Matsumoto. 2004. Applying conditional random fields to Japanese morphological analysis. In *Proc of EMNLP*. pages 230–237.

Philip Meyer. 2009. *The vanishing newspaper : saving journalism in the information age*. University of Missouri Press, Columbia.

Improved Abusive Comment Moderation with User Embeddings

John Pavlopoulos
Prodromos Malakasiotis
Juli Bakagianni
Straintek, Athens, Greece
{ip, mm, jb}@straintek.com

Ion Androutsopoulos
Department of Informatics
Athens University of Economics
and Business, Greece
ion@aueb.gr

Abstract

Experimenting with a dataset of approximately 1.6M user comments from a Greek news sports portal, we explore how a state of the art RNN-based moderation method can be improved by adding user embeddings, user type embeddings, user biases, or user type biases. We observe improvements in all cases, with user embeddings leading to the biggest performance gains.

1 Introduction

News portals often allow their readers to comment on articles, in order to get feedback, engage their readers, and build customer loyalty. User comments, however, can also be abusive (e.g., bullying, profanity, hate speech), damaging the reputation of news portals, making them liable to fines (e.g., when hosting comments encouraging illegal actions), and putting off readers. Large news portals often employ moderators, who are frequently overwhelmed by the volume and abusiveness of comments.[1] Readers are disappointed when non-abusive comments do not appear quickly online because of moderation delays. Smaller news portals may be unable to employ moderators, and some are forced to shut down their comments.[2]

In previous work (Pavlopoulos et al., 2017a), we introduced a new dataset of approx. 1.6M manually moderated user comments from a Greek sports news portal, called Gazzetta, which we made publicly available.[3] Experimenting on that dataset and the datasets of Wulczyn et al. (2017), which contain moderated English Wikipedia comments, we showed that a method based on a Recurrent Neural Network (RNN) outperforms DETOX

(Wulczyn et al., 2017), the previous state of the art in automatic user content moderation.[4] Our previous work, however, considered only the texts of the comments, ignoring user-specific information (e.g., number of previously accepted or rejected comments of each user). Here we add *user embeddings* or *user type embeddings* to our RNN-based method, i.e., dense vectors that represent individual users or user types, similarly to word embeddings that represent words (Mikolov et al., 2013; Pennington et al., 2014). Experiments on Gazzetta comments show that both user embeddings and user type embeddings improve the performance of our RNN-based method, with user embeddings helping more. User-specific or user-type-specific *scalar biases* also help to a lesser extent.

2 Dataset

We first discuss the dataset we used, to help acquaint the reader with the problem. The dataset contains Greek comments from Gazzetta (Pavlopoulos et al., 2017a). There are approximately 1.45M training comments (covering Jan. 1, 2015 to Oct. 6, 2016); we call them G-TRAIN (Table 1). An additional set of 60,900 comments (Oct. 7 to Nov. 11, 2016) was split to development set (G-DEV, 29,700 comments) and test set (G-TEST, 29,700).[5] Each comment has a gold label ('accept', 'reject'). The user ID of the author of each comment is also available, but user IDs were not used in our previous work.

When experimenting with *user type* embeddings or biases, we group the users into the fol-

---

[1]See, for example, https://goo.gl/WTQyio.

[2]See https://goo.gl/2eKdeE.

[3]The portal is http://www.gazzetta.gr/. Instructions to download the dataset will become available at http://nlp.cs.aueb.gr/software.html.

[4]Two of the co-authors of Wulczyn et al. (2017) are with Jigsaw, who recently announced Perspective, a system to detect toxic comments. Perspective is not the same as DETOX (personal communication), but we were unable to obtain scientific articles describing it.

[5]The remaining 1,500 comments are not used here. Smaller subsets of G-TRAIN and G-TEST are also available (Pavlopoulos et al., 2017a), but are not used in this paper. The Wikipedia comment datasets of Wulczyn et al. (2017) cannot be used here, because they do not provide user IDs.

Proceedings of the 2017 EMNLP Workshop on Natural Language Processing meets Journalism, pages 51–55
Copenhagen, Denmark, September 7, 2017. ©2017 Association for Computational Linguistics

Dataset/Split	Gold Label		Comments Per User Type				Total
	Accepted	Rejected	Green	Yellow	Red	Unknown	
G-TRAIN	960,378 (66%)	489,222 (34%)	724,247 (50%)	585,622 (40%)	43,702 (3%)	96,029 (7%)	1.45M
G-DEV	20,236 (68%)	9,464 (32%)	14,378 (48%)	10,964 (37%)	546 (2%)	3,812 (13%)	29,700
G-TEST	20,064 (68%)	9,636 (32%)	14,559 (49%)	10,681 (36%)	621 (2%)	3,839 (13%)	29,700

Table 1: Comment statistics of the dataset used.

Dataset/Split	Individual Users Per User Type				Total
	Green	Yellow	Red	Unknown	
G-TRAIN	4,451	3,472	251	21,865 → 1	8,175
G-DEV	1,631	1,218	64	1,281 → 1	2,914
G-TEST	1,654	1,203	67	1,254 → 1	2,925

Table 2: User statistics of the dataset used.

lowing types. $T(u)$ is the number of training comments posted by user (ID) u. $R(u)$ is the ratio of training comments posted by u that were rejected.

Red: Users with $T(u) > 10$ and $R(u) \geq 0.66$.
Yellow: $T(u) > 10$ and $0.33 < R(u) < 0.66$.
Green: $T(u) > 10$ and $R(u) \leq 0.33$.
Unknown: Users with $T(u) \leq 10$.

Table 2 shows the number of users per type.

3   Methods

RNN: This is the RNN-based method of our previous work (Pavlopoulos et al., 2017a). It is a chain of GRU cells (Cho et al., 2014) that transforms the tokens $w_1 \ldots, w_k$ of each comment to the hidden states $h_1 \ldots, h_k$ ($h_i \in \mathbb{R}^m$). Once h_k has been computed, a logistic regression (LR) layer estimates the probability that comment c should be rejected:

$$P_{\text{RNN}}(reject|c) = \sigma(W_p h_k + b) \qquad (1)$$

σ is the sigmoid function, $W_p \in \mathbb{R}^{1 \times m}$, $b \in \mathbb{R}$.[6]

ueRNN: This is the RNN-based method with *user embeddings* added. Each user u of the training set with $T(u) > 10$ is mapped to a user-specific embedding $v_u \in \mathbb{R}^d$. Users with $T(u) \leq 10$ are mapped to a single 'unknown' user embedding. The LR layer is modified as follows; v_u is the embedding of the author of c; and $W_v \in \mathbb{R}^{1 \times d}$.

$$P_{ue\text{RNN}}(reject|c) = \sigma(W_p h_k + W_v v_u + b) \qquad (2)$$

teRNN: This is the RNN-based method with *user type embeddings* added. Each user type t is mapped to a user type embedding $v_t \in \mathbb{R}^d$. The LR layer is modified as follows, where v_t is the embedding of the type of the author of c.

$$P_{te\text{RNN}}(reject|c) = \sigma(W_p h_k + W_v v_t + b) \qquad (3)$$

ubRNN: This is the RNN-based method with *user biases* added. Each user u of the training set with $T(u) > 10$ is mapped to a user-specific bias $b_u \in \mathbb{R}$. Users with $T(u) \leq 10$ are mapped to a single 'unknown' user bias. The LR layer is modified as follows, where b_u is the bias of the author of c.

$$P_{ub\text{RNN}}(reject|c) = \sigma(W_p h_k + b_u) \qquad (4)$$

We expected *ub*RNN to learn higher (or lower) b_u biases for users whose posts were frequently rejected (accepted) in the training data, biasing the system towards rejecting (accepting) their posts.

tbRNN: This is the RNN-based method with *user type biases*. Each user type t is mapped to a user type bias $b_t \in \mathbb{R}$. The LR layer is modified as follows; b_t is the bias of the type of the author.

$$P_{tb\text{RNN}}(reject|c) = \sigma(W_p h_k + b_t) \qquad (5)$$

We expected *tb*RNN to learn a higher b_t for the red user type (frequently rejected), and a lower b_t for the green user type (frequently accepted), with the biases of the other two types in between.

In all methods above, we use 300-dimensional word embeddings, user and user type embeddings with $d = 300$ dimensions, and $m = 128$ hidden units in the GRU cells, as in our previous experiments (Pavlopoulos et al., 2017a), where we tuned all hyper-parameters on 2% held-out training comments. Early stopping evaluates on the same held-out subset. User and user type embeddings are randomly initialized and updated by backpropagation. Word embeddings are initialized to the WORD2VEC embeddings of our previous work (Pavlopoulos et al., 2017a), which were pretrained on 5.2M Gazzetta comments. Out of vocabulary words, meaning words not encountered or encountered only once in the training set and/or words with no initial embeddings, are mapped (during both training and testing) to a single randomly initialized word embedding, updated by backpropagation. We use Glorot initialization (Glorot and

---

[6]In our previous work (Pavlopoulos et al., 2017a), we also considered a variant of RNN, called *a*-RNN, with an attention mechanism. We do not consider *a*-RNN here to save space.

System	G-DEV	G-TEST
*ue*RNN	**80.68** ($\pm$**0.11**)	**80.71** ($\pm$**0.13**)
*ub*RNN	80.54 ($\pm$0.09)	80.53 ($\pm$0.08)
*te*RNN	80.37 ($\pm$0.05)	80.41 ($\pm$0.09)
*tb*RNN	80.33 ($\pm$0.12)	80.32 ($\pm$0.05)
RNN	79.40 ($\pm$0.08)	79.24 ($\pm$0.05)
*u*BASE	67.61	68.57
*t*BASE	63.16	63.82

Table 3: AUC scores. Standard error in brackets.

Bengio, 2010) for other parameters, cross-entropy loss, and Adam (Kingma and Ba, 2015).[7]

***u*BASE:** For a comment c authored by user u, this baseline returns the rejection rate $R(u)$ of the author's training comments, if there are $T(u) > 10$ training comments of u, and 0.5 otherwise.

$$P_{u\text{BASE}}(reject|c) = \begin{cases} R(u), & \text{if } T(u) > 10 \\ 0.5, & \text{if } T(u) \leq 10 \end{cases}$$

***t*BASE:** This baseline returns the following probabilities, considering the user type t of the author.

$$P_{t\text{BASE}}(reject|c) = \begin{cases} 1, & \text{if } t \text{ is Red} \\ 0.5, & \text{if } t \text{ is Yellow} \\ 0.5, & \text{if } t \text{ is Unknown} \\ 0, & \text{if } t \text{ is Green} \end{cases}$$

4 Results and Discussion

Table 3 shows the AUC scores (area under ROC curve) of the methods considered. Using AUC allows us to compare directly to the results of our previous work (Pavlopoulos et al., 2017a) and the work of Wulczyn et al. (2017). Also, AUC considers performance at multiple classification thresholds t (rejecting comment c when $P(reject|c) \geq t$, for different t values), which gives a more complete picture compared to reporting precision, recall, or F-scores for a particular t only. Accuracy is not an appropriate measure here, because of class imbalance (Table 1). For methods that involve random initializations (all but the baselines), the results are averaged over three repetitions; we also report the standard error across the repetitions.

User-specific information always improves our original RNN-based method (Table 3), but the best results are obtained by adding user embeddings (*ue*RNN). Figure 1 visualizes the user embeddings learned by *ue*RNN. The two dimensions of Fig. 1 correspond to the two principal components of the user embeddings, obtained via PCA. The colors and numeric labels reflect the rejection rates $R(u)$ of

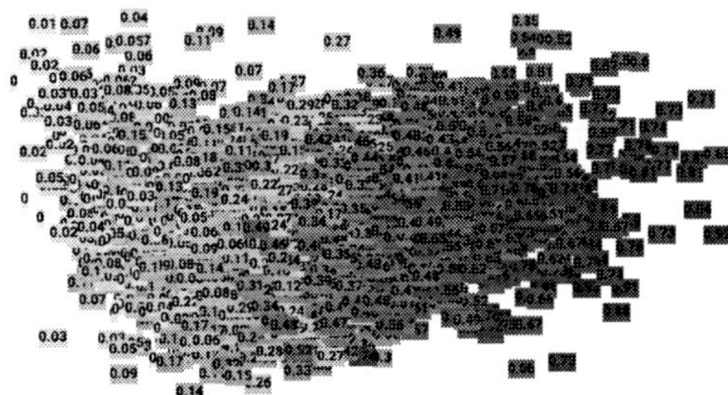

Figure 1: User embeddings learned by *ue*RNN (2 principal components). Color represents the rejection rate $R(u)$ of the user's training comments.

the corresponding users. Moving from left to right in Fig. 1, the rejection rate increases, indicating that the user embeddings of *ue*RNN capture mostly the rejection rate $R(u)$. This rate (a single scalar value per user) can also be captured by the simpler user-specific biases of *ub*RNN, which explains why *ub*RNN also performs well (second best results in Table 3). Nevertheless, *ue*RNN performs better than *ub*RNN, suggesting that user embeddings capture more information than just a user-specific rejection rate bias.[8]

Three of the user types (Red, Yellow, Green) in effect also measure $R(u)$, but in discretized form (three bins), which also explains why user type embeddings (*te*RNN) also perform well (third best method). The performance of *tb*RNN is close to that of *te*RNN, suggesting again that most of the information captured by user type embeddings can also be captured by simpler scalar user-type-specific biases. The user type biases b_t learned by *tb*RNN are shown in Table 4. The bias of the Red type is the largest, the bias of the Green type is the smallest, and the biases of the Unknown and Yellow types are in between, as expected (Section 3). The same observations hold for the average user-specific biases b_u learned by *ub*RNN (Table 4).

Overall, Table 3 indicates that user-specific information (*ue*RNN, *ub*RNN) is better than user-type information (*te*RNN, *tb*RNN), and that embeddings (*ue*RNN, *te*RNN) are better than the scalar biases (*ub*RNN, *tb*RNN), though the differences are small. All the RNN-based methods outperform the two baselines (*u*BASE, *t*BASE), which do not consider the texts of the comments.

Let us provide a couple of examples, to illustrate the role of user-specific information. We en-

---

[7]We used Keras (http://keras.io/) with the TensorFlow back-end (http://www.tensorflow.org/).

[8]We obtained no clear clusterings with tSNE (van der Maaten and Hinton, 2008).

User Type	b_t of *tb*RNN	average b_u of *ub*RNN
Green	$-0.471\,(\pm0.007)$	$-0.180\,(\pm0.024)$
Yellow	$0.198\,(\pm0.015)$	$0.058\,(\pm0.022)$
Unknown	$0.256\,(\pm0.021)$	$0.312\,(\pm0.011)$
Red	$1.151\,(\pm0.013)$	$0.387\,(\pm0.023)$

Table 4: Biases learned and standard error.

countered a comment saying just "Ooooh, down to Pireaus…" (translated from Greek), which the moderator had rejected, because it is the beginning of an abusive slogan. The rejection probability of RNN was only 0.34, presumably because there are no clearly abusive expressions in the comment, but the rejection probability of *ue*RNN was 0.72, because the author had a very high rejection rate. On the other hand, another comment said "Indeed, I know nothing about the filth of Greek soccer." (translated, apparently not a sarcastic comment). The original RNN method marginally rejected the comment (rejection probability 0.57), presumably because of the 'filth' (comments talking about the filth of some sport or championship are often rejected), but *ue*RNN gave it a very low rejection probability (0.15), because the author of the comment had a very low rejection rate.

5   Related work

In previous work (Pavlopoulos et al., 2017a), we showed that our RNN-based method outperforms DETOX (Wulczyn et al., 2017), the previous state of the art in user content moderation. DETOX uses character or word n-gram features, no user-specific information, and an LR or MLP classifier. Other related work on abusive content moderation was reviewed extensively in our previous work (Pavlopoulos et al., 2017a). Here we focus on previous work that considered user-specific features and user embeddings.

Dadvar et al. (2013) detect cyberbullying in YouTube comments, using an SVM and features examining the content of each comment (e.g., second person pronouns followed by profane words, common bullying words), but also the profile and history of the author of the comment (e.g., age, frequency of profane words in past posts). Waseem et al. (2016) detect hate speech tweets. Their best method is an LR classifier, with character n-grams and a feature indicating the gender of the author; adding the location of the author did not help.

Cheng et al. (2015) predict which users will be banned from on-line communities. Their best system uses a Random Forest or LR classifier, with features examining the average readability and sentiment of each user's past posts, the past activity of each user (e.g., number of posts daily, proportion of posts that are replies), and the reactions of the community to the past actions of each user (e.g., up-votes, number of posts rejected). Lee et al. (2014) and Napoles et al. (2017) include similar user-specific features in classifiers intended to detect high quality on-line discussions.

Amir et al. (2016) detect sarcasm in tweets. Their best system uses a word-based Convolutional Neural Network (CNN). The feature vector produced by the CNN (representing the content of the tweet) is concatenated with the user embedding of the author, and passed on to an MLP that classifies the tweet as sarcastic or not. This method outperforms a previous state of the art sarcasm detection method (Bamman and Smith, 2015) that relies on an LR classifier with hand-crafted content and user-specific features. We use an RNN instead of a CNN, and we feed the comment and user embeddings to a simpler LR layer (Eq. 2), instead of an MLP. Amir et al. discard unknown users, unlike our experiments, and consider only sarcasm, whereas moderation also involves profanity, hate speech, bullying, threats etc.

User embeddings have also been used in: conversational agents (Li et al., 2016); sentiment analysis (Chen et al., 2016); retweet prediction (Zhang et al., 2016); predicting which topics a user is likely to tweet about, the accounts a user may want to follow, and the age, gender, political affiliation of Twitter users (Benton et al., 2016).

Our previous work (Pavlopoulos et al., 2017a) also discussed how machine learning can be used in *semi-automatic* moderation, by letting moderators focus on 'difficult' comments and automatically handling comments that are easier to accept or reject. In more recent work (Pavlopoulos et al., 2017b) we also explored how an attention mechanism can be used to highlight possibly abusive words or phrases when showing 'difficult' comments to moderators.

6   Conclusions

Experimenting with a dataset of approx. 1.6M user comments from a Greek sports news portal, we explored how a state of the art RNN-based moderation method can be improved by adding user embeddings, user type embeddings, user biases, or user type biases. We observed improvements in all cases, but user embeddings were the best.

We plan to compare *ue*RNN to CNN-based methods that employ user embeddings (Amir et al., 2016), after replacing the LR layer of *ue*RNN by an MLP to allow non-linear combinations of comment and user embeddings.

Acknowledgments

This work was funded by Google's Digital News Initiative (project ML2P, contract 362826).[9] We are grateful to Gazzetta for the data they provided. We also thank Gazzetta's moderators for their feedback, insights, and advice.

References

S. Amir, B. C. Wallace, H. Lyu, P. Carvalho, and Mario J. M. J. Silva. 2016. Modelling context with user embeddings for sarcasm detection in social media. In *Proceedings of CoNLL*, pages 167–177, Berlin, Germany.

D. Bamman and N.A. Smith. 2015. Contextualized sarcasm detection on Twitter. In *Proc. of the 9th International Conference on Web and Social Media*, pages 574–577, Oxford, UK.

A. Benton, R. Arora, and M. Dredze. 2016. Learning multiview embeddings of Twitter users. In *Proc. of ACL*, pages 14–19, Berlin, Germany.

H. Chen, M. Sun, C. Tu, Y. Lin, and Z. Liu. 2016. Neural sentiment classification with user and product attention. In *Proc. of EMNLP*, pages 1650–1659, Austin, TX.

J. Cheng, C. Danescu-Niculescu-Mizil, and J. Leskovec. 2015. Antisocial behavior in online discussion communities. In *Proc. of the International AAAI Conference on Web and Social Media*, pages 61–70, Oxford University, England.

K. Cho, B. van Merrienboer, C. Gulcehre, D. Bahdanau, F. Bougares, H. Schwenk, and Y. Bengio. 2014. Learning phrase representations using RNN encoder–decoder for statistical machine translation. In *EMNLP*, pages 1724–1734, Doha, Qatar.

M. Dadvar, D. Trieschnigg, R. Ordelman, and F. de Jong. 2013. Improving cyberbullying detection with user context. In *ECIR*, pages 693–696, Moscow, Russia.

X. Glorot and Y. Bengio. 2010. Understanding the difficulty of training deep feedforward neural networks. In *Proc. of the International Conference on Artificial Intelligence and Statistics*, pages 249–256, Sardinia, Italy.

D. P. Kingma and J. Ba. 2015. Adam: A method for stochastic optimization. In *ICLR*, San Diego, CA.

J.-T. Lee, M.-C. Yang, and H.-C. Rim. 2014. Discovering high-quality threaded discussions in online forums. *Journal of Computer Science and Technology*, 29(3):519–531.

J. Li, M. Galley, Chris C. Brockett, G. Spithourakis, J. Gao, and B. Dolan. 2016. A persona-based neural conversation model. In *Proc. of ACL*, pages 994–1003, Berlin, Germany.

L. J. P. van der Maaten and G. E. Hinton. 2008. Visualizing data using t-SNE. *Journal of Machine Learning Research*, 9:2579–2605.

T. Mikolov, W.-t. Yih, and G. Zweig. 2013. Linguistic regularities in continuous space word representations. In *NAACL-HLT*, pages 746–751, Atlanta, GA.

C. Napoles, A. Pappu, and J. Tetreault. 2017. Automatically identifying good conversations online (yes, they do exist!). In *Proc. of the International AAAI Conference on Web and Social Media*.

J. Pavlopoulos, P. Malakasiotis, and Androutsopoulos I. 2017a. Deep learning for user comment moderation. In *Proc. of the ACL Workshop on Abusive Language Online*, Vancouver, Canada.

J. Pavlopoulos, P. Malakasiotis, and Androutsopoulos I. 2017b. Deeper attention to abusive user content moderation. In *EMNLP*, Copenhagen, Denmark.

J. Pennington, R. Socher, and C. Manning. 2014. GloVe: Global vectors for word representation. In *EMNLP*, pages 1532–1543, Doha, Qatar.

Z. Waseem and D. Hovy. 2016. Hateful symbols or hateful people? Predictive features for hate speech detection on Twitter. In *Proc. of NAACL Student Research Workshop*, pages 88–93, San Diego, CA.

E. Wulczyn, N. Thain, and L. Dixon. 2017. Ex machina: Personal attacks seen at scale. In *WWW*, pages 1391–1399, Perth, Australia.

Q. Zhang, Y. Gong, J. Wu, H. Huang, and X. Huang. 2016. Retweet prediction with attention-based deep neural network. In *Proc. of the International on Conference on Information and Knowledge Management*, pages 75–84, Indianapolis, IN.

---

[9]See https://digitalnewsinitiative.com/.

Incongruent Headlines: Yet Another Way to Mislead Your Readers

Sophie Chesney[†], **Maria Liakata**[‡], **Massimo Poesio**[†] and **Matthew Purver**[†]

[†]Cognitive Science Research Group
School of Electronic Engineering and Computer Science
Queen Mary University of London, UK
`{initial.lastname}@qmul.ac.uk`

[‡]Department of Computer Science
University of Warwick, Coventry, UK
`m.liakata@warwick.ac.uk`

Abstract

This paper discusses the problem of incongruent headlines: those which do not accurately represent the information contained in the article with which they occur. We emphasise that this phenomenon should be considered separately from recognised problematic headline types such as clickbait and sensationalism, arguing that existing natural language processing (NLP) methods applied to these related concepts are not appropriate for the automatic detection of headline incongruence, as an analysis beyond stylistic traits is necessary. We therefore suggest a number of alternative methodologies that may be appropriate to the task at hand as a foundation for future work in this area. In addition, we provide an analysis of existing data sets which are related to this work, and motivate the need for a novel data set in this domain.

1 Introduction

The problem of mis- and disinformation in the media is the subject of much recent attention. This is often given the general label 'fake news' – but this term can refer to a number of distinct concepts, from fabricated or manipulated content to satire (Wardle, 2017), each of which might have very different requirements for a computational treatment. In this paper we highlight a specific problem within this realm, that of headline incongruence, show that it is distinct from problems considered within NLP so far, and discuss how it might be approached. Consider (1), taken from the *Express*

UK online newspaper[1] (Ecker et al., 2014):

(1) **Headline:** Air pollution now leading cause of lung cancer
Evidence within article: "We now know that outdoor air pollution is not only a major risk to health in general, but also *a* leading *environmental* cause of cancer deaths." Dr. Kurt Straif, of IARC [emphasis added]

As Ecker et al. (2014) highlight, this headline misleads the reader by overstating the claim made later in the article. First, omitting 'environmental' from the headline radically generalises the claim: a leading environmental cause may not be the leading cause, above all other causes. Second, omitting the indefinite determiner 'a' (as is common in English 'headlinese', Mårdh, 1980) allows a salient reading with an implicit definite article 'the', further exaggerating the claim.

The headline therefore significantly misrepresents the findings reported in the article itself. While the article reports these accurately, even quoting another source contradicting the exaggerated claim (*"...although air pollution increases the risk of developing lung cancer by a small amount, other things have a much bigger effect on our risk, particularly smoking"*), these nuances are lost in the headline. This seems particularly dangerous in the light of experimental work into reader behaviour: Ecker et al. (2014) show that even after reading the article in full, a reader is likely to be left with their initial impression gained from the headline; and Gabielkov et al. (2016) found that c.60% of shared URLs on Twitter are not clicked on before sharing, suggesting that in

---

[1]Tom Rawle (2013): http://www.express.co.uk/lifestyle/health/437473/Air-pollution-now-leading-cause-of-lung-cancer

Proceedings of the 2017 EMNLP Workshop on Natural Language Processing meets Journalism, pages 56–61
Copenhagen, Denmark, September 7, 2017. ©2017 Association for Computational Linguistics

many cases only headlines are read. Automatic detection of these misleading cases could therefore directly impact the spread of misinformation.

Indeed, the phenomenon is particularly noticeable on social media, partly due to the practice of using different headlines online. Official posts on social media from some sources include a different headline in the social media post preview than on the article itself, as demonstrated by (2), taken from the *Independent*'s Facebook page.

(2) **Social media post copy:** Enjoy it while you can
Social media headline[2]: Scientists have predicted the end of sex
Article headline[3]: Sex will be made unnecessary by 'designer babies', professor says
Evidence within article: Professor Henry Greely believes that in as little as 20 years, most children will be conceived in a laboratory, rather than through sexual intercourse.

This example shows a gradual increase in accuracy and detail, from the misleading social media post to the evidence within the article itself. The social media headline is incongruent with the details of the story, and this is exaggerated further when combined with the rest of the post. This clearly demonstrates that social media can be used to carefully market stories by exaggerating and twisting key elements of a story in the headline in conjunction with copy in the post itself.

It is important to highlight, however, that this phenomenon is not limited to social media, nor to particular sectors of the press (e.g. tabloid press, press from certain political leanings). We found examples from across the political spectrum, as well as across multiple reputable mainstream sources cross-lingually. Consider examples (3)-(8),[4] which discuss a recent announcement by Volvo Cars on the production of electric cars. As with (1), the headlines consistently exaggerate the claims made in the original press release (8), varying from outright incongruence (3) to subtle quantifier scope ambiguity that leaves interpretation open (6)-(8).

(3) **Dagens Industri***[5]: Volvo stops developing cars with internal combustion engines

(4) **Independent (Social media headline)**[6]: Petrol cars are dead, say Volvo

(5) **Sveriges Radio***[7]: Volvo becomes electric car brand

(6) **Göteborgs Posten***[8]: Volvo to only make electric cars

(7) **Reuters**[9]: Geely's Volvo to go all electric with new models from 2019

(8) **Volvo Cars Press Release**[10]: Volvo Cars to go all electric
Evidence from official press release: Volvo Cars, the premium car maker, has announced that every Volvo it launches from 2019 will have an electric motor, marking the historic end of cars that *only* have an internal combustion engine.

The story, which, from the headlines suggests that Volvo Cars will completely stop production of cars with internal combustion engines and only produce electric vehicles, circulated in the mainstream and automotive press. In fact, in-article evidence makes clear that, although all new vehicles produced after 2019 will contain some electric element, many will still contain some petrol or diesel component. Importantly, Volvo Cars CEO Håkan Samuelsson is quoted to say, "this announcement marks the end of the *solely* combustion engine-powered car", a nuance which is lost in the headlines above. Interestingly, these examples illustrate that headline incongruence can occur even in sources widely considered as reliable and reputable, such as Reuters (7), as well as in the very source of the story, as in the case of Volvo Cars' own press release (8).

Here, we consider whether existing definitions and NLP techniques can be applied to this phenomenon, and if not, how we may define it and approach its detection computationally. This has ap-

---

[2]https://www.facebook.com/TheIndependentOn-line/posts/10154972799736636

[3]Will Worley (2016): http://www.independent.co.uk/news/science/sex-unnecessary-designer-babies-stanford-professor-says-a6957636.html

[4]Examples labelled with * are translated from Swedish, and independently verified by a native speaker.

[5]Håkan Matson (2017): http://www.di.se/bil/volvo-slutar-tillverka-bilar-med-forbranningsmotorer/

[6]https://www.facebook.com/TheIndependentOn-line/posts/10154981271001636

[7]http://sverigesradio.se/sida/artikel.aspx?programid=83&artikel=6732573

[8]Ida Johansson (2017): http://www.gp.se/nyheter/ekonomi/volvo-ska-bara-tillverka-elbilar-1.4413878

[9]Niklas Pollard (2017): https://uk.reuters.com/article/us-volvocars-geely-electric-idUKKBN19Q0BJ

[10]https://www.media.volvocars.com/global/en-gb/media/pressreleases/210058/volvo-cars-to-go-all-electric

plications within news aggregation, as a means of weighting articles and informing readers, as well as potential in the incentivisation of journalistic values.

2 Existing Definitions

These cases, then, do not involve misinformation or fabricated content within the article, but rather properties of the headline and its relation to the content. In this section, we examine existing work into the description and classification of problematic types of headline.

2.1 Clickbait

Headlines have traditionally been characterised as short, 'telegram'-like, and maximally informative summaries of the article with which they appear (Van Dijk, 1988; Cotter, 2010). They appear to follow a particular condensed grammar commonly referred to as 'headlinese' (Mårdh, 1980; De Lange, 2008), and are often carefully constructed to attract the attention of a reader (Bell, 1984; Ecker et al., 2014). In extreme cases this results in 'clickbait'-style headlines, characteristic of tabloids and online-native digital media sites such as *Buzzfeed*[11], expressly designed to withhold information to entice the reader to read on, or in most cases, to click. A recent press release by Facebook[12] describes clickbait as *"headlines that intentionally leave out crucial information, or mislead people, forcing people to click to find out the answer"* – see (9)-(11):

(9) You'll Never Believe Who Tripped and Fell on the Red Carpet. . . (Facebook)

(10) Here's What Happens When You Put A Few Little Kids In A Room With 2 Dolls In 2 Different Colors. (Chen et al., 2015)

(11) Which Real Housewife Are You Based On Your Birth Month (Chakraborty et al., 2016)

Clickbait shows characteristic stylistic and lexical features: 'forward-referencing', heavy use of demonstrative pronouns, adverbs, interrogatives, and imperatives (Blom and Hansen, 2015), as well as extensive use of personal pronouns (e.g. 'you'), numbers, and celebrity references (Chen et al., 2015). These features can therefore be used within standard NLP methodologies: Chakraborty et al.

[11]www.buzzfeed.com

[12]https://newsroom.fb.com/news/2017/05/news-feed-fyi-new-updates-to-reduce-clickbait-headlines/

(2016) achieved 93% classification accuracy on a corpus including 7,500 English clickbait headlines using a set of 14 such features in a Support Vector Machine (SVM) classifier.

Returning to our example (1), however, although the headline does withhold information and thereby misleads, it does not fulfil our expectation of a clickbait headline. Most importantly, it does not 'force' the reader to click to find out the conclusions of the story, but rather delivers a *misleading* conclusion up front in the headline which (likely purposefully) misinforms the reader on the details in order to frame the facts in a certain light. Consequently, it lacks the typical observable features of clickbait (e.g. forward-referencing, demonstrative pronouns, numbers, etc.), and is therefore unlikely to be detected through these stylometric means. It is therefore rather more subtle than archetypal clickbait as targeted by the methods suggested by Chen et al. (2015); Chakraborty et al. (2016).

2.2 Sensationalism

Some examples labelled as clickbait, however, have a different approach to engaging readers. Chen et al. (2015) also identify the use of affective language and action words, associated with emotional engagement, as in (12):

(12) The first lady of swearing! How a ten-year-old Michelle Obama lost out on a 'best camper' award because she wouldn't stop cursing (Daily Mail, Chen et al., 2015)

While Chen et al. (2015) refer to this example as 'clickbaiting', this arguably introduces a complexity and inconsistency into their definition. This example does not *force* the reader to click by withholding information or using leading language, but instead uses techniques more traditionally considered as *sensationalism*, to dramatise an otherwise non-dramatic story.

Though many definitions exist, sensationalism can be considered as "the presentation of stories in a way that is intended to provoke public interest or excitement, *at the expense of accuracy*" (Oxford Dictionary Online). Sensationalist news is generally considered negatively in the journalism literature (see e.g. Wang and Cohen, 2009), as content which "triggers emotion for the reader (Vettehen et al., 2008) and treats an issue in a predominantly tabloid-like way" (Kilgo et al., 2016). Although traditionally associated with certain topics e.g. sex, scandal, crime and disaster (Grabe et al., 2001; Vettehen et al., 2008), recent work suggests that it is now just as likely with political stories (Kilgo et al., 2016). Examples (13)-(15) (Molek-Kozakowska, 2013, originally *Daily Mail*) show the characteristic use of exaggeration, emotive language, and punctuation, and cover a range of topics including health, crime, and education:

(13) A sausage a day could lead to cancer: Pancreatic cancer warning over processed meat

(14) Rise of the hugger mugger: Sociable thieves who cuddle while they rob

(15) £100 to play truant! Schools accused of bribing worst pupils to stay away when Ofsted inspectors call

Molek-Kozakowska (2013) views sensationalism as a *discourse strategy* used to repackage information in a more exciting, extraordinary or interesting way, via the presence of several discourse *illocutions* (e.g. exposing, speculating, generalising, warning, and extolling).[13] Based on this view, Hoffman and Justicz (2016) propose a method for automatic sensationalism detection in scientific reporting, training a supervised Maximum Entropy classifier on a corpus of 500 annotated news records, with bag-of-words TF.IDF document vectorisation[14]. They achieve an average accuracy of 73% over 200 validation instances. Crucially, headline and article were not treated separately, so any nuances between the two components will not be captured in this model.

Again, though, while our example (1) does satisfy several aspects of the definitions of sensationalism discussed here (e.g. warning, use of emotive content), it does not do so through the typical stylistic traits seen in (13)-(15). The vocabulary is not particularly inflammatory or emotive, nor is the structure typical of sensationalism. This defines the precise difficulty with the detection of incongruence in headlines this paper aims to highlight: incongruent headlines do not necessarily adhere to an identifiable style in their surface form, but rather must be identified in relation to the text they represent. This presents significant problems for the NLP approaches so far discussed.

---

[13]As Molek-Kozakowska (2013) used only one news source (the *Daily Mail*), this list may be specific to this particular newspaper's voice and/or the knowledge, subjectivity and demographic range of the annotators.

[14]See Hoffman and Justicz (2016, Appendices 1-4).

3 Incongruent Headlines: Suggested Methodology

The relationship between a headline and the article with which it appears can be conceptualised in a number of ways. We propose novel methods of incongruence detection which would explore varying aspects of the phenomenon, based on existing work in other areas. It is clear from the cross-source examples (3)-(8) that relying on source information alone is unlikely to be sufficient in determining headline incongruence, given that this phenomenon does not seem to be strictly limited to one section of the press. However, in conjunction with other methodology, the source of the headline-article pair may well prove to be a useful feature in the broader classification process, which we will explore experimentally in future work.

Arguably, the task of headline incongruence detection is best approached in parts: to analyse complex relationships between a headline and an entire news article is likely to be extremely difficult, not least because of their very different lengths and levels of linguistic complexity. This could therefore be facilitated with the extraction of key quotes (Pouliquen et al., 2007) or claims (Vlachos and Riedel, 2015; Thorne and Vlachos, 2017). Alternatively, one could automatically generate the statistically 'best' headline for an article using existing title and headline generation and summarisation methods (e.g. Banko et al. (2000); Zajic et al. (2002); Dorr et al. (2003)), and evaluate how far away the existing headline is from this in terms of a number of criteria, such as lexical choices, syntactic structure, length, tonality (sentiment or emotion), and so on.

It may also be interesting to explore existing work on argument analysis: for example, Stab and Gurevych (2017) explore methods for the identification of arguments supported by insufficient evidence. This could be viewed as very close to the task of the detection of incongruent headlines, where the headline represents an argument which is not supported by claims in the text. Further, we could approach incongruence as a semantic issue and look to existing work on contradiction (De Marneffe et al., 2008), contrast (Harabagiu et al., 2006) and entailment recognition (Levy et al., 2013). In doing so, we may well discover several sub-types of incongruence which may fall into different semantic categories.

Finally, stance detection (Augenstein et al., 2016; Mohammad et al., 2016) has been applied in the Fake News Challenge (FNC-1)[15] as a means of exploring whether different articles agree or disagree with a given headline or claim, to aid in the task of fact checking. Stance is certainly relevant to task of incongruence detection, but we argue that it is not sufficient for our task, as the headline-article relation may be incongruent in ways separate from (dis)agreement. Beyond the headline-article pair itself, however, stance detection could be used to analyse engagement and interaction with an article on social media, given that early indications suggest that users are compelled to alert others when they notice that a headline is misleading.

4 Existing Data

A number of data sets are available which address related tasks, but none seem directly suited to the incongruence problem. The Clickbait Challenge[16] released a data set of 2495 social media posts (titles, articles and social media copy), labelled on a four-point scale (not/slightly/considerably/heavily clickbaiting) through crowdsourcing. Although precise guidelines for the annotation process are not provided, it seems that the organisers follow a definition of clickbait similar to those discussed in Section 2.1, in which posts are "designed to entice readers into clicking an accompanying link". As already emphasised, this differs from the concept of headline incongruence described here, and we do not expect this annotation to be useful for our task; however, as a source of paired titles and articles it may provide useful raw data.

Piotrkowicz et al. (2016) present a corpus of 11,980 *Guardian News* headlines automatically annotated with news values (prominence, sentiment, superlativeness, proximity, surprise, and uniqueness). Although this corpus does not contain a target class in line with headline incongruence, it may provide useful insight in the feature extraction process.

The Fake News Challenge (FNC-1) has released a corpus of headline-article pairs which are annotated with one of the following four stances:

Agrees: *The body text agrees with the headline.*
Disagrees: *The body text disagrees with the headline.*

Discusses: *The body text discuss the same topic as the headline, but does not take a position.*
Unrelated: *The body text discusses a different topic than the headline.*

Built on the data set described in Ferreira and Vlachos (2016), which is collected from rumour tracking website, Emergent[17], the corpus contains approximately 50,000 annotated headline-body pairs. A manual analysis of the first 50 body IDs led to a number of observations on the applicability of this data set to the problem of headline incongruence. Firstly, the 'headline' in a pair is the claim from the original post on the website, and is as such not necessarily a gold-standard headline. In addition, a single 'headline' can occur with multiple article bodies, and vice versa, which means that the original relation between the two is not captured. In our task, we are particularly interested in how a headline is utilised to (mis)represent the information in an article; it is therefore important that the data we use reflects these subtle connections and disconnections, a feature that may be lost when pairing a headline (or claim) with an article body at random. The *unrelated* class in this data set is therefore unlikely to be relevant, as it appears to reflect a random shuffling of headline-body pairs. The *disagree* class represents contradictions between headline and body, which is too strong a notion of incongruence for our purposes; disagreement represents a direct contrast, whereas incongruence can be a subtle exaggeration or misrepresentation of facts but need not represent an opposing view. If this data set contains incongruent headline-body pairs by our definition, it appears that they are not in line with the existing labels, therefore it cannot be used in its current form.

5 Conclusions

The paper discusses incongruent headlines and how we may approach their automatic detection using existing NLP methods, motivated by experimental evidence on reader behaviour (Ecker et al., 2014; Gabielkov et al., 2016). We emphasise that headline incongruence, as seen in example (1), cannot be approached through methodology applied to related concepts like clickbait and sensationalism, as these use headline-specific stylometric features, and do not consider any deeper semantic relation between headline and text that

---

[15]http://www.fakenewschallenge.org/
[16]http://www.clickbait-challenge.org/
[17]http://www.emergent.info/

would be critical to the task at hand. We consequently suggest a number of potential approaches for this task, based on existing work in summarisation and headline generation, stance detection, claim and quote extraction, as well as argument analysis. Finally, we discuss a number of existing data sets, but demonstrate that, in their current forms, none are appropriate for the task discussed here. This therefore motivates the need for a novel data set in this domain, which lays the foundation for the next stages of our future work.

References

I. Augenstein, A. Vlachos, and K. Bontcheva. 2016. Any-target stance detection on twitter with autoencoders. In *Proc. SemEval*.

M. Banko, V. O. Mittal, and M. J. Witbrock. 2000. Headline generation based on statistical translation. In *Proc. ACL*.

A. Bell. 1984. 'Good copy-bad news'. the syntax and semantics of news editing. *Applied Sociolinguistics* pages 73–116.

J. N. Blom and K. R. Hansen. 2015. Click bait: Forward-reference as lure in online news headlines. *Journal of Pragmatics* 76:87–100.

A. Chakraborty, B. Paranjape, S. Kakarla, and N. Ganguly. 2016. Stop clickbait: Detecting and preventing clickbaits in online news media. In *Proc. IEEE/ACM ASONAM*.

Y. Chen, N. Conroy, and V. Rubin. 2015. Misleading online content: Recognizing clickbait as false news. In *Proc. ACM Multimodal Deception Detection*.

C. Cotter. 2010. News talk. *Investigating the Language of Journalism. CUP, Cambridge* .

J. De Lange. 2008. *Article Omission in Headlines and Child Language: A Processing Approach*. Netherlands Graduate School of Linguistics.

M.-C. De Marneffe, A. N. Rafferty, and C. D. Manning. 2008. Finding contradictions in text. In *ACL*.

B. Dorr, D. Zajic, and R. Schwartz. 2003. Hedge trimmer: A parse-and-trim approach to headline generation. In *Proc. HLT-NAACL*.

U. K. Ecker, S. Lewandowsky, E. P. Chang, and R. Pillai. 2014. The effects of subtle misinformation in news headlines. *Journal of Experimental Psychology: Applied* 20(4):323.

W. Ferreira and A. Vlachos. 2016. Emergent: a novel data-set for stance classification. In *NAACL-HLT*.

M. Gabielkov, A. Ramachandran, A. Chaintreau, and A. Legout. 2016. Social Clicks: What and Who Gets Read on Twitter? In *ACM SIGMETRICS / IFIP Performance 2016*.

M. E. Grabe, S. Zhou, and B. Barnett. 2001. Explicating sensationalism in television news: Content and the bells and whistles of form. *Journal of Broadcasting & Electronic Media* 45(4):635–655.

S. Harabagiu, A. Hickl, and F. Lacatusu. 2006. Negation, contrast and contradiction in text processing. In *AAAI*.

S. J. Hoffman and V. Justicz. 2016. Automatically quantifying the scientific quality and sensationalism of news records mentioning pandemics: validating a maximum entropy machine-learning model. *Journal of Clinical Epidemiology* 75:47–55.

D. K. Kilgo, S. Harlow, V. García-Perdomo, and R. Salaverría. 2016. A new sensation? an international exploration of sensationalism and social media recommendations in online news publications. *Journalism* .

O. Levy, T. Zesch, I. Dagan, and I. Gurevych. 2013. Recognizing partial textual entailment. In *ACL*.

I. Mårdh. 1980. *Headlinese: On the grammar of English front page headlines*, volume 58. Liberläromedel/Gleerup.

S. M. Mohammad, S. Kiritchenko, P. Sobhani, X. Zhu, and C. Cherry. 2016. Semeval-2016 task 6: Detecting stance in tweets. *Proceedings of SemEval* 16.

K. Molek-Kozakowska. 2013. Towards a pragma-linguistic framework for the study of sensationalism in news headlines. *Discourse & Communication* 7(2):173–197.

A. Piotrkowicz, V. Dimitrova, and K. Markert. 2016. Automatic extraction of news values from headline text. In *Proceedings of EACL*.

B. Pouliquen, R. Steinberger, and C. Best. 2007. Automatic detection of quotations in multilingual news. In *Proc. RANLP*.

C. Stab and I. Gurevych. 2017. Recognizing insufficiently supported arguments in argumentative essays. In *Proc. EACL*.

J. Thorne and A. Vlachos. 2017. An extensible framework for verification of numerical claims.

T. A. Van Dijk. 1988. *News as discourse*. Revised edition. Routledge (2013).

P. H. Vettehen, K. Nuijten, and A. Peeters. 2008. Explaining effects of sensationalism on liking of television news stories: The role of emotional arousal. *Communication Research* 35(3):319–338.

A. Vlachos and S. Riedel. 2015. Identification and verification of simple claims about statistical properties. In *Proc. EMNLP*.

T.-L. Wang and A. A. Cohen. 2009. Factors affecting viewers perceptions of sensationalism in television news: A survey study in Taiwan. *Issues and Studies* 45(2):125–157.

C. Wardle. 2017. Fake news. it's complicated. *First Draft News* Retrieved from https://firstdraft-news.com/fake-news-complicated/ on 04/05/2017.

D. Zajic, B. Dorr, and R. Schwartz. 2002. Automatic headline generation for newspaper stories. In *Workshop on Automatic Summarization*.

Unsupervised Event Clustering and Aggregation from Newswire and Web Articles

Swen Ribeiro
LIMSI, CNRS
Univ. Paris-Sud
Université Paris-Saclay
swen.ribeiro@limsi.fr

Olivier Ferret
CEA, LIST,
Gif-sur-Yvette,
F-91191 France.
olivier.ferret@cea.fr

Xavier Tannier
LIMSI, CNRS
Univ. Paris-Sud
Université Paris-Saclay
xavier.tannier@limsi.fr

Abstract

In this paper, we present an unsupervised pipeline approach for clustering news articles based on identified event instances in their content. We leverage press agency newswire and monolingual word alignment techniques to build meaningful and linguistically varied clusters of articles from the Web in the perspective of a broader event type detection task. We validate our approach on a manually annotated corpus of Web articles.

1 Introduction

In the context of news production, an event is the characterization of a significant enough change in a space-time context to be reported as newsworthy content. This definition fits with definitions proposed in other contexts such as the ACE 2005 and TAC KBP Event evaluations or work such as (Cybulska and Vossen, 2014; Mitamura et al., 2015), which generally view each event as "something that happens at a particular place and time", implying changes in the state of the world and involving participants. In accordance with ontologies about events such as the Simple Event Model (SEM) ontology (van Hage et al., 2011), events can be categorized into different *types*, for example "elections" or "earthquakes", gathering multiple real-life *instances*, for example the "2017 UK General Election" or the "2012 French Presidential Election". These *instances* are reported by journalists through varying textual *mentions*. Event extraction is a challenging task that has received increasing interest in the past years through many formulations such as event identification or

event detection. It is also an important subtask of larger NLP applications such as document summarization and event schema induction. Several approaches have been used to tackle the different aspects of this task, particularly in an unsupervised fashion, from linguistic pipelines (Filatova et al., 2006; Huang et al., 2016) to topic modeling approaches (Chambers and Jurafsky, 2011; Cheung et al., 2013) and more recently neural networks (Nguyen et al., 2016). While the definition and granularity of an event varies with the task and objectives at hand, most event identification systems exploit *mentions* to produce *type*-level representations.

We propose to address the unsupervised event extraction task through two subtasks: first, unsupervised event instance extraction and second, event type extraction. This paper will focus on our efforts regarding the first step, *e.g.* unsupervised event instance extraction. In this perspective, we present a method based on clustering algorithms leveraging news data from different sources. We believe that this first step might act as a bridge between the surface forms that are mentions and the more abstract concept of *instances* and *types* of events. Moreover, the context of this work is the ASRAEL project, which aims at providing operational tools for journalists, and this instance/type segmentation seems relevant in the perspective of further event-driven processing developments.

Our clustering approach considers three dimensions: time, space and content. A content alignment system is adapted from Sultan et al. (2014) and a time and space-aware similarity function is proposed in order to aggregate articles about the same event.

We work with a large collection of English news

62

Proceedings of the 2017 EMNLP Workshop on Natural Language Processing meets Journalism, pages 62–67
Copenhagen, Denmark, September 7, 2017. ©2017 Association for Computational Linguistics

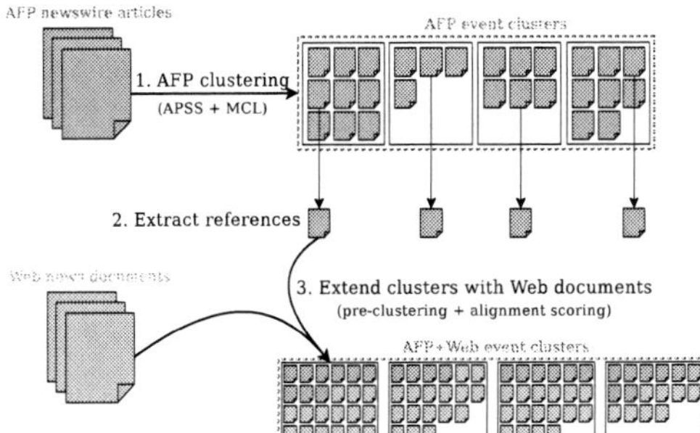

Figure 1: Overview of the system.

and Web articles, where each article describes an event: the main topic of the article is a specific event, and other older events are mentioned in order to put it into perspective. Thus, we consider an event associated with an article.

Our system's objective is to build clusters of articles describing the same exact real-life event, *e.g* the same event *instance*. We adopt two definitions of the relation "same event" (strict and loose) and evaluate through these two definitions.

2 Two-step Clustering

Our approach is structured as a pipeline including a two-step clustering with an additional filtering step at the end. The first step leverages an homogeneous corpus of news articles for building focused and "clean" clusters corresponding to event instances. The second step exploits these focused clusters for clustering documents coming from the Web that are more noisy but also more likely to bring new information about the considered events. Figure 1 illustrates this pipeline.

2.1 Corpora

The first clustering step (represented in blue on Figure 1) is performed on a corpus from Agence France-Presse (AFP) news agency. Each news article comes with several metadata providing additional information about its time-space context of creation, such as its UTC time-stamp, and its content, through International Press Telecommunications Council (IPTC) NewsCodes. NewsCodes are a standard subject taxonomy created and maintained by the IPTC, with a focus on text.

From the 1,400+ existing NewsCodes, we selected 72 that can be viewed as event types[1], cov-

ering as many event types as possible without overlapping with one another, and retrieved all news articles tagged with at least one of these NewsCodes. This resulted in a corpus of about 52,000 documents for the year 2015.

The second clustering step (in orange on Figure 1) takes as input news articles crawled from a list of Web news feeds in English. We used a corpus of 1.3 million Web news articles published in 2015, from about 20 different Web news sites (3,700 documents/day in average) including the RSS feeds of the New-York Times, the BBC or the Wall Street Journal.

In both corpora, we process only the title and first paragraph (usually one or two sentences) of the documents, under the assumption that they follow the journalistic rule of the 5Ws: the lead of an article must provide information about *what*, *when*, *where*, *who* and *why*.

2.2 Approach

2.2.1 Press Agency Clustering

The first clustering step computes the similarity matrix of the AFP news by the means of the All Pairs Similarity Search (APSS) algorithm (Bayardo et al., 2007) and applies to it the Markov Clustering (MCL) algorithm (van Dongen, 2000). News are represented by a bag-of-word representation including the lemmatized form of their nouns, adjectives and verbs.

The similarity function between two documents d_1 and d_2 is the following:

$$sim(d_1, d_2) = \frac{cos(d_1, d_2)}{e^{\delta/24}}$$

where $cos(d_1, d_2)$ is the cosine similarity and δ is the difference between the documents creation times (in hours). This time decay ensures that two similar but different events, occurring at different moments, will not be grouped together. Only similarities above a threshold τ have been considered[2].

This first step yields small and instance-focused clusters of press agency news articles only. While they can be considered high quality content, they are quite homogeneous and lack variety in their wording, and could not be used for broader tasks such as event type-level detection. An example of output for this step is provided in Figure 2.

---

[1] A user-friendly tree visualization of all the NewsCodes is available at http://show.newscodes.org/index.html?newscodes=subj.

[2] A grid search led to $\tau = 0.5$.

Hundreds dead in Nepal quake, avalanche triggered on Everest. A massive 7.8 magnitude earthquake killed hundreds of people Saturday as it ripped through large parts of Nepal, toppling office blocks and towers in Kathmandu and triggering an avalanche that hit Everest base camp.

Nepal quake kills 1,200, sparks deadly Everest avalanche. A massive earthquake killed more than 1,200 people Saturday as it tore through large parts of Nepal, toppling office blocks and towers in Kathmandu and triggering a deadly avalanche at Everest base camp.

Hundreds dead in Nepal quake, deadly avalanche on Everest. A massive 7.8 magnitude earthquake killed more than 900 people Saturday as it ripped through large parts of Nepal, toppling office blocks and towers in Kathmandu and triggering a deadly avalanche that hit Everest base camp.

Figure 2: 3 of 5 AFP news articles clustered together. While they indeed cover the same event instance, there are few wording variations between them, limiting their interest for broader event detection and assimilated tasks.

2.2.2 Web Article Extension

In this step, we aim to alleviate the lack of variability of our AFP news article clusters by leveraging their high focus to aggregate Web documents about the same event instances.

To do so, we identify the first article published in each AFP cluster (using the time-stamp) and retrieve all Web articles in the next 24 hours. This is based on the assumption that press agencies are a primary source of trustworthy information for most news feeds, so it would be rare to find mentions of an event instance before an article was released, especially in an international context. We call this article the "reference".

We first perform a first "coarse-grain" agglomeration by performing low-threshold cosine similarity-based clustering between the AFP reference and all Web articles for the given 24-hour timespan. This results in smaller subsets of data to feed the next module in the pipeline.

We then use the monolingual word alignment system described in Sultan et al. (2014). This system performs a word-to-word alignment between two sentences by applying a series of alignment modules focusing each on a specific type of linguistic units. The alignment process starts with n-grams of words (with n $\geqslant$ 2) including at least one content word. Then, named entities are considered, followed by content words and finally, stopwords. While alignment of n-grams of words and named-entities is based only on string matching (exact match for n-grams, partial for named entities as the system uses Stanford NER to resolve acronyms and matching partial mentions), the system also relies on contextual evidence for other linguistic units, e.g: syntactic dependencies and textual neighborhood. Textual neighborhood is defined as a window of the next and previous 3 content words surrounding each word being considered for an alignment. The system then computes a similarity score between each candidate pair available based on this evidence, and selects the highest scored pair for a given word as the chosen alignment. We adapted the system to better fit our needs by extending the stopword list, first aligning unigram exact matches and using the absence of matching content words or named entities as an early stopping condition of the alignment process.

For each AFP cluster, we perform alignment between the reference (earliest article) and each Web article from the subset. This allows us to build a word alignment matrix where each column contains the words in a document and each line shows how each word of the reference has aligned across all documents.

We then compute a score for each document, taking into account how many words in a document have been aligned with the reference, and how many times a reference word has found an alignment across all documents.

Figure 3 illustrates how this score is computed. We first build the binary alignment matrix B where columns represent documents and rows represent term alignments. If a term i (out of M aligned terms) from document j (out of N documents) has been aligned with a term from the reference, then $B_{i,j} = 1$, otherwise $B_{i,j} = 0$. We then compute a weight for each alignment, leading to a vector $Align$ such as for each term i:

$$Align_i = \sum_{j=0}^{N} B_{i,j}$$

The absolute alignment score of each document j is then:

$$s_j = \sum_{i=0}^{M} W_{i,j}$$

where $W = B \times Align$. Finally, we normalize these by the scores that the reference itself would have obtained.

Once we have scored the documents of a cluster, we sort them and find the greatest gap between

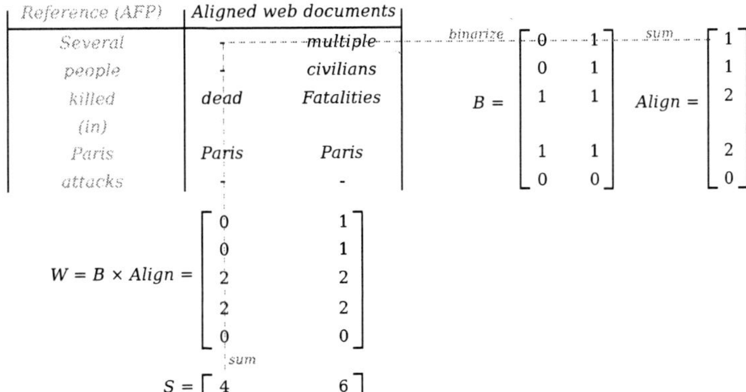

Figure 3: Document scoring.

two consecutive scores (scree test). Only the best-ranked documents before this elbow value are kept as event instance driven document clusters.

3 Evaluation and Results

In our evaluation, we focus on assessing the quality of the clusters produced at the end of the alignment filtering step. We performed our experiments on the AFP and Web data for the whole year 2015. Considering that the AFP corpus sometimes develops more "France-" and "Europe-centric" content while our Web corpus is more "Anglo-Saxon-centered", we need to ensure that we evaluate on event instances that are covered in both corpora, which is the case in the resulting outputs of the coarse-grain agglomeration phase, by construction. We therefore selected 12 of these "pre-clusters" of event instances, based on the notable events of the year 2015 as per Wikipedia[3]. This selection is described in Table 1. The Web articles in these intermediary outputs are sorted by descending order of their cosine similarity to the AFP reference. This ordering will serve as a baseline to evaluate the capacity of the alignment module to produce more relevant clusters, the documents processed at both steps being the same.

We ran AFP clustering and "coarse-grain" agglomeration, identified the resulting intermediary outputs that corresponded to our 12 selected event instances (content and time-stamp wise). We then ran the alignment phase, picked the 50 best-ranked Web articles in each cluster obtained from the selected outputs and tagged them manually with a relevance attribute as follows:

- 0: The document is not related to the refer-

France seizes passports of would-be jihadists. *February 23rd*	Protesters clash with police in St Louis, Mo., USA. *August 20th*
Cyclone Pam hit Vanuatu archipelago. *March 15th*	Facebook vows to combat racist content on German platform. *September 14th*
UK General Election campaign start. *March 30th*	Wildfires rampage across northern California. *September 14th*
Magnitude 7.9 earthquake hits Nepal. *April 25th*	Paris Attacks. *November 13th*
Pakistan police kill head of anti-Shiite group. *July 7th*	Swedish police arrest man for plotting terror attack. *November 20th*
ISIS Truck bombing in Baghdad market. *August 13th*	Typhoon Melor causes heavy flooding in Philippines. *December 16th*

Table 1: The 12 events of our gold standard.

ence event considered;
- 1: The document has a *loose* relation to the reference event;
- 2: The document has a *strict* relation to the reference event.

We define *strict* and *loose* relation as follows: a *strict* relation means that the document is focused on the event and differ from the reference news article only by its wording or additional/missing information; a *loose* relation designates a document that is not focused on the event, but provides a news that is so specific to this event that its mention is core to the overall information provided. Examples of strict and loose relations are provided in Figure 4.

This distinction was introduced when facing two particular types of documents: death toll updates and responsibility claims for terrorist attacks. In both cases, the causal events (attack or natural disaster) are first released as they are in-

---

[3]https://en.wikipedia.org/wiki/2015

Magnitude 7.5 earthquake hits Nepal: USGS. A powerful 7.5 magnitude earthquake struck Nepal on Saturday, the United States Geological Survey said, with strong tremors felt across the Himalayan nation and parts of India.

101 dead as 7.8 quake hits Nepal, causing big damage. A powerful earthquake struck Nepal Saturday, killing at least 71 people as the violently shaking earth, collapsed houses, leveled centuries-old temples and triggered avalanches in the Himalayas.

Nepal quake toll reaches 688: government. KATHMANDU (Reuters) - The death toll from a powerful earthquake that struck Nepal on Saturday has risen to 688, a senior home ministry official told Reuters, with 181 people killed in the capital Kathmandu.

Figure 4: Examples of strict and loose relations. The first text is from the reference news article, the second one is assessed as "strict" relation, the third one as a "loose" relation.

formation of their own. Afterwards, death tolls and claims become stand-alone newsworthy content and are updated independently, yet remaining tightly connected to their causal event.

We use the same metrics as described in Glavaš and Šnajder (2013): mean R-precision (*R-prec.*) and mean average precision (*MAP*) are computed over the complete ordering of all the documents in the cluster with:

$$\textit{R-prec} = \frac{r}{R}$$

where r = number of relevant retrieved documents and R = total number of relevant documents to retrieve. Average Precision (AP) is given by:

$$AP = \frac{\sum_{k=1}^{n} (P(k) * rel(k))}{R}$$

where k = rank of the document, $P(k)$ is the precision at cut-off k and $rel(k) = 1$ if document k is relevant, 0 otherwise. We also compute precision, recall and F-score after applying the elbow splitting to evaluate it separately.

Our results are detailed in Table 2 by distinguishing for each reference (strict or loose) the figures with (*align*) and without (*no align*) the use of our final alignment algorithm. From that perspective, Table 2 clearly shows the interest of this last step, with a significant increase of both MAP and R-precision when the final alignment algorithm is applied. This increase is particularly noticeable for R-precision, which emphasizes the ability of this last step to rerank the Web documents in a relevant way. Unsurprisingly, the strict reference is globally more difficult than the loose one, especially for precision: as *loose* documents are close

	Strict		**Loose**	
	no align	**align**	**no align**	**align**
MAP	58.6	62.2	63.7	66.9
R-prec.	50.2	60	56.5	63.5
Precision	–	70.7	–	77.1
Recall	–	80.3	–	76.3
F-score	–	75.2	–	77.7

Table 2: Performance of our event instance clustering system. Average values for the 12 events.

to *strict* documents, the overall system tends to select more false positives with the *strict* reference. Logically, the *loose* reference makes recall decrease, but very slightly.

From a qualitative perspective, we observed several phenomena. Sometimes, the journalistic coverage of an event extends greatly from the time-space context of the mentioned instance, which tends to have a negative impact on precision. For example, in our corpus, the 13 November terrorist attacks of Paris have caused many official reactions worldwide as well as actions taken through social media that have been covered on their own, all in a very short period of time. Moreover, the event itself might be complex in nature: while the event "Paris Attacks" can be restricted to the city of Paris on one particular night (unified time-space context), it is in fact composite, consisting in multiple attacks of different natures (shootings and bombings). For our system, this results in clusters of abnormal sizes (700+ documents clustered in this case, against an usual maximum of 100+). In such cases, the number of annotated documents in the gold standard can be too low, which is an obstacle to the correct evaluation of the output. These abnormal clusters also have another characteristic: being composed of significantly more documents, the distribution of their alignment scores tends to be smoother, making the scree-test less reliable.

4 Conclusion and Perspectives

In this paper, we introduced an unsupervised pipeline aiming at producing event instance driven clusters of news articles. To do so, we leverage homogeneous high-quality news agency articles to identify event instances and find linguistic variations in their expression from Web news articles. Our experimental results validate our approach as a groundwork for future extensions in the broader task of grouping events according to their type and inducing a shared representation of each type of event by identifying and generalizing the participants of events.

5 Acknowledgment

This work has been partially funded by French National Research Agency (ANR) under project AS-RAEL (ANR-15-CE23-0018). We would like to thank the French News Agency (AFP) for providing us with the corpus.

References

Roberto J. Bayardo, Yiming Ma, and Ramakrishnan Srikant. 2007. Scaling up all pairs similarity search. In *16th International World Wide Web Conference (WWW'07)*. pages 131–140.

Nathanael Chambers and Dan Jurafsky. 2011. Template-based information extraction without the templates. In *Proceedings of the 49th Annual Meeting of the Association for Computational Linguistics (ACL 2011)*. Portland, Oregon, USA, pages 976–986.

Jackie Chi Kit Cheung, Hoifung Poon, and Lucy Vanderwenden. 2013. Probabilistic frame induction. In *Proceedings of NAACL-HLT 2013*. Atlanta, Georgia, USA, pages 837–846.

Agata Cybulska and Piek Vossen. 2014. Using a Sledgehammer to Crack a Nut? Lexical Diversity and Event Coreference Resolution. In *Ninth International Conference on Language Resources and Evaluation (LREC'14)*. Reykjavik, Iceland.

Elena Filatova, Vasileios Hatzivassiloglou, and Kathleen McKeown. 2006. Automatic creation of domain templates. In *Proceedings of the COLING/ACL 2006 Main Conference Poster Sessions*. pages 207–214.

Goran Glavaš and Jan Šnajder. 2013. Recognizing identical events with graph kernels. In *51st Annual Meeting of the Association for Computational Linguistics (ACL 2013)*. Sofia, Bulgaria, pages 797–803.

Lifu Huang, Taylor Cassidy, Feng Xiaocheng, Heng Ji, Clare R. Voss, Jiawei Han, and Avirup Sil. 2016. Liberal event extraction and event schema induction. In *Proceedings of the 54th Annual Meeting of the Association for Computational Linguistics (ACL 2016)*. Berlin, Germany, pages 258–268.

Teruko Mitamura, Yukari Yamakawa, Susan Holm, Zhiyi Song, Ann Bies, Seth Kulick, and Stephanie Strassel. 2015. Event Nugget Annotation: Processes and Issues. In *3rd Workshop on EVENTS: Definition, Detection, Coreference, and Representation*. Denver, Colorado, pages 66–76.

Thien Huu Nguyen, Kyunghyun Cho, and Ralph Grishman. 2016. Joint event extraction via recurrent neural networks. In *Proceedings of NAACL-HLT 2016*. San Diego, California, USA, pages 300–309.

Md Arafat Sultan, Steven Bethard, and Tamara Summer. 2014. Back to Basics for Monolingual Alignment: Exploiting Word Similarity and Contextual Evidence. *Transactions of the Association for Computational Linguistics (TACL)* 2:219–230.

Stijn van Dongen. 2000. *Graph Clustering by Flow Simulation*. Ph.D. thesis, University of Utrecht.

Willem Robert van Hage, Véronique Malaisé, Roxane Segers, Laura Hollink, and Guus Schreiber. 2011. Design and use of the simple event model (sem). *Web Semantics: Science, Services and Agents on the World Wide Web* 9(2):128–136.

Semantic Storytelling, Cross-lingual Event Detection and other Semantic Services for a Newsroom Content Curation Dashboard

Julian Moreno-Schneider, Ankit Srivastava,
Peter Bourgonje, David Wabnitz[*], Georg Rehm

DFKI GmbH, Language Technology Lab, Alt-Moabit 91c, 10559 Berlin, Germany
[*]Kreuzwerker GmbH, Ritterstraße 12-14, 10969 Berlin, Germany
Corresponding author: georg.rehm@dfki.de

Abstract

We present a prototypical content curation dashboard, to be used in the newsroom, and several of its underlying semantic content analysis components (such as named entity recognition, entity linking, summarisation and temporal expression analysis). The idea is to enable journalists (a) to process incoming content (agency reports, twitter feeds, reports, blog posts, social media etc.) and (b) to create new articles more easily and more efficiently. The prototype system also allows the automatic annotation of events in incoming content for the purpose of supporting journalists in identifying important, relevant or meaningful events and also to adapt the content currently in production accordingly in a semi-automatic way. One of our long-term goals is to support journalists building up entire storylines with automatic means. In the present prototype they are generated in a backend service using clustering methods that operate on the extracted events.

1 Introduction

Journalists write and distribute news articles based on information collected from different sources (news agencies, media streams, other news articles etc.). In order to produce a high-quality piece, a fair bit of research is needed on the topic and domain at hand. Facts have to be checked, requiring at least basic domain knowledge, different view points considered and information from multiple sources combined in a sensible way. In short, much research is needed to arrive at a piece of content that combines new and surprising information with a decent context of the event reported upon. While the amount of available, especially digital information is increasing on a daily basis, the journalist's ability to read all this information is decreasing in the little time available. This calls for tools that support journalists in processing large amounts of incoming information.

There are differences in journalistic reporting, depending on the event being covered. News about a event with global relevance, such as a war, differs from news about the inauguration of a local cultural centre. When looking at the available source material, the amount of background information, also its diversity, differs significantly in both cases. Coverage for the global event depends on a much larger amount of readily available information while the local event coverage depends on smaller amounts of data that may need a bit of effort in tracking them down (the name of local news sources for example). To address this difference in research requirements we describe a prototypical approach for cross-lingual semantic analysis, especially event detection, ultimately aimed at supporting journalists through semantic storytelling, based on two data sets.

Section 2 briefly describes the content curation dashboard, while Section 3 focuses upon semantic storytelling. Section 4 describes the use cases and sketches the results of initial experiments on news data. Section 5 concludes the paper.

Proceedings of the 2017 EMNLP Workshop on Natural Language Processing meets Journalism, pages 68–73
Copenhagen, Denmark, September 7, 2017. ©2017 Association for Computational Linguistics

2 The Content Curation Dashboard

One of the partner companies involved in our joint technology transfer project (Rehm and Sasaki, 2015) to introduce curation technologies to different sectors, is currently designing and developing an extension for the open source newsroom software Superdesk.[1] Superdesk is a production environment for journalists that specialises on the creation of content, i. e., the play-out and rendering of the content is taken care of by other parts of a larger system. Our Superdesk extension allows the semantic processing of incoming news streams to enable several smart features, e. g., keyword alerts, content exploration, identifying related content, among others. The tool also allows the visualisation and annotation of news documents using additional information sources, databases and knowledge graphs such as Linked Data. The idea is to allow rich faceted search scenarios so that the journalist has fine-grained mechanisms for locating the needle in a potentially very large haystack of digital data. Faceted search includes entities, topics, sentiment values and genres, complemented with semantic information from external sources (DBpedia) enabling higher semantic search precision based on extracted information than would be possible with keyword based search.

Visualisation includes menus that show the annotated entities and their frequencies next to a set of related documents. Example screens of the content curation dashboard are shown in Figure 1. The Superdesk extension and the underlying semantic technologies mainly operate on the (1) ingest view and the (2) authoring view. The first view allows to ingest multiple incoming content channels into the production environment; our semantic tools can automatically analyse the content using, for example, named entity recognition, sentiment analysis, topic detection, classification (e. g., IPTC topics) and others, so that journalists can tailor the incoming news feed exactly to their liking and current topics. In the second view, the semantic tools are used to support the authoring process, to add and modify annotations, to recommend related content potentially to be linked to in the new article.

While Superdesk is a specialised newsroom software, journalists also often use Content Management Systems such as Symphony to automate day-to-day work (e. g., file and document man-

---

[1] https://www.superdesk.org

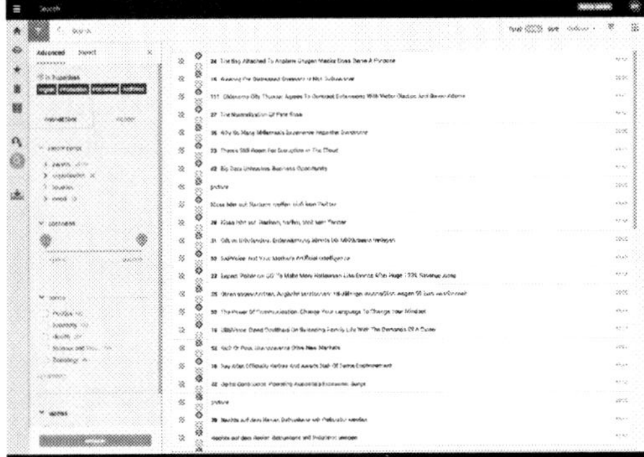

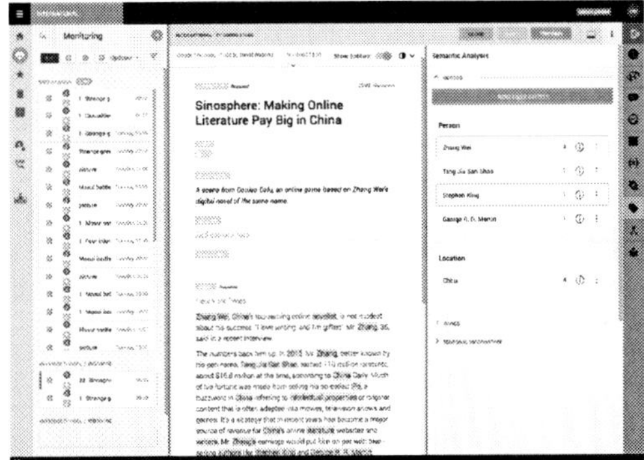

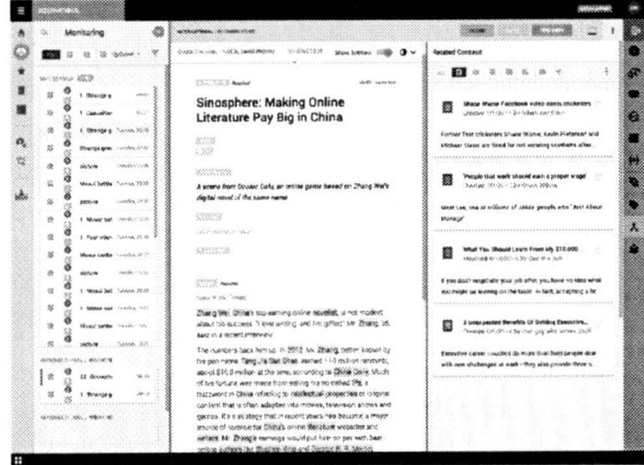

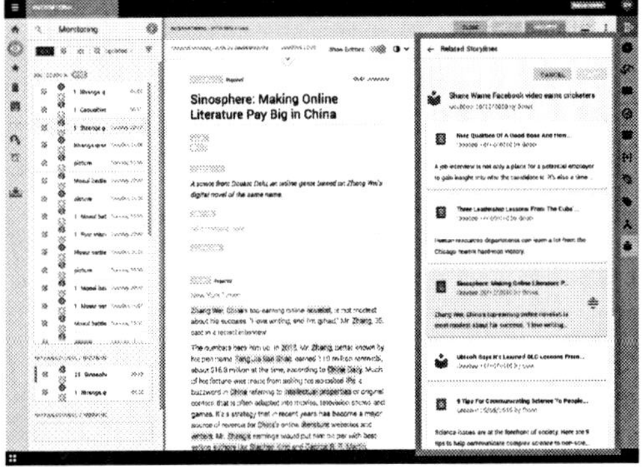

Figure 1: The Content Curation Dashboard

agement).[2] For document exploration proper IR systems (mainly ElasticSearch) have gained popularity through user-friendly wrappers such as Kibana,[3] which offers visualisation of maps and timelines, or Kibi,[4] which offers richer visualisation capabilities (graphs, charts).

We want to enable journalists interactively to put together a story based on extensive semantic content enrichment. In our various use cases, different parts of the content function as atomic building blocks (sentences, paragraphs, documents). In the use case of the present paper we focus, for now, upon document level building blocks for generating stories, i. e., documents can be rearranged, included and deleted from a storyline. In a later stage we plan to use smaller content components with which we will experiment towards the generation of news articles based on multiple story paths, automatically generated with the help of semantic annotations.

Currently our technology allows us to generate "semantic fingerprints" which enable suggestions as to where the currently edited article would fit in either an existing storyline or recommend a new one based on content currently being readied for production and further enhanced by related content. Generally, it would enable journalists to work more in smaller update increments to a developing story or storyline without having to retell a story time and again. Storylines, in that sense, can be thought of as a container, pulling related stories together. By providing for a semi-automatic arrangement of stories within a storyline (e. g., by suggesting that a story fits in a certain slot within a chronological order of related events or in a certain slot in an existing narrative), journalists can be alleviated of the need to be aware of these relationships and to manage them. Consumers of news articles get the benefit of additional context and navigational tools provided by articles being arranged in storylines as well as enjoying a more efficient news consumption experience.

3   Semantic Storytelling for Journalists

In our current prototype we attempt to generate a set of potential storylines from a collection of incoming news documents. A storyline is a set of building blocks that, through their combination (temporal, geographical, semantic, etc.) form a story. In several use cases, the atomic building blocks are documents; we use a more fine-grained approach in which events are the building blocks of storylines, i. e., a set of entities governed by a trigger element (normally a verb) and which together represent an occurring action in the text.

The linguistic processing is done by a semantic annotation pipeline that creates a layer of named entities, temporal expressions and other information on top of the document collection, also augmented with event detection (Bourgonje et al., 2016a,b). For example, in the sentence "Barack Obama visited Ukraine last summer and had a meeting with Petró Poroshenko" there are two persons (Barack Obama, Petró Poroshenko), one location (Ukraine) and one temporal expression (last summer). There are also two trigger verbs: "visited" and "meet". Therefore, there are two events in this sentence: [visited, Barack Obama, Ukraine, last summer] and [meet, Barack Obama, Petró Poroshenko]. The sentence "Vladimir Putin will meet next summer with president Petró Poroshenko in Moscow" contains one event: [meet, Vladimir Putin, Petró Poroshenko, Moscow, next summer]. Events in German or English texts are extracted using cross-lingual event detection (Section 3.1). Then, storylines are created from combinations of annotated events using three clustering techniques to obtain related and similar information in the collection. In the Superdesk extension (Section 2), storylines are still composed of a set of related documents. Once completed, the extension will also operate on the more fine-grained event-centric approach.

Work related to our rather general, domain-independent storytelling concept typically concentrates on very specific objectives. A few systems focus on providing content for entertainment purposes (Wood, 2008; Poulakos et al., 2015). Other researchers focus on specific domains, e. g., storytelling in gaming (Gervás, 2013), for recipes (Cimiano et al., 2013)or weather reports (Belz, 2008), requiring knowledge about characters, actions, locations, events, or objects that exist in this particular domain (Riedl and Young, 2010; Turner, 2014). Regarding news, (Shahaf and Guestrin, 2010) describe methods for navigating within a new topic using hidden connections. They automatically find links between news articles through the extraction of links between entities. (Vossen

---

[2]https://symphony.com

[3]https://www.elastic.co/products/kibana

[4]https://siren.solutions/kibi/

et al., 2015) handle news streams through a formal model for representing storylines. They also describe a first implementation and visualisation that helps inspecting the generated structures.

3.1 Cross-lingual Event Detection

We implemented a cross-lingual event detection system, i.e., we automatically translate non-English documents to English using Moses (Koehn et al., 2007) and detect events in the translated documents using a state-of-the-art event extraction system based on (Yang and Mitchell, 2016), trained on the English section of ACE 2005 (Doddington et al., 2004). The cross-lingual detection of events encompasses a pipeline that ends up with a list of annotated events in every document (Rehm et al., 2017b).

3.2 Semantic Storytelling

Extracted events themselves are not useful to a journalist who works on a set of documents. They have to be analysed further, summarised, rearranged and then presented in a way that speeds up (human) access and understanding. In a previous approach (Schneider et al., 2016) we focused upon template-filling, using the results of relation extraction to fill (biography) templates to present these as content pieces to the knowledge worker. In the present paper, events serve the same purpose, delivering content pieces for a news article.

These general clusters of events can provide the logical text structure of a new journalistic piece. We can also cluster documents based on the temporal dimension grouping together events that happened in the same period of time (e. g., a war or an award ceremony), or based on locations, using latitude and longitude coordinates. Another option is traditional semantic clustering, obtaining sets of documents that talk about the same events and entities. To get semantically related events, we cluster documents based on the entities that appear in the events (entity frequency). Our interpretation of semantically related events are events that share entities as their participants (subject and object). The cluster information for the two previous examples is shown in Table 1. Once the documents are clustered, their events are grouped and ranked by frequency. In the previous example there were three events, one document with two events and one document with one event: $d1 = \{ev1, ev2\}$ and $d2 = \{ev3\}$. If both documents are in the same cluster, and considering that we use the clusters as storylines, the resulting set of events in this storyline will be $\{ev1, ev2, ev3\}$.

3.3 Visualisation

To get a better understanding of the data set, the analysis results, the extracted events and to prepare attaching the semantic storytelling back-end to the newsroom content curation dashboard, we implemented an experimental visualisation prototype (Figure 2). This prototype provides access to the full set of semantic analysis information and can be used interactively to explore and evaluate the system. The map shows locations involved in extracted events with highlighted annotations. The slider below the map can be used to filter events by time. Additional details and case studies can be found in (Rehm et al., 2017a; Schneider et al., 2017). We will explore if we can integrate part of this prototype tool into the Superdesk extension.

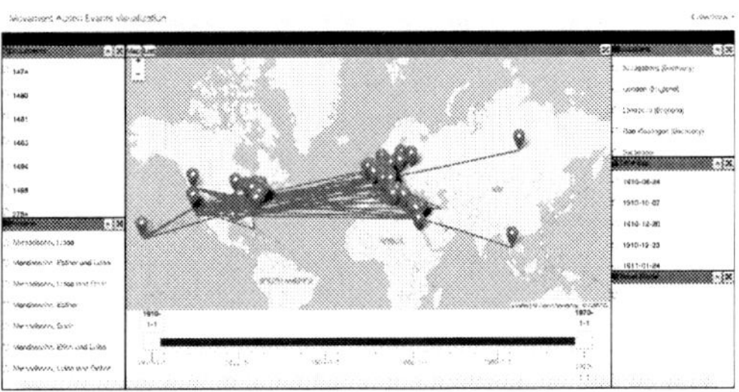

Figure 2: The experimental visualisation tool

4 Evaluation

We performed a qualitative evaluation of several generated storylines (clusters).[5] We apply the storytelling generation approach in two journalistic use cases: domain-specific web-crawled global news and general domain regional news. While the basic steps in both cases are the same (collecting relevant information, checking facts, writing an article, etc.), there are differences that make these two cases special: the "global news" articles are in English and were collected online while the "regional news" articles are in German, distributed by a news agency, so language usage and also register/style is different. We applied several clustering algorithms to both data sets using fixed and free cluster sizes; EM provides a rather balanced distribution along clusters.

---

[5]We would have performed the evaluation with the Superdesk extension but are still in the process of fully integrating the current prototype.

	Obama	Petró	Summer	Putin	Moscow	Ukraine
Document $d1$	1	1	1	0	0	1
Document $d2$	0	1	1	1	1	0

Table 1: Using the frequencies of extracted events as features for a clustering algorithm

4.1 Global News: Obama's Trips

For the global news case we used a data set that consists of news articles on the trips of Barack Obama (487 files, 24,387 sentences, 897,630 tokens).[6] All documents are English online news, which is why boilerplate cleaning was applied.[7]. The storytelling backend annotated a total of 61,718 entity mentions and 6,752 event triggers. After clustering using EM and the 50 most frequent entities as features, we obtain five clusters, i.e., five storylines. The number of documents contained in each storyline is: 4, 4, 19, 19, 16. The number of events included in each cluster is: 472, 1027, 2525, 3785, 2638. In the first cluster, there are three documents talking about trips to Asia (China, Vietnam, Istanbul) and only one to Germany; the documents in the second cluster are grouped together because of remaining HTML tags after the boilerplate cleaning; the third cluster is semantically more diverse and contains documents talking about trips to South America (Cuba, Argentina, Colombia) and Asia (Beijing, Bangkok, Philippines), but there are some unrelated documents talking about wars (Syria, Second World War) and trips to the UK (London); the fourth cluster contains mainly documents talking about trips to Europe to the G20 Summit; the last cluster groups documents mentioning different places (Brazil, Egypt, Afghanistan, Japan, etc). Considering the topic diversity, this approach seems to be an interesting initial point for the automatic generation of semantic content for stories in large collections with topic heterogeneity.

4.2 Regional News

For the second use case we analyse a German general domain regional news collection (1,037 articles, 716,885 words, avg. number of words 691.3), provided by one of our project partner companies. The storytelling system, working on the automat-

ically translated English documents, annotated a total of 61,054 entity mentions and 2,571 event triggers. The discrepancy in the number of events between the two data sets can be attributed to different writing styles as well as the fact that the latter was translated automatically. After the clustering process using EM and the 50 most frequent entities as features, we obtain five storylines (with 34, 17, 113, 25, 35 documents, and 4167, 2529, 11885, 2930, 3284 events, respectively). After manually evaluating the documents and events we can summarise that the automatic translation of the documents, performed with an MT system that had not been domain-adapted, has had a negative impact on the performance of the event extraction system and, therefore, the clustering results.

5 Conclusions and Future Work

We present a system based on three main components: (1) a cross-lingual event detection module; (2) a storyline generation component that can determine related events; (3) a newsroom content curation dashboard prototype that helps journalists in the process of analysing large document collections. Regarding the manual evaluation of the generated storylines, we observe that the storyline generator clearly unveils inherent semantic relatedness as a basic property of the documents in the global news data set, while demonstrating documents in the local news data set to be rather unrelated. Further improvement of the storyline generation and event detection system is foreseen for future work, especially regarding deeper and more fine-grained filtering of the extracted events in order to minimise the number of events included in a storyline. A future version of the newsroom curation dashboard will be able to suggest, to the journalist, event-based storylines. We will also include additional visualisation, as well as more linked data sources. In the semantic backend, additional processing modules will be included, especially coreference resolution to improve the coverage of extracted entity mentions.

---

[6]Based on a list of links to news articles in https://en.wikipedia.org/wiki/List_of_international_presidential_trips_made_by_Barack_Obama

[7]https://github.com/kohlschutter/boilerpipe

Acknowledgments

The authors wish to thank the anonymous reviewers for their helpful feedback. The project "Digitale Kuratierungstechnologien" is supported by the German Federal Ministry of Education and Research, Wachstumskern-Potenzial (no. 03WKP45). http://www.digitale-kuratierung.de.

References

Anja Belz. 2008. Automatic Generation of Weather Forecast Texts Using Comprehensive Probabilistic Generation-space Models. *Natural Language Engineering* 14(4):431–455.

Peter Bourgonje, Julian Moreno-Schneider, Jan Nehring, Georg Rehm, Felix Sasaki, and Ankit Srivastava. 2016a. Towards a Platform for Curation Technologies: Enriching Text Collections with a Semantic-Web Layer. In H. Sack, G. Rizzo, N. Steinmetz, D. Mladenic, S. Auer, and C. Lange, editors, *The Semantic Web*. Springer, number 9989 in LNCS, pages 65–68.

Peter Bourgonje, Julian Moreno Schneider, Georg Rehm, and Felix Sasaki. 2016b. Processing Document Collections to Automatically Extract Linked Data: Semantic Storytelling Technologies for Smart Curation Workflows. In A. Gangemi and C. Gardent, editors, *Proc. of the 2nd Int. Workshop on NLG and the Semantic Web (WebNLG 2016)*. ACL, Edinburgh, UK, pages 13–16.

Philipp Cimiano, Janna Lüker, David Nagel, and Christina Unger. 2013. Exploiting Ontology Lexica for Generating Natural Language Texts from RDF Data. In *Proc. of the 14th European Workshop on NLG*. ACL, Sofia, Bulgaria, pages 10–19.

George Doddington, Alexis Mitchell, Mark Przybocki, Lance Ramshaw, Stephanie Strassel, and Ralph Weischedel. 2004. The automatic content extraction (ace) program – tasks, data, and evaluation. In *Proc. of LREC 2004*. ELRA, Lisbon, Portugal.

Pablo Gervás. 2013. Stories from Games: Content and Focalization Selection in Narrative Composition. In *I Spanish Symposium on Entertainment Computing*. Universidad Complutense de Madrid, Spain.

P. Koehn, H. Hoang, A. Birch, C. Callison-Burch, R. Zens, M. Federico, N. Bertoldi, C. Dyer, B. Cowan, W. Shen, C. Moran, O. Bojar, A. Constantin, and E. Herbst. 2007. Moses: Open Source Toolkit for Statistical Machine Translation. ACL, Prague, CZ, pages 177–180.

Steven Poulakos, Mubbasir Kapadia, Andrea Schüpfer, Fabio Zünd, Robert Sumner, and Markus Gross. 2015. Towards an Accessible Interface for Story World Building. In *AAAI Conf. on AI and Interactive Digital Entertainment*. pages 42–48.

Georg Rehm, Jing He, Julian Moreno Schneider, Jan Nehring, and Joachim Quantz. 2017a. Designing User Interfaces for Curation Technologies. In S. Yamamoto, editor, *Human Interface and the Management of Information: Information, Knowledge and Interaction Design, 19th Int. Conf., HCI Int. 2017*. Springer, Vancouver, CA, number 10273 in LNCS, pages 388–406. Part I.

Georg Rehm and Felix Sasaki. 2015. Digitale Kuratierungstechnologien – Verfahren für die effiziente Verarbeitung, Erstellung und Verteilung qualitativ hochwertiger Medieninhalte. In *Proc. of GSCL 2015*. pages 138–139.

Georg Rehm, Julian Moreno Schneider, Peter Bourgonje, Ankit Srivastava, Jan Nehring, Armin Berger, Luca König, Sören Räuchle, and Jens Gerth. 2017b. Event Detection and Semantic Storytelling: Generating a Travelogue from a large Collection of Personal Letters. In T. Caselli, B. Miller, M. van Erp, P. Vossen, M. Palmer, E. Hovy, and T. Mitamura, editors, *Proc. of the Events and Stories in the News Workshop*. ACL, Vancouver, CA.

Mark Owen Riedl and Robert Michael Young. 2010. Narrative Planning: Balancing Plot and Character. *J. Artif. Int. Res.* 39(1):217–268.

Julian Moreno Schneider, Peter Bourgonje, Jan Nehring, Georg Rehm, Felix Sasaki, and Ankit Srivastava. 2016. Towards Semantic Story Telling with Digital Curation Technologies. In L. Birnbaum, O. Popescu, and C. Strapparava, editors, *Proc. of NLP meets Journalism (NLPMJ 2016)*. NY.

Julian Moreno Schneider, Peter Bourgonje, and Georg Rehm. 2017. Towards User Interfaces for Semantic Storytelling. In S. Yamamoto, editor, *Human Interface and the Management of Information: Information, Knowledge and Interaction Design, 19th Int. Conf, HCI Int. 2017*. Springer, Vancouver, CA, number 10274 in LNCS, pages 403–421. Part II.

Dafna Shahaf and Carlos Guestrin. 2010. Connecting the dots between news articles. In *Proc. of 16th ACM SIGKDD Int. Conf. on Knowledge Discovery and Data Mining*. ACM, New York, NY, USA, KDD '10, pages 623–632.

S.R. Turner. 2014. *The Creative Process: A Computer Model of Storytelling and Creativity*. Taylor & Francis.

Piek Vossen, Tommaso Caselli, and Yiota Kontzopoulou. 2015. Storylines for Structuring Massive Streams of News. In *Proc. of 1st Workshop on Computing News StoryLines (CNewS 2015), co-located with ACL 2015 and ACL-IJCNLP 2015*. Bejing, China.

Mark D. Wood. 2008. Exploiting Semantics for Personalized Story Creation. In *Proc. of Int. Conf. on Semantic Computing*. Washington, DC, ICSC '08, pages 402–409.

Bishan Yang and Tom Mitchell. 2016. Joint extraction of events and entities within a document context. In *Proc. of NAACL 2016*. ACL, pages 289–299.

Deception Detection in News Reports in the Russian Language:

Lexics and Discourse

Dina Pisarevskaya
dinabpr@gmail.com

Abstract

Different language markers can be used to reveal the differences between structures of truthful and deceptive (fake) news. Two experiments are held: the first one is based on lexics level markers, the second one on discourse level is based on rhetorical relations categories (frequencies). Corpus consists of 174 truthful and deceptive news stories in Russian. Support Vector Machines and Random Forest Classifier were used for text classification. The best results for lexical markers we got by using Support Vector Ma-chines with rbf kernel (f-measure 0.65). The model could be developed and be used as a preliminary filter for fake news detection.

1 Introduction

The research field of deception detection in news reports and automated fact checking arose in natural language processing (NLP) rather recently. It can be applied for linguistic expertise, fact checking tools for newsrooms and news aggregators, tools for users.

We get information from different sources and should evaluate the reliability to avoid rumours, hoaxes and deceptive (fake) information in news reports. The word 'post-truth' was chosen as the Oxford Dictionaries Word of the Year 2016 and points that objective facts can be less influential than appeals to emotion and personal belief. It regards political and other news of our 'post-truth era'. In the media community, key persons pay attention to the value of truth in journalism, to the necessity of fact checking, to the threat of fake news and to the need for technical systems that would help diminish the problem: Almar Latour (The Wall Street Journal, 2016), sir Tim Berners-Lee (worldwide web inventor, 2017), Tim Cook (Apple, 2017), and Mark Zuckerberg (Facebook, 2016).

There are three types of fake news: serious fabrications, large-scale hoaxes and humorous fakes (Rubin et al., 2015a). OpenSources (www.opensources.co) suggests more news types, fake news among them. They are understood as fabricated information, disseminated deceptive content, or grossly distorted actual news reports. This definition corresponds to serious fabrications.

In social media, people participate in the propagation of the news that they find interesting. Algorithmic ranking, social bubbles and group polarization may lead to intentional or unintentional viral spread of unreliable news. Big amounts of news reports with misinformation spread caused by political reasons in 2016 in the USA (presidential election) (Allcott and Gentzkow, 2017). For the Russian language the problem of fake news is already vital since 2014 (Russian-Ukrainian discourse).

2 Related Work

Data science companies, academics, media organizations are working on computational fact checking for English: on fake news detection and real-time detection algorithms. In 2016, Google gave funding to FactMata and Full Fact project to develop automated fact checking tools. FactMata's (UK) project is devoted to fact checking and claim validation by known statistical databases. The Full Fact (UK) is developing an automated fact checking helper, using the logic of question answering machines: facts from social media will be parsed, compared with curated known-true facts

Proceedings of the 2017 EMNLP Workshop on Natural Language Processing meets Journalism, pages 74–79
Copenhagen, Denmark, September 7, 2017. ©2017 Association for Computational Linguistics

and determined as true or false. Tracer News system (0.84 accuracy) is a noise filter for journalists to discover breaking news in Twitter (Liu et al., 2016): machine learning models for noise filtering and event detection are implemented, NLP is also used. "Fake News" Classifier (www.classify.news) allows to score the veracity of an article by entering its URL. The corpus articles are based on OpenSources labels. The tool focuses on NLP techniques and considers both content (bag of words; multinomial Naive Bayes classifier) and context (sentiment analysis, capitalization and punctuation usage; Adaptive Boosting). HeroX Fact Check Challenge (https://herox.com/factcheck/community) (2016-2017) and FakeNewsChallenge (http://www.fakenewschallenge.org/) (2017) competitions were held to help to create fact checking systems.

As to the winners of HeroX Fact Check Challenge, Fact Scan (1st place) can check several types of claims automatically, such as numerical, position, quote and object property claims. Claim Buster (2nd place) is also able to check simple statements; it can match claims, and it is based on knowledge bases. As regards FakeNewsChallenge, the teams focused on the headline-text body relationships. Talos Intelligence team (1st place) used the ensemble classifier (gradient-boosted decision trees and deep convolutional neural network). Word embeddings, based on Google News pretrained vectors, were used for the neural network. Such features are informative for decision trees: the number overlapping words between the headline and body text; similarities measured between the word count, bigrams and trigrams; similarities measured after TF-IDF weighting and singular value decomposition. UCL Machine Reading system (3rd place) is based on lexical and similarity features fed through a multi-layer perceptron with one hidden layer. Features for checking headline-text body consistency contain three elements: a bag-of-words term frequency vector of the headline; a bag-of-words term frequency vector of the body; the cosine similarity of TF-IDF vectors of the headline and the text body.

Fake news may be identified on different levels. Usually they are combined, from lexics and semantics to syntax. Most studies focus on lexics and semantics and some syntax principles; discourse and pragmatics have rarely been considered (Rubin et al., 2015b) due to their complexity.

On lexics level, stylistic features (part of speech (POS), length of words, subjectivity terms etc.) can be extracted that help to apart tabloid news (they are similar to fake news) with 0.77 accuracy (Lex et al., 2010). Numbers, imperatives, names of media persons can be extracted from news headlines (Clark, 2014); the numbers of these keywords can be used as features for classification with SVMs or Naive Bayes Classifier (Lary et al., 2010). Psycholinguistics lexicons, for instance LIWC (Pennebaker and Francis, 1999), can be used in performing binary text classifications for truthful vs deceptive texts (0.70 accuracy) (Mihalcea and Strapparava, 1999) — for example, methods can be based on frequency of affective words or action words. On syntax level, Probability Context Free Grammars can be used (0.85-0.91 accuracy) (Feng et al., 2012). On pragmatics level, pronouns with antecedents in text are more often used in fake news' headlines (Blom and Hansen, 2015). On discourse level, rhetorical structures are used (Rubin et al., 2015b): vector space modeling application predicts whether a report is truthful or deceptive (0.63 accuracy) for English. Corpus consists of seriously fabricated news stories. So rhetorical structures and discourse constituent parts and their coherence relations are possible deception detection markers in English news.

As to facts in the described event, in (Sauri and Pustejovsky, 2012) model is based on grammatical fact description structures in English and kindred languages. It is implemented in De Facto, a factuality profiler for eventualities based on lexical types and syntax constructions. The FactBank, annotated corpus in English, was also created. FactMinder, a fact checking and analysis assistant based on information extraction, can help to find relevant information (Goasdoué et al., 2013). Knowledge networks like Wikipedia can be used for simple fact checking questions (Ciampaglia et al., 2015).

In (Hardalov et al., 2016) the combined approach for automatically distinguishing credible from fake news, based on different features and combining different levels, is presented: there are linguistic (n-gram), credibility-related (capitalization, punctuation, pronoun use, sentiment polarity), and semantic (embeddings and DBPedia data) features. The accuracy is from 0.75 to 0.99 on 3 different datasets.

The impact of different features on deception detection was studied in recent works (Fitzpatrick et al., 2015; Rosso et al., 2017).

There are no automated deception detection tools for news reports for Russian, although the field of deception detection in written texts is studied on the Russian Deception Bank (226 texts). The majority of research parameters are related to POS tags, lexical-semantic group, and other frequencies of LIWC lexicon words. The classifier's accuracy is 0.68 (Litvinova et al., 2017). Hence, we should base the research for Russian on the experience of methods for other languages, keeping in mind linguistics, social and cultural circumstances.

3 Research Objective

The aim is to reveal differences between fake and truthful news reports using markers from different linguistics levels. We use POS tags, length of words, sentiment terms, punctuation on the lexics level. Deception detection requires understanding of complex text structures, so we use Rhetorical Structures Theory (RST) relations as markers on the discourse level. In two experiments we shall classify the texts from the definite corpus.

4 Data Collection Principles

There are no sources that contain verified samples of fake and truthful news for Russian, although the problem of fake news is annually discussed on conference "Media Literacy, Media Ecology, Media Education: Digital Media for the Future" (Moscow). There are no Factbanks, unbiased fact checking websites, crowdsourcing projects, lists of truthful/deceptive sources. We can rely only on the presented facts, on the factuality.

The daily manual monitoring of news lasted 24 months (June 2015-June 2017). Online newspapers in Russian were used as sources. For balance, texts were from diverse sources: well-known news agencies' websites, local or topic-based news portals, online newspapers from different countries. News source mention was not included in text annotations to avoid biases. Blogs and social media texts, analytic journalism stories based on opinions (not on facts) were not taken. We selected only serious fabrications. News stories were carefully analyzed in retrospect when the factuality was already known, to avoid biased evaluation. In case of mutual contradictions in the reports about the same event, a re-

port was added to fake cases if at the same time period in online media existed reports with unproven facts and with their truthful refutation. So it was an intended fake and not a journalist's mistake caused by lack of facts.

5 Corpus Details and Data Analysis

The corpus consists of news reports about 48 different topics, with equal number of truthful and deceptive texts to each topic (not more than 12 texts for one topic). It contains 174 texts. The whole number of tokens is 33049. The mean length of texts is 189.04 tokens, the median length is 168.5 tokens. The whole number of rhetorical relations in corpus is 3147. Mean number of rhetorical relations in text is 18.09, the median number is 16.5.

The corpus size is conventional for the initial research on the field of automated deception detection, especially if we use the discourse level of language analysis, because it still requires manual annotation. Discourse parsers exist most notably for English (RASTA, SPADE, HILDA, CODRA etc.), and researchers do not use them even for English corpora when they need precise results. For comparison, the dataset in the paper which describes automated deception detection for news reports, based on RST, includes 144 news reports that were tagged manually (Rubin et al., 2015b). Corpus in the research about the impact of discourse markers on argument units classification (Eckle-Kohler et al., 2015) consists of 88 documents, predominantly news texts.

We used the following 18 normalized lexical markers for each text: average length of tokens; type-token ratio; frequency of adverbs; frequency of adjectives; frequency of pronouns-adverbs; frequency of numerals-adjectives; frequency of pronouns-adjectives; frequency of conjunctions; frequency of interjections; frequency of numerals; frequency of particles; frequency of nouns; frequency of pronouns-nouns; frequency of verbs; frequency of all punctuation marks; frequency of quotations; frequency of exclamation marks; frequency of lemmas from a sentiment lexicon.

All POS tags were obtained with MyStem tool for Russian which is for free use (some form words were excluded from the analysis). We collected seriously fabricated news reports, so we do not take capitalization as a feature. As there are no tools for sentiment polarity for Russian for free use, we use frequencies of lemmas from a list of

5000 sentiment words from reviews (Chetviorkin and Loukachevitch, 2012).

As to the discourse part, RST framework (Mann and Thompson, 1988) represents text as an hierarchical tree. Some parts are more essential (nucleus) than others (satellite). Text segments are connected to each other with relations. The theory pretends to be universal for all languages, so we chose it for our research. There are no discourse parsers for Russian: tagging and validation were made manually. We used UAM CorpusTool for discourse-level annotation. We based the research on the "classic" set by Mann and Thompson and added to it some more types: so, we created 4 types of Evidence according to the precision of source of information mention. News reports usually have a definite template, so a rather small number of relations was used. We have 33 relation types: 'Circumstance', 'Reason', 'Evidence1', 'Evidence2', 'Evidence3', 'Evidence4', 'Contrast', 'Restatement', 'Disjunction', 'Unconditional', 'Sequence', 'Motivation', 'Summary', 'Comparison', 'Non-Volitional Cause', 'Antithesis', 'Volitional Cause', 'Non-Volitional Result', 'Joint', 'Elaboration', 'Background', 'Solution', 'Evaluation', 'Interpretation', 'Concession', 'Means', 'Conjunction', 'Volitional Result', 'Justify', 'Condition', 'Exemplify', 'Otherwise', 'Purpose'. To avoid subjectivity of annotators' interpretation, we had 2 annotators and tried to solve this problem by preparing a precise manual for tagging and by developing consensus-building procedures. We selected Krippendorff's unitized alpha (0.78) as a measure of inter-annotator agreement.

The first dataset is based on statistics data about frequencies of lexical markers for each news report. The second one is based on statistics data about types of RST relations and their frequencies for each news report. In fact, we have a 'bag of relation types', disregarding their order.

We selected two supervised learning methods for texts classification and machine learning: Support Vector Machines (SVMs) and Random Forest, both realized in scikit-learn library for Python. SVMs were used with linear kernel and with rbf kernel. In both experiments (for both datasets) we used 10-fold cross-validation for estimator performance evaluation.

The baseline for all experiments is 50%, because there is the equal number of truthful and deceptive texts in the corpus.

6 Statistical Procedures

The results of two experiments are presented in Table 1.

	Precision	Accuracy	Recall	F-measure
Support Vector Machines, rbf kernel, 10-fold cross-validation				
Lexical features	**0.62**	**0.64**	**0.73**	**0.65**
Discourse features	0.56	0.54	0.52	0.51
Support Vector Machines, linear kernel, 10-fold cross-validation				
Lexical features	0.62	0.61	0.62	0.60
Discourse features	0.54	0.53	0.51	0.50
Random Forest Classifier, 10-fold cross-validation				
Lexical features	0.58	0.56	0.47	0.50
Discourse features	0.62	0.57	0.52	0.54

Table 1: Results for lexical and discourse features

We can evaluate that for the first one the classification task is solved better by SVMs (rbf kernel). The most significant features are: average length of tokens, frequency of sentiment words, frequency of particles, frequency of verbs. It was checked with Student's t-test. Although the results of the first experiment are better, for the second one the classification task is solved better by Random Forest Classifier. The most significant rhetorical relation types among discourse features are disjunction/conjunction, non-volitional cause, evaluation, elaboration. Non-volitional cause, elaboration, evaluation, conjunction are more typical for deceptive texts. Probably authors of fake news pay more attention to the causation, because they want to explain an event with the internal logic, without any inconsistencies.

7 Discussion

Automated deception detection seems to be a promising and methodologically challenging research topic, and further measures should be taken to find features for deception/truth detection in automated news verification model for Russian.

The model should be developed, learned and tested on larger data collections with different topics. We should use a complex approach and combine lexics and discourse methods, also combining them with other linguistics and statistical methods. For instance, n-grams, word embeddings, psycholinguistics features; syntactic level features on top of sequences of discourse relations should be studied. 'The trees' - hierarchies of RST relation types in texts should also be considered, to get better results. The extrapolation of the existing model to all possible news reports in Russian would be incorrect. But it can already be used as a preliminary filter for fake news detection. Results of its work should be double-checked, especially for suspicious instances. The model is also restricted by the absence of tools and corpora for Russian, as typical for NLP tasks for Russian. The guidelines for gathering a corpus of obviously truthful/deceptive news should also be improved.

8   Conclusions

News verification and automated fact checking tend to be very important issues in our world, with its information warfare. The research is initial. We collected a corpus for Russian (174 news reports, truthful and fake). We held two experiments, for both we applied SVMs algorithm (linear/rbf kernel) and Random Forest to classify the news reports into 2 classes: truthful/deceptive. We used 18 markers on lexics level, mostly frequencies of POS tags in texts. On discourse level we used frequencies of RST relations in texts. The classification task in the first experiment is solved better by SVMs (rbf kernel) (f-measure 0.65). The model based on RST features shows best results with Random Forest Classifier (f-measure 0.54) and should be modified. In the next research, the combination of different deception detection markers for Russian should be taken in order to make a better predictive model.

References

H. Allcott and M. Gentzkow. 2017. Social Media and Fake News in the 2016 Election. In *Journal of Economic Perspectives*. Vol. 31-2: 211-236.

J.N. Blom and K.R. Hansen. 2015. Click bait: Forward-reference as lure in online news headlines. *Journal of Pragmatics*, 76: 87-100.

I.I. Chetviorkin and N.Y. Loukachevitch. 2012. Extraction of Russian Sentiment Lexicon for Product Meta-Domain. In *Proceedings of COLING 2012: Technical Papers*: 593–610.

GL Ciampaglia, P. Shiralkar, LM Rocha, J. Bollen, F. Menczer, and A. Flammini. 2015. *Computational Fact Checking from Knowledge Networks*. PLoS ONE 10(6): e0128193. https://doi.org/10.1371/journal.pone.0128193

R. Clark. 2014. *Top 8 Secrets of How to Write an Upworthy Headline*, Poynter, URL: http://www.poynter.org/news/media-innovation/255886/top-8-secrets-of-how-to-write-an-upworthy-headline/

J. Eckle-Kohler, R. Kluge, I. Gurevych. 2015. On the Role of Discourse Markers for Discriminating Claims and Premises in Argumentative Discourse, In *Proceedings of the 2015 Conference on Empirical Methods in Natural Language Processing (EMNLP)*: 2236-2242.

S. Feng, R. Banerjee, and Y. Choi. 2012. Syntactic Stylometry for Deception Detection. In *Proceedings 50th Annual Meeting of the Association for Computational Linguistics, Association for Computational Linguistics*, Vol. 2: Short Papers: 171–175.

E. Fitzpatrick, J. Bachenko, and T. Fornaciari. 2015. *Automatic Detection of Verbal Deception. Synthesis Lectures on Human Language Technologies.* Morgan & Claypool Publishers.

F. Goasdoué, K. Karanasos, Y. Katsis, J. Leblay, I. Manolescu, and S. Zampetakis. 2013. Fact Checking and Analyzing the Web. In *SIGMOD - ACM International Conference on Management of Data*, Jun 2013, New York, United States.

M. Hardalov, I. Koychev, P. Nakov. 2016. In Search of Credible News. In *Artificial Intelligence: Methodology, Systems, and Applications*: 172-180.

D.J. Lary, A. Nikitkov, and D. Stone. 2010. *Which Machine-Learning Models Best Predict Online Auction Seller Deception Risk?* American Accounting Association AAA Strategic and Emerging Technologies.

E. Lex, A. Juffinger, and M. Granitzer. 2010. Objectivity classification in online media. In *Proceedings of the 21st ACM conference on Hypertext and hypermedia*: 293-294.

O. Litvinova, T. Litvinova, P. Seredin, Y. Lyell. 2017. Deception Detection in Russian Texts. In *Proceedings of the Student Research Workshop at the 15th Conference of the European Chapter of the Association for Computational Linguistics*: 43-52.

X. Liu, Q. Li, A. Nourbakhsh, R. Fang, M. Thomas, K. Anderson, R. Kociuba, M. Vedder, S. Pomerville, R. Wudali, R. Martin, J. Duprey, A. Vachher, W. Keenan, and S. Shah. 2016. Reuters Tracer: A

Large Scale System of Detecting & Verifying Real-Time News Events from Twitter. In *Proceedings of the 25th ACM International on Conference on Information and Knowledge Management*. Indianapolis, Indiana, USA, October 24-28, 2016: 207-216.

W.C. Mann and S.A. Thompson. 1988. *Rhetorical Structure Theory: Toward a Functional Theory of Text Organization*, Text, vol. 8, no.3: 243-281.

R. Mihalcea and C. Strapparava. 1999. The Lie Detector: Explorations in the Automatic Recognition of Deceptive Language. In *Proceedings 47th Annual Meeting of the Association for Computational Linguistics*, Singapore: 309-312.

J. Pennebaker and M. Francis. 1999. *Linguistic inquiry and word count: LIWC*, Erlbaum Publishers.

P. Rosso and L. Cagnina. 2017. Deception Detection and Opinion Spam. In: *A Practical Guide to Sentiment Analysis*, Cambria, E., Das, D., Bandyopadhyay, S., Feraco, A. (Eds.), Socio-Affective Computing, vol. 5, Springer-Verlag: 155-171.

V.L. Rubin, N.J. Conroy, and Y. Chen. 2015a. *Deception Detection for News: Three Types of Fakes*. Conference: ASIS T2015, At St. Louis, MO, USA.

V.L. Rubin, N.J. Conroy, and Y.C. Chen. 2015b. *Towards News Verification: Deception Detection Methods for News Discourse*. In Proceedings of the Hawaii International Conference on System Sciences (HICSS48) Symposium on Rapid Screening Technologies, Deception Detection and Credibility Assessment Symposium, January 5-8, 11 pages.

R. Sauri and J. Pustejovsky. 2012. Are You Sure That This Happened? Assessing the Factuality Degree of Events in Text. In *Computational Linguistics*: 1-39.

Fake News Detection using Stacked Ensemble of Classifiers

James Thorne   Mingjie Chen   Giorgos Myrianthous
Jiashu Pu   Xiaoxuan Wang   Andreas Vlachos
Department of Computer Science
University of Sheffield, UK
`{j.thorne,mchen33,gmyrianthous1,ppu1,xwang130,a.vlachos}`
`@sheffield.ac.uk`

Abstract

Fake news has become a hotly debated topic in journalism. In this paper, we present our entry to the 2017 Fake News Challenge which models the detection of fake news as a stance classification task that finished in 11th place on the leader board. Our entry is an ensemble system of classifiers developed by students in the context of their coursework. We show how we used the stacking ensemble method for this purpose and obtained improvements in classification accuracy exceeding each of the individual models' performance on the development data. Finally, we discuss aspects of the experimental setup of the challenge.

1 Introduction

The distribution of news on social media is an influential factor in the public's political attitudes (Allcott and Gentzkow, 2017). Social networks offer platforms in which information and articles may be shared without fact-checking or moderation. Moderating user-generated content on social media presents a challenge due to both volume and variety of information posted. In particular, highly partisan fabricated materials on social media, *fake news*, is believed to be an influencing factor in recent elections (DiFranzo and Gloria-Garcia, 2017). Misinformation spread through fake news has attracted significant media attention recently and current approaches rely on manual annotation by third parties (Heath, 2016) to notify users that shared content may be untrue.

One of the challenges in detecting misinformation is that there does not yet exist a unified definition of fake news and the criteria required to label an article as true or false. As a consequence,

there is no community-wide shared task in order to compare the various approaches proposed. Until recently, the evaluations related to fake news have had relatively little adoption. Even though there is valid criticism that shared tasks have the risk of focusing the community on a particular task definition and dataset, shared definition and evaluation platforms such as those developed for example by the CoNLL shared tasks[1] have largely stimulated progress.

The 2017 *Fake News Challenge*[2] (FNC) aims to provide a community-wide shared task and evaluation platform in order to stimulate progress in fake news detection. Acknowledging the complexity of the task even for human experts and following the task decomposition proposed by Silverman (2015), they propose to address a subtask in fake news detection, namely stance classification. Stance classification is the labeling of whether an article agrees with, disagrees with or simply discusses a 'fact'. It can be considered to be a form of textual entailment (Dagan et al., 2006), while it also bears similarity with stance classification in the context of sentiment analysis (e.g. Mohammad et al. (2016)) and . Stance classification serves as a first step in compiling lists of articles that corroborate or refute claims made on social media, allowing end-users to make a better informed judgment.

In this paper, we discuss our entry to the fake news challenge: an ensemble comprising five individual systems developed by students in the context of their natural language processing module at The University of Sheffield. We used stacking (Wolpert, 1992) as our ensembling technique as it has been applied successfully in other tasks (e.g. Riedel et al. (2011)) and show that it increases the ensemble score above the performance of any of

---

[1]`http://www.conll.org/previous-tasks`
[2]`http://fakenewschallenge.org`

80

Proceedings of the 2017 EMNLP Workshop on Natural Language Processing meets Journalism, pages 80–83
Copenhagen, Denmark, September 7, 2017. ©2017 Association for Computational Linguistics

the individual classifiers. Furthermore, we evaluate system accuracy against the upper performance bound of our ensemble, assuming a perfect oracle selecting the correct member of the ensemble to return the prediction.

2 The Fake News Challenge

The fake news challenge is a text classification task: given a headline and article body - the classifier must first predict whether the two are related and if so, must then further assign a stance label - whether the headline agrees with, disagrees with or is discussed by (observing) the article.

The evaluation for the FNC is as follows: for each stance, 0.25 points are available for correctly classifying whether the article and headline are related. A further 0.75 points are available for correctly labeling the relationship between a related headline-article pair. We report percentage scores as a proportion against the maximum possible score for correctly labeling a dataset.

The task dataset is derived from the Emergent project (Silverman, 2015) and is an extension of the stance classification task proposed by Ferreira and Vlachos (2016). It consists of 49972 labeled stances (headline and body pairs) constructed from 2582 articles and is publicly available on the organizers' website. In the FNC baseline, the organizers provide a dataset split between training data and hold-out development evaluation dataset (proportions: 0.8 training, 0.2 dev). The article bodies in this dataset split are disjoint, however, the headlines were not. An additional blind test set containing 25413 stances from 904 articles was used for evaluating the final solution. This was not made available until the competition closed and the winners were announced.

The official baseline (Galbraith et al., 2017) makes heavy use of task-specific feature engineering and applies a gradient boosted decision tree classifier to the fake news challenge dataset - achieving a score of 79.5% on the dev dataset. Features included in this approach include ngram overlap between the headline and article and the presence of refuting words (such as *fake* or *debunk*) in the headline or the article. While this baseline was good in distinguishing between the related/unrelated classes, the recall for the disagree label was poor.

The classification accuracy of the baseline is limited by the range of features used. While fur-

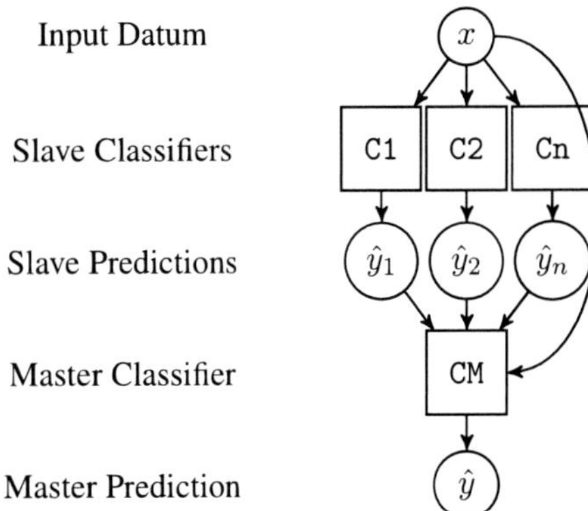

Figure 1: Stacked ensemble classification architecture where circle nodes represent data, rectangles represent classifiers and arrows indicate data flow

ther feature engineering may be used to improve performance of the classifier, this requires human effort and judgment and biases the classifier to the domain in which the features were observed. Zeng et al. (2017) applied and compared three recurrent neural models which negate the need for feature engineering. While these have high FNC scores, they don't necessarily capture the aspects of the task that manually engineered features do. Bird et al. (2017) combine a deep convolutional network with feature engineering through an evenly weighted ensemble of two classifiers. Riedel et al. (2017) simply use term-frequency vectors and the tf-idf cosine similarity as features for a shallow multi-layer perceptron.

3 Our Solution

We present our solution to the Fake News Challenge, a stacked ensemble of five independent classifiers developed by students in the context of the natural language processing module assignments. The stacked ensemble is a two-layer classifier architecture that leverages predictions from weaker slave classifiers as features in a stronger master classifier. The architecture is illustrated in Figure 1. We provide an overview of the five slave classifiers (C1-C5) and master classifier (CM) used in the ensemble:

C1: Concatenate average word2vec vectors for headline and article body, cosine similarity between headline and article body tf-idf vectors and counts of refuting words. 4-way classification using a (300,8) multi-layer perceptron (MLP) with ReLU activation function.

C2: Average word2vec embeddings for headline words and article words excluding stop words, indicator features for punctuation, word overlap, counts of refuting words. 4-way classification using a (1010,6) MLP with ReLU activation function.

C3: 4-way classification using one-vs-all logistic regression with L2 regularization over word unigram and bigram tf-idf vectors.

C4: Concatenate word2vec embeddings for headline and article words. 4-way classification using (256,128,128) MLP with dropout probabilities of (0.5,0.3,0.1) between layers and ReLU activation function.

C5: Official FNC baseline classifier

CM: Gradient boosted decision tree classifier using as features the values predicted from C1-C5 and all the features from the FNC baseline classifier.

The master classifier is trained using 2 fold cross validation using the following regime: The dataset is randomly split into two equal sizes. Two instances of C1-C5 are instantiated and are trained independently on each data fold. The predictions are concatenated to the original input data to form one dataset - the master training data used to train CM. New instances of C1-C5 are trained on the entire original training dataset and used to provide input to CM at test time.

4 Results

We present the results for our stacked ensemble and slave classifiers trained and evaluated on the fake news challenge baseline data split (dev) and the final test set in Table 1. In the dev setup, the training set contains 40350 stances over 1345 unique articles and we evaluated on 9622 stances over 336 unique articles. The article bodies were disjoint between the training and development sets.

Because the test dataset was blinded, the risk of building a biased system was mitigated against.

System	Dev %	Test %
Official Baseline[3]	79.53	75.20
SOLAT in the SWEN[4]	-	82.02
Athene[5]	-	81.97
UCL Machine Reading[6]	-	81.72
C1	88.09	75.77
C2	86.68	75.08
C3	87.48	77.99
C4	87.36	58.69
C5	79.25	75.22
Our Ensemble (CM)	90.05	78.04
CM Upper Limit	*97.25*	*90.89*

Table 1: FNC score comparison on development evaluation dataset. The performance difference between C5 and the official baseline is caused by different k-fold training regimen.

However, the classification difficulty of the test set was far greater than that of the development data split which impacted results. In the development data split, article bodies were disjoint but there was some overlap between article headlines. In the training set, both article bodies and headlines were entirely disjoint. The more successful entries for this competition, such as Riedel et al. (2017), built their own entirely disjoint development split and used this for cross-validation. We found that cross-validating against the development split yielded classifiers that were not able to generalize to the unseen articles in the test set, harming the classification accuracy.

On the development dataset, the ensemble classifier yielded an absolute improvement by at least 1.6% over any of the individual constituent slave classifiers. This performance gain, however, did not transfer to the blind test set.

The CM upper limit uses a scoring oracle that awards FNC score if at least one of the slave classifiers correctly labels the input stance. This acts as a measure that describes the maximum possible score that CM could give assuming that it always selected a correct label from one of the slaves. In this case, the upper limit was 90.89% - exceeding the top ranked system. While this result is encouraging, it highlights the need to build a stronger master classifier less prone to over-fitting and more resilient to the noisy predictions made by the slaves.

The performance of some of the slave classifiers (the student projects C1-4) was variable and

---

[3](Galbraith et al., 2017)
[4](Bird et al., 2017)
[5](Hanselowski et al., 2017)
[6](Riedel et al., 2017)

highly dependent on the network topology, feature selection and dataset/split. The most resilient classifier, C5, used entirely non-lexical features whereas C4, which used only averaged word vectors and a large network topology, suffered the greatest loss in performance on the unseen test data.

The best performing system (Bird et al., 2017) is an ensemble of a convolutional neural model and a decision tree classifier. This system simply averaged the two predictions with equal weighting. The master meta-classifier in our entry leverages additional information about which slave predictions to favor given a certain headline and article pair. While the two classifiers in (Bird et al., 2017) are strong, further improvements could be obtained by incorporating stacking.

5 Conclusions

In this paper, we presented a stacked ensemble of 5 classifiers developed by students. The performance gains observed in the development set did not materialize in the competition though due to a much more difficult blind test set. One factor limiting our assessment of the ability our model(s) to generalize is the overlap of headlines between the training and development evaluation dataset. Future evaluations could consider temporal splits, i.e. deriving training, development and test sets from articles from different periods, which would also mimic to an extent how these models might be used in practice.

Acknowledgements

We would like to thank the challenge organizers, Dean Pomerleau and Delip Rao, for their efforts in this community-wide event. We are looking forward to future versions of the challenge addressing more issues in fake news detection. Andreas Vlachos is supported by the EU H2020 SUMMA project (grant agreement number 688139).

References

Hunt Allcott and Matthew Gentzkow. 2017. Social media and fake news in the 2016 election. Technical report, National Bureau of Economic Research.

Sean Bird, Doug Sibley, and Yuxi Pan. 2017. Talos targets disinformation with Fake News Challenge victory .

Ido Dagan, Oren Glickman, and Bernardo Magnini. 2006. The pascal recognising textual entailment challenge. In *Machine learning challenges. evaluating predictive uncertainty, visual object classification, and recognising tectual entailment*, Springer, pages 177–190.

Dominic DiFranzo and Kristine Gloria-Garcia. 2017. Filter Bubbles and Fake News. *XRDS* 23(3):32–35. https://doi.org/10.1145/3055153.

William Ferreira and Andreas Vlachos. 2016. Emergent : a novel data-set for stance classification. *Naacl2016* (1):1163–1168. https://doi.org/10.18653/v1/N16-1138.

Byron Galbraith, Humza Iqbal, HJ van Veen, Delip Rao, James Thorne, and Yuxi Pan. 2017. Baseline FNC implementation. http://github.com/fakenewschallenge/fnc-1-baseline.

Andreas Hanselowski, Avinesh PVS, Benjamin Schiller, and Felix Caspelherr. 2017. Description of the system developed by Team Athene in the FNC-1 .

Alex Heath. 2016. Facebook is going to use snopes and other fact-checkers to combat and bury 'fake news'. http://businessinsider.com/facebook-will-fact-check-label-fake-news-in-news-feed-2016-12. [Online; accessed 01-June-2017].

Saif M Mohammad, Svetlana Kiritchenko, Parinaz Sobhani, Xiaodan Zhu, and Colin Cherry. 2016. SemEval-2016 Task 6: Detecting Stance in Tweets pages 31–41.

Benjamin Riedel, Isabelle Augenstein, George Spithourakis, and Sebastian Riedel. 2017. A simple but tough-to-beat baseline for the Fake News Challenge stance detection task. *CoRR* abs/1707.03264. http://arxiv.org/abs/1707.03264.

Sebastian Riedel, David McClosky, Mihai Surdeanu, Christopher D. Manning, and Andrew McCallum. 2011. Model combination for event extraction in bionlp 2011. In *Proceedings of the Natural Language Processing in Biomedicine NAACL 2011 Workshop (BioNLP '11)*.

Craig Silverman. 2015. Lies, damn lies and viral content. http://towcenter.org/research/lies-damn-lies-and-viral-content/.

David H Wolpert. 1992. Stacked generalization. *Neural networks* 5(2):241–259.

Qi Zeng, Quan Zhou, and Shanshan Xu. 2017. Neural stance detectors for fake news challenge.

From Clickbait to Fake News Detection:
An Approach based on Detecting the Stance of Headlines to Articles

Peter Bourgonje, Julian Moreno Schneider, Georg Rehm
DFKI GmbH, Language Technology Lab
Alt-Moabit 91c, 10559 Berlin, Germany
{peter.bourgonje,julian.moreno_schneider,georg.rehm}@dfki.de

Abstract

We present a system for the detection of
the stance of headlines with regard to their
corresponding article bodies. The approach can be applied in fake news, especially clickbait detection scenarios. The
component is part of a larger platform for
the curation of digital content; we consider veracity and relevancy an increasingly important part of curating online information. We want to contribute to the
debate on how to deal with fake news and
related online phenomena with technological means, by providing means to separate
related from unrelated headlines and further classifying the related headlines. On
a publicly available data set annotated for
the stance of headlines with regard to their
corresponding article bodies, we achieve a
(weighted) accuracy score of 89.59.

1 Introduction

With the advent of social media and its increasingly important role as a provider and amplifier
of news, basically anyone, anywhere, can produce and help circulate content for other people
to read. Traditional barriers to publishing content (like a press to print newspapers or broadcasting time for radio or television) have disappeared,
and with this, at least part of traditional quality
control procedures have disappeared as well. Basic journalistic principles like source verification,
fact checking and accountability can be easily by-
passed or simply ignored by individuals or organ-
isations publishing content on Twitter, Facebook
or other social networks. The impact of this situation is illustrated by the predominance of terms
like "trolls", "fake news", "post-truth media" and
"alternative facts". There is evidence that these de-

velopments and their effects are not harmless but
can have a significant impact on real-world events,
which is illustrated by a description of the role of
social media in the 2016 US presidential election
by (Allcott and Gentzkow, 2017), and by a study
on the effectiveness and debunking strategies of
rumours surrounding the Affordable Care Act by
(Berinsky, 2017).

While the cause of this situation may have its
roots in many different aspects of modern society, and hence needs to be approached from several different angles, we aim to make a contribution from the angle of Language Technology and
Natural Language Processing. We consider fully-
automated procedures for fact-checking, clickbait
detection or fake news classification not feasible
at this point (Rehm, 2017), but aim to support the
community by providing means of detecting articles or pieces of news that need to be approached
with caution, where a human has to make final
decisions (on credibility, legitimacy etc.), but is
aided by a set of tools. The approach described
in this paper can serve as the back-end of such a
smart set of tooling around fact-checking and can
augment news coming from both traditional and
non-traditional (social media) sources. We envi-
sion the resulting set of tools as a collection of
expert tools for specific job profiles (like a journalist or a news editor), or in the shape of a simple browser plug-in, flagging unverified or dubious
content to the end user.

The work presented in this paper was carried
out under the umbrella of a two-year research and
technology transfer project, in which a research
centre collaborates with four SME partners that
face the challenge of having to process, analyse
and make sense of large amounts of digital content. The companies cover four different use cases
and sectors (Rehm and Sasaki, 2015) including
journalism. For these partners we develop a plat-

84

Proceedings of the 2017 EMNLP Workshop on Natural Language Processing meets Journalism, pages 84–89
Copenhagen, Denmark, September 7, 2017. ©2017 Association for Computational Linguistics

form that provides access to language and knowledge technologies (Bourgonje et al., 2016a,b). The services are integrated by the SME partners into their own in-house systems or those of clients.

In this paper, we aim to contribute to a first step in battling fake news, often referred to as stance detection, where the challenge is to detect the stance of a claim with regard to another piece of content. Our experiments are based on the setup of the first Fake News Challenge (FNC1).[1]. In FNC1, the claim comes in the form of a headline, and the other piece of content is an article body. This step may seem, and, in fact, is, a long way from automatically checking the veracity of a piece of content with regard to some kind of ground truth. But the problem lies exactly in the definition of the truth, and the fact that it is sensitive to bias. Additionally, and partly because of this, annotated corpora, allowing training and experimental evaluation, are hard to come by and also often (in the case of fact checker archives) not freely available. We argue that detecting whether a piece of content is related or not related to another piece of content (e. g., headline vs. article body) is an important first step, which would perhaps best be described as clickbait detection (i. e., a headline not related to the actual article is more likely to be clickbait). Following the FNC1 setup, the further classification of related pieces of content into more fine-grained classes provides valuable information once the "truth" (in the form of a collection of facts) has been established, so that particular pieces of content can be classified as "fake" or, rather, "false". Since this definitive, resolving collection of facts is usually hard to come by, the challenge of stance detection can be put to use combining the outcome with credibility or reputation scores of news outlets, where several high-credibility outlets disagreeing with a particular piece of content point towards a false claim. Stance detection can also prove relevant for detecting political bias: if authors on the same end of the political spectrum are more likely to agree with each other, the (political) preference of one author can be induced once the preference of the other author is known. Additionally, the stances of utterances towards a specific piece of content can provide hints on its veracity. (Mendoza et al., 2010) show that the propagation of tweets regarding crisis situations (like natural disasters) differs based on their content: tweets spreading news are affirmed by related tweets, whereas tweets spreading rumours are mostly questioned or denied. In this paper we propose a solution that involves the human-in-the-loop. We think that our approach can be a valuable part of solving the problem described above. The rest of this paper is divided into five sections. Section 2 reviews related work, Section 3 describes the data set used, Section 4 explains our approach in detail and Section 5 provides an evaluation. Our conclusions are presented in Section 6.

2 Related Work

The suggestion of using Language Technologies (NLP, NLU etc.) to design solutions for modern online media phenomena such as "fake news", "hate speech", "abusive language", etc. is receiving rapidly growing interest in the form of shared tasks, workshops and conferences. The awareness that LT can contribute to solutions related to these topics is present. Yet, at the same time, it is being acknowledged that the problem is much more complex than anything that can be solved by exploiting current state of the art techniques alone. The effect known as "belief perseverance" or "continued influence effect" (Wilkes and Leatherbarrow, 1988) and its influence on modern media and politics is described by (Nyhan and Reifler, 2015), who state that reasoning based on facts that have shown to be false, remains in place until an alternative line of reasoning has been offered. The credibility of a politician stepping down due to bribery accusations is not restored after only rejecting this explanation (by a letter from the prosecutors). In addition, an alternative explanation (like being named president of a university, but not being able to disclose this until the predecessor has stepped down) has to be provided. Another socio-psychological contribution on the topic of "fake news" and its consumption is presented by (Marchi, 2012) who report on a survey among teenagers and their news consumption habits. Although they have a slightly different definition of "fake news" than the one we use in this paper, the study presents a relevant overview of the consumption of news and the important aspects with different social groups. The authors claim that "authenticity" is highly valued among teenagers consuming news, hence their explained preference for blogs, satirical shows,

---

[1]http://www.fakenewschallenge.org

or basically anything other than traditional media outlets, which they consider "identical", lacking contextual information and any authenticity. The acknowledgment that teenagers increasingly rely on news coming from non-traditional news sources underlines the need for new ways of dealing with challenges related to these alternative sources. (Conroy et al., 2015) present a useful overview of recent approaches towards "fake news" detection using NLP and network analyses. The authors include several state-of-the-art figures and acknowledge the fact that these numbers are domain-dependent, which is why it is difficult to arrive at a state-of-the-art figure independent of a specific use case and data set. From an NLP perspective, the challenge of dealing with this problem is further exemplified by the fact that annotated data is hard to find, and, if present, exhibits rather low inter-annotator agreement. Approaching the "abusive language" and "hate speech" problem from an NLP angle (Bourgonje et al., 2017), (Ross et al., 2016) introduce a German corpus of tweets and annotate it for hate speech, resulting in figures for Krippendorff's α between 0.18 and 0.29, (Waseem, 2016) compare amateur (CrowdFlower) annotations and expert annotations on an English corpus of Tweets and report figures for Cohen's Kappa of 0.14, (Van Hee et al., 2015) use a Dutch corpus annotated for cyberbullying and report Kappa scores between 0.19 and 0.69, and (Kwok and Wang, 2013) investigate English racist tweets and report an overall inter-annotator agreement of only 33%.

An approach similar to ours is described by (Ferreira and Vlachos, 2016), who introduce a data set and three-class classification ("for", "against", "observing"). In addition to a logistic regression classifier, the authors exploit dependency parse graphs, a paraphrase database (Pavlick et al., 2015) and several other features, to arrive at an accuracy of 73%. Another related approach is described by (Augenstein et al., 2016), who apply stance detection methods on the SemEval 2016 Task 6 data set. Their focus is on learning stances towards a topic in an unsupervised and weakly supervised way using a neural network architecture. (Babakar and Moy, 2016) present a useful and recent overview of fact checking approaches.

3 Data Set

Our experiments are conducted on the dataset released by the organisers of the first Fake News Challenge (FNC1) on stance detection. The data set is based on the work of (Ferreira and Vlachos, 2016) and can be downloaded from the corresponding GitHub page, along with a baseline implementation for this task, achieving a score of 79.53.[2] The data consists of a set of headlines and articles that are combined with each other (multiple times, in different combinations) and annotated for one of four classes: "unrelated", "agree", "disagree", "discuss", indicating the stance of the headline towards the content of the article (see Table 1).

Unique headlines	1.648	
Unique articles	1.668	
Annotated pairs	49.972	100%
Class: unrelated	36.545	73%
Class: discuss	8.909	18%
Class: agree	3.678	7%
Class: disagree	840	2%

Table 1: Key figures of the FNC-1 data set

The FNC1 scoring method consists of first verifying whether a particular combination of headline and article has been correctly classified as "unrelated" (the corresponding class) or "related" (one of the classes "agree", "disagree" or "discuss"). Getting this binary classification correct amounts up to 25% of the final, weighted score. The remaining 75% of the score consists of correctly classifying headline article pairs in the three remaining classes. The setup of our system adheres to this scoring method, and hence applies several classifiers sequentially, as explained in Section 4.

4 Approach and Methods

In line with the scoring system of the challenge, we first apply a procedure to decide whether a particular headline/article combination is related or unrelated. This is done based on n-gram matching of the lemmatised input (headline or article), using the CoreNLP Lemmatiser (Manning et al., 2014). The number of matching n-grams (where $n = 1..6$) in the headline and article is multiplied by length and IDF value of the matching n-gram

---

[2]https://github.com/FakeNewsChallenge/fnc-1

(n-grams containing only stop words or punctuation are not considered), then divided by the total number of n-grams. If the resulting score is above some threshold (we established 0.0096 as the optimal value), the pair is taken to be related.

A formal definition is provided in Equation 1: considering a headline and an article represented by two arrays (H and A) of all possible lemmatised n-grams when $n \in [1,6]$, $h(i)$ and $a(i)$ being the ith element of arrays H and A, $len(\cdot)$ being a function that computes the length in tokens of a string (n-gram), TF_T^k being the frequency of appearance of term k in array T and IDF^k being the inverse document frequency of term k in all the articles.

$$sc = \frac{\sum_{i=1}^{len(H)} TF^{h(i)} * IDF^{h(i)}}{len(H) + len(A)} \qquad (1)$$

where

$$TF^{h(i)} = \{(TF_H^{h(i)} + TF_A^{H(i)}) * len(h(i))\} \qquad (2)$$

As shown in Table 1, the majority of "related" instances are of the class "discuss" and simply assigning this class to all "related" instances leads to an accuracy of 61.51 already (for this portion of the data set), as shown in the "Majority vote" column. To improve upon this baseline and to further classify the related pairs into "agree", "disagree" or "discuss", we use Mallet's Logistic Regression classifier implementation (McCallum, 2002) trained on headlines only (without lemmatisation or stop word removal), using the three classes. This resulted in a weighted score of 79.82 (column "3-class classifier"). In subsequent experiments, we introduced a (relative) confidence threshold: if the distance between the best scoring class and the second-best scoring class is above some threshold (we established 0.7 as the optimal value), the best-scoring class is assigned to the pair. If the difference was below the threshold, we used three binary classifiers to decide between the best scoring class and the second-best scoring class (i. e., one binary classifier for "agree"-"disagree", one for "agree"-"discuss" and one for "discuss"-"disagree"). These classifiers are trained on both the headline and the article (joined together, without lemmatisation or stop word removal). The results are shown in the column "Combined classifiers" in Table 2.

This setup leads to the best results on the data set. In other experiments we used more linguisti-cally motivated features, some of them inspired by the work of (Ferreira and Vlachos, 2016). From rather basic ones (like a question mark at the end of a headline to detect "disagree" instances) to more sophisticated ones (like extracting a dependency graph, looking for negation-type typed dependencies and calculate their normalised distance to the root node of the graph, and compare this value for headline and article), but these did not improve upon the final weighted score reported in Table 2.

5 Evaluation

The first step of deciding whether a headline/article pair is related or not is done based on n-gram matching (of lemmatised n-grams). This procedure is rule-based and only relies on finding an optimal value for the threshold, based on the data. To arrive at an optimal value, we used all data and did not separate it into training and test sets. Since the subsequent classification methods are based on machine learning, the following evaluation figures are the result of 50-fold cross-validation, with a 90-10 division of training and test data, respectively.

Considering that the combination of headlines and article bodies has been performed randomly with many obviously unrelated combinations, the relatedness score of 93.27 can be considered relatively low.[3] Upon manual investigation of the cases classified as "unrelated" (but that were in fact of the "agree", "disagree" or "discuss" class), we found that the vast majority had headlines with different wordings that were not matching after lemmatisation. One concrete example with the headline "Small Meteorite Hits Managua" in its article body mentions "the Nicaraguan capital" but not "Managua" and "a chunk of an Earth-passing asteroid" instead of "small meteorite". To improve the approach for cases such as this one, we propose to include more sophisticated techniques to capture word relatedness in a knowledge-rich way as an important part of future work. The other way round, cases classified as related that were in fact annotated as "unrelated" contained words in the headline that were frequently mentioned in the article body. One example with the headline "SHOCK CLAIM: PGA Golfer Says Tiger Woods Is Suspended For Failed Drug Test" was combined

---

[3]The variation for this row in Table 2 is due to different runs (on different, random splits of the data).

	Majority vote	3-class classifier	Combined classifiers
Relatedness score	93.27	93.26	93.29
Three-class score	61.51	75.34	88.36
Weighted score	69.45	79.82	**89.59**

Table 2: Results of 50-fold cross-validation

with an article body about the divorce of Tiger Woods and Elin Nordegren. Here, we suggest, as part of future work, to include event detection, to move away from entity-based representations and put more focus on the event actually reported.

After deciding on relatedness, we are left with (on average) 1,320 instances. For the three-class classification of this set, we obtained (on average) 686 cases that scored above the scoring difference threshold and were assigned their class by this three-class Logistic Regression classifier. Of these, 642 were correct, resulting in an accuracy of 93.64 for this portion of the data set (i. e., "related"). The average number of cases where the scoring difference was below the threshold (634) were classified using the three binary classifiers. This resulted in 544 correctly classified instances, and a score of 85.83 for this section of the data set. Putting these scores together, the weighted score and the individual components are shown in Table 2, i. e., the relatedness score for the binary decision "related" or "unrelated" (25% of the weighted score) and the three-class score for the classification of "related" instances into "agree", "disagree" or "discuss" (75% of the weighted score). To get an idea of the effect of the first stage's error rate on the second stage of processing, we re-ran the experiments taking the "related" vs. "unrelated" information from the annotations directly. This resulted in a three-class score of 89.82, i. e., a 1.46 drop in accuracy due to classification errors in the first stage.

While these numbers look promising for initial steps towards tackling the challenge that fake news poses globally, we acknowledge that at least the 25% of the score (the relatedness score of 93.27) is not directly applicable in a real world scenario, since the data set was artificially boosted by randomly combining headlines and article bodies – a headline such as "Isis claims to behead US journalist" is combined with an article on who is going to be the main actor in a biopic on Steve Jobs. Although this headline/article pair was (obviously) tagged as "unrelated", this is not something that is usually encountered in a real-world scenario. For the more fine-grained classification of articles that have been classified as "related", the three-way classification is a relevant first step, but other classes may need to be added to the set, or a more detailed division may need to be made in order to take the next steps in tackling the fake news challenge. Additionally, we see the integration of known facts and general discourse knowledge (possibly through Linked Data), and the incorporation of source credibility information as important and promising suggestions for future research.

6 Conclusions

We present a system for stance detection of headlines with regard to their corresponding article bodies. Our system is based on simple, lemmatisation-based n-gram matching for the binary classification of "related" vs. "unrelated" headline/article pairs. The best results were obtained using a setup where the more fine-grained classification of the "related" pairs (into "agree", "disagree", "discuss") is carried out using a Logistic Regression classifier at first, then three binary classifiers with slightly different training procedures for the cases where the first classifier lacked confidence (i. e., the difference between the best and second-best scoring class was below a threshold). We improve on the accuracy base line set by the organisers of the FNC1 by over 10 points and scored 9th place (out of 50 participants) in the actual challenge. As described in Section 1, the approach explained in this article can be part of the set of services needed by a fact-checking tool (Rehm, 2017). The first, binary classification of "related" vs. "unrelated" can be exploited for clickbait detection. The more fine-grained classification of related headlines can specifically support in the detection of political bias and rumour veracity (Srivastava et al., 2017).

Acknowledgments

The authors wish to thank the anonymous reviewers for their helpful feedback. The project "Digitale Kuratierungstechnologien" is supported by the German Federal Ministry of Education and Research, Wachstumskern-Potenzial (no. 03WKP45). http://www.digitale-kuratierung.de.

References

Hunt Allcott and Matthew Gentzkow. 2017. Social media and fake news in the 2016 election. Working Paper 23089, National Bureau of Economic Research.

Isabelle Augenstein, Tim Rocktäschel, Andreas Vlachos, and Kalina Bontcheva. 2016. Stance detection with bidirectional conditional encoding. *CoRR*, abs/1606.05464.

Mevan Babakar and Will Moy. 2016. The State of Automated Factchecking.

Adam J. Berinsky. 2017. Rumors and health care reform: Experiments in political misinformation. *British Journal of Political Science*, 47(2):241–262.

Peter Bourgonje, Julian Moreno-Schneider, Jan Nehring, Georg Rehm, Felix Sasaki, and Ankit Srivastava. 2016a. Towards a Platform for Curation Technologies: Enriching Text Collections with a Semantic-Web Layer. In *The Semantic Web*, number 9989 in LNCS, pages 65–68. Springer.

Peter Bourgonje, Julian Moreno Schneider, and Georg Rehm. 2017. Automatic Classification of Abusive Language and Personal Attacks in Various Forms of Online Communication. In *Language Technologies for the Challenges of the Digital Age: Proc. of GSCL 2017*, Berlin.

Peter Bourgonje, Julian Moreno Schneider, Georg Rehm, and Felix Sasaki. 2016b. Processing Document Collections to Automatically Extract Linked Data: Semantic Storytelling Technologies for Smart Curation Workflows. In *Proc. of the 2nd Int. Workshop on NLG and the Semantic Web (WebNLG 2016)*, pages 13–16, Edinburgh, UK.

Niall J. Conroy, Victoria L. Rubin, and Yimin Chen. 2015. Automatic deception detection: Methods for finding fake news. In *Proc. of the 78th ASIS&T Annual Meeting*, ASIST '15, pages 82–82.

W. Ferreira and A. Vlachos. 2016. Emergent: a novel data-set for stance classification. The 15th Annual Conference of the North American Chapter of the Association for Computational Linguistics: Human Language Technologies. ACL.

Irene Kwok and Yuzhou Wang. 2013. Locate the hate: Detecting tweets against blacks. In *Proc. of the 27th AAAI Conf. on AI*, pages 1621–1622.

Christopher D. Manning, Mihai Surdeanu, John Bauer, Jenny Finkel, Steven J. Bethard, and David Mc-Closky. 2014. The Stanford CoreNLP Toolkit. In *ACL*, pages 55–60.

R. Marchi. 2012. With facebook, blogs, and fake news, teens reject journalistic objectivity. *Journal of Communication Inquiry*, 36(3):246–262.

Andrew Kachites McCallum. 2002. Mallet: A machine learning for language toolkit.

Marcelo Mendoza, Barbara Poblete, and Carlos Castillo. 2010. Twitter Under Crisis: Can We Trust What We RT? In *Proc. of the First Workshop on Social Media Analytics*, pages 71–79.

Brendan Nyhan and Jason Reifler. 2015. Displacing misinformation about events: An experimental test of causal corrections. *Journal of Exp. Political Science*, 2(01):81–93.

Ellie Pavlick, Pushpendre Rastogi, Juri Ganitkevitch, Benjamin Van Durme, and Chris Callison-Burch. 2015. PPDB 2.0: Better paraphrase ranking, fine-grained entailment relations, word embeddings, and style classification. In *Proc. of the 53rd Annual Meeting of the ACL, Beijing, China, Volume 2: Short Papers*, pages 425–430.

Georg Rehm. 2017. An Infrastructure for Empowering Internet Users to handle Fake News and other Online Media Phenomena. In *Language Technologies for the Challenges of the Digital Age: Proc. of GSCL 2017*, Berlin.

Georg Rehm and Felix Sasaki. 2015. Digitale Kuratierungstechnologien – Verfahren für die effiziente Verarbeitung, Erstellung und Verteilung qualitativ hochwertiger Medieninhalte. In *Proc. of GSCL 2015*, pages 138–139.

Björn Ross, Michael Rist, Guillermo Carbonell, Benjamin Cabrera, Nils Kurowsky, and Michael Wojatzki. 2016. Measuring the Reliability of Hate Speech Annotations: The Case of the European Refugee Crisis. In *Proc. of NLP4CMC III: 3rd Workshop on NLP for CMC*, pages 6–9.

Ankit Srivastava, Georg Rehm, and Julian Moreno Schneider. 2017. DFKI-DKT at SemEval-2017 Task 8: Rumour Detection and Classification Using Cascading Heuristics. In *Proc. of SemEval-2017*, pages 477–481, Vancouver, Canada. ACL.

Cynthia Van Hee, Els Lefever, Ben Verhoeven, Julie Mennes, Bart Desmet, Guy De Pauw, Walter Daelemans, and Veronique Hoste. 2015. Detection and fine-grained classification of cyberbullying events. In *Proc. of the Int. Conf. Recent Advances in NLP*, pages 672–680.

Zeerak Waseem. 2016. Are You a Racist or Am I Seeing Things? Annotator Influence on Hate Speech Detection on Twitter. In *Proc. of the 1st Workshop on NLP and Computational Social Science*, pages 138–142.

A. L. Wilkes and M. Leatherbarrow. 1988. Editing episodic memory following the identification of error. *The Quarterly Journal of Exp. Psychology*, 40(2):361–387.

'Fighting' or 'Conflict'? An Approach to Revealing Concepts of Terms in Political Discourse

Linyuan Tang and **Kyo Kageura**

Graduate School of Interdisciplinary Information Studies / Interfaculty Initiative in Information Studies
The University of Tokyo, Tokyo, Japan
linyuan-tang@g.ecc.u-tokyo.ac.jp, kyo@p.u-tokyo.ac.jp

Abstract

Previous work on the epistemology of fact-checking indicated the dilemma between the needs of binary answers for the public and ambiguity of political discussion. Determining concepts represented by terms in political discourse can be considered as a Word-Sense Disambiguation (WSD) task. The analysis of political discourse, however, requires identifying precise concepts of terms from relatively small data. This work attempts to provide a basic framework for revealing concepts of terms in political discourse with explicit contextual information. The framework consists of three parts: 1) extracting important terms, 2) generating concordance for each term with stipulative definitions and explanations, and 3) agglomerating similar information of the term by hierarchical clustering. Utterances made by Prime Minister Abe Shinzo in the Diet of Japan are used to examine our framework. Importantly, we revealed the conceptual inconsistency of the term *Sonritsu-kiki-jitai*. The framework was proved to work, but only for a small number of terms due to lack of explicit contextual information.

1 Introduction

In October 2016, in the process of diet deliberations on assigning Japan's Self-Defense Forces members to U.N. operations in South Sudan, Japanese Prime Minister Abe Shinzo stated that the 'fighting' between the government and rebel forces were not to be considered as a 'military conflict'[1], according to the definition of 'conflict' under Japanese peacekeeping law.

When domain-specific jargons are used, the ambiguity between common usage and domain-specific usage becomes inevitable. In addition, the case above illustrates that the task of political discourse analysis is different from other scientific discourse analysis. In contrast to other scientific domains, terms used by political figures tend to be vague and ambiguous due to their unwillingness to explain their opinions or statements sufficiently clearly to the public. Although social scientists may derive certain implications from the ambiguities, an intentional misuse of terms by a political figure, which is difficult to recognize, could lead the public to misinterpretation.

As a prerequisite for fact-checking, therefore, it is essential to reveal concepts represented by terms in political discourse. As we cannot expect politicians to do this, it is necessary for the public and/or journalists to disambiguate concepts of terms. Automatic processing of political texts, namely word sense disambiguation (WSD), has a potential to assist this process.

The procedure of WSD can be summarized as: 'given a set of words, a techique is applied which makes use of one or more sources of knowledge to associate the most appropriate senses with words in context' (Navigli, 2009). WSD in general relies on knowledge; without knowledge, not only computers but also human beings cannot understand word sense. The unwillingness of political figures to clarify the meaning of their utterances causes at least two difficulties in WSD specific to political discourse.

First, there exist few political domain-specific dictionaries or corpora that could serve as a knowl-

---

[1] As in English, there are also various verbal expressions (*Sentō*, *Shōtotsu*, etc.) of the act of fighting in Japanese. *Sentō* is the term that generally thought to be parallel to 'military conflict' as well as 'military fighting'.

Proceedings of the 2017 EMNLP Workshop on Natural Language Processing meets Journalism, pages 90–94
Copenhagen, Denmark, September 7, 2017. ©2017 Association for Computational Linguistics

edge base, which is desirable for WSD. Generally, in order to facilitate communication, a dictionary defines standard usage and a corpus exhibits practical usage of terms. On the other hand, political figures almost always create specific usage of terms to escape from common understanding.

Second, every term in political discourse could have a peculiar concept. It is well known in Japan that most utterances made in the Diet are drafted by bureaucrats, and there are always subtle nuances present in bureaucratese. If necessary, political figures would make every single term be independent of its synonyms, hyponyms and hypernyms, even when the terms share a similar surface word form[2]. Therefore, unlike the tasks of document summarization or simplification, when revealing the concept of a term made by political figures, information loss is relatively less acceptable.

The first difficulty could be overcome by creating a domain-specific knowledge base or applying unsupervised disambiguation or word sense induction (WSI) methods. However, knowledge provided by political knowledge bases, which is necessary for further research, could sometimes obstruct the analysis, because concepts of terms can vary across political figures and scenarios. WSI, on the other hand, while it is also necessary for further research, suffers from a more practical problem, i.e., it identifies sense clusters rather than assigning a sense to a word, and 'a significant gap still exists between the results of these techniques and the gold standard of manually compiled word sense dictionaries' (Denkowski, 2009).

In view of the urgent need for an accessible and straightforward approach to practical WSD for political discourse, this ongoing research provides a springboard by introducing a framework to reveal concepts of terms using only explicit contextual information. The method we propose copes with the balance of the needs of knowledge and the attention to the specific usages of terms by creating a concordance that serves as a temporary knowledge base. On the other hand, it deals with precision of concept generation by keeping as much information as possible.

We collected utterances made by Prime Ministers of Japan in the Diet deliberations as target discourses. The concept-revealing framework consists of three parts. First, we applied widely-used tf-idf method to weigh terms and acquired nouns with ranks by their importance. Second, we generated a concordance for each of the important terms in order to collect their stipulative definitions and explanations offered in the document. Thirdly, focusing on the similarity of concepts rather than the quantity of clusters, we agglomerated similar information by hierarchical clustering.

Theoretically, as our approach extracts information from given documents without summarization or simplification, concepts of terms will surely be revealed. Given this, we will show, instead of emphasizing the overall results, an important observation obtained from the concept of *Sonritsu-kiki-jitai*[3] which was identified as one of the most important terms used by Prime Minister Abe Shinzo. Specifically, conceptual inconsistency exists not only between the speaker and the audience, but also in the same speaker's utterances.

2   Related work

The controversy among Uscinski and Butler (2013), Amazeen (2015), and Uscinski (2015) over the epistemology of fact-checking illustrated issues on the methodology of fact-checking.

Uscinski and Butler (2013) made five methodological criticisms against fact-checking methods: selection effects, confounding multiple facts or picking apart a whole, causal claims, predicting the future, and inexplicit selection criteria. These challenges were related to 'the naïve political epistemology at work in the fact-checking branch of journalism' (Uscinski and Butler, 2013).

Amazeen (2015) critized Uscinski and Butler (2013) for their overgeneralization of the selection effects and failure to offer supportive empirical quantification. She also demonstrated that there was a high level of consistency among multiple fact-checkers, and argued that fact-checking is important as long as 'unambiguous practices of deception' continue (Amazeen, 2015).

The rejoinder then from Uscinski (2015) argued that Amazeen's attempt to infer the accuracy of fact-checks failed because of fact-checkers' possible political biases, and she also ignored the distinction between facts and claims. Fact-checking was therefore still a 'continuation of politics by

---

[2]In the example above, according to the government, *Sentō* (fighting) is not defined while *Sentō-kōi* (act of fighting) is defined by the law, so that these two terms have different meanings and only the latter can be used.

[3]An armed attack against foreign country resulting in threatening Japan's survival.

means of journalism' rather than being an 'counterweight to political untruths' (Uscinski, 2015).

Although the discussion was mainly about the epistemological disagreement over so-called "truth" between journalists and social scientists, it did indicate the dilemma between 'the needs of citizens, politicians, and therefore journalists for clear-cut binary answers' (Uscinski, 2015) and ambiguity of most politcal discussion, which suggests the necessity of a novel perspective on fact-checking, focusing on how political figures performed their language rather then what really occurred.

3 Approach

3.1 Dataset

We assembled a corpus of utterances made by prime ministers of Japan at the Plenary Session of the Diet from 1996 to 2016, from the Diet Record[4]. The corpus of 2605 fulltext discourses includes utterances from 11 prime ministers, 47 sessions. We selected utterances of Abe Shinzo, the incumbent Japanese Prime Minister, as our targets. The target utterances include 427 fulltext discourses from 6 sessions (16469 sentences, 9715 types, 492505 tokens). We used the rest of the corpus as supplementary materials to weigh the terms.

3.2 Procedure

3.2.1 Term extraction

We firstly seperated 2605 discourses into 47 documents in accordance with sessions of the Diet (6 target documents for Prime Minister Abe). After data cleansing, we used *ChaSen*[5](A Japanese morphological analyzer) to convert each document into a bag of its nouns. Nominal verbs were also included.

We then ranked nouns to obtain the most important terms in each document. We applied the tf-idf model because it is one of the most popular term-weighting schemes and is empirically useful.

3.2.2 Concordance generation

For each important term in the document, a list of all the instances of the term was generated if the term co-occurred with a stipulation expression such as *to-ha, to-tēgi* (both of the phrases represent 'be defined as')[6]. An instance of a term was a sentence which consists of the term and its context. All the instances of a term formed its concordance. The term's concept was constructed with only these instances.

3.2.3 Concept clustering

We converted every entry in the concordance into a vector for calculating the similarity of the term's contextual information. We applied tf-idf model instead of word embedding. Word embeddings contain biases in their geometry that reflect stereotypes present in broader society, and word embeddings not only reflect such stereotypes but can also amplify them (Bolukbasi et al., 2016). On the other hand, tf-idf has no semantic representation of words. In order to cope with potential subtle nuances in the utterances of political figures, a non-semantic representation is preferable to a semantic one. We then generated a hierarchy of clusters of the entries with Ward's method. Even though clustering approaches in WSI are usually non-hierarchical (Navigli, 2009; Denkowski, 2009), the reason for applying a hierarchical clustering instead of a non-hierarchical one is that we focused on the similarity of entries rather than the quantity of concepts.

Finally, by eliminating duplicated entries[7]and combining the remainder manually, we were able to acquire concepts of terms which are constructed with explicit stipulative definitions and explanations offered in documents. The revealed concept was therefore entirely contextual and independent of that which we have already known about.

4 Results

We treated the top 100 out of 8298 (3568 proper nouns) nouns as important terms. Three of them are explicitly defined in Prime Minister Abe's utterances: *Sekkyokuteki-hēwa-syugi* (Proactive pacifism), *Sonritsu-kiki-jitai*, and *Rikken-syugi* (Constitutionalism). *Sekkyokuteki-hēwa-syugi* was ranked as the 17th most important term among all the nouns. The cluster dendrogram of 68 sentences which were in the term's concordance is shown in figure 1. *Sonritsu-kiki-jitai* was ranked as the 24th most important term among all the

---

[4]http://kokkai.ndl.go.jp

[5]http://chasen-legacy.osdn.jp

[6]Besides these two phrases, various expressions are used to define terms. Since there haven't been a comprehensive summary of definition/stipulation expressions yet, we may not be able to extract all the potential defined terms.

[7]Most utterances were repeated twice at the House of Representatives and the House of Councilors.

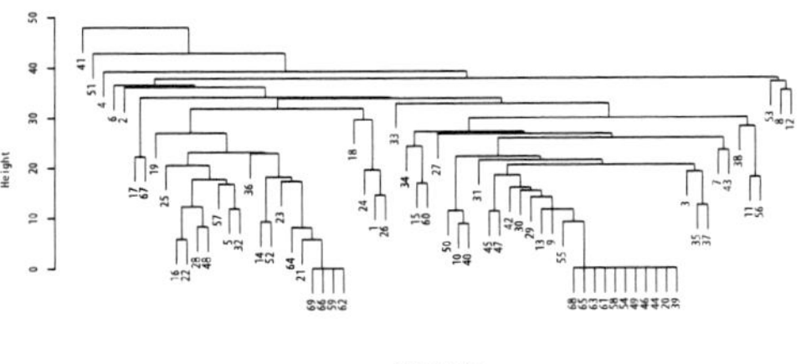

Figure 1: Cluster dendrogram of *Sekkyokuteki-hēwa-syugi*

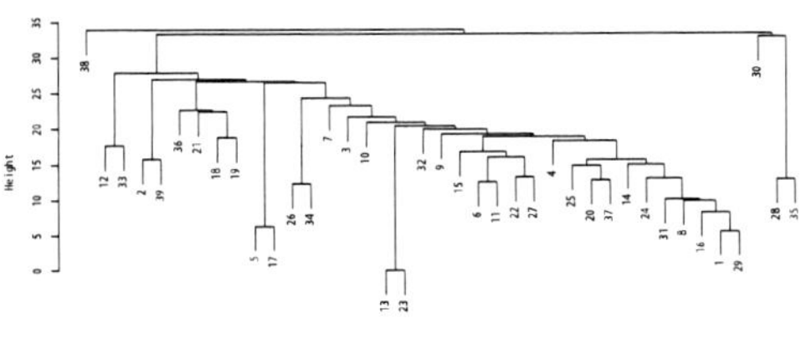

Figure 2: Cluster dendrogram of *Sonritsu-kiki-jitai*

nouns. The clustering result of 39 sentences is shown in figure 2. *Rikken-syugi* was ranked as the 72nd most important term among all the nouns. The clustering result of 22 sentences is shown in figure 3. Few terms were defined in utterances of Prime Ministers (15 terms in total).

Mutually contradictory explanations were found in the concordance of *Sonritsu-kiki-jitai*. Specifically, this term is currently translated to 'an armed attack against foreign country resulting in threatening Japan's survival', and is defined as a situation that 'an armed attack against Japan or a foreign country that is in a close relationship with Japan occurs, and as a result, threatens Japan's survival and poses **a clear danger** to fundamentally overturn people's right to life, liberty and pursuit of happiness' by the Ministry of Foreign Affairs of Japan. The

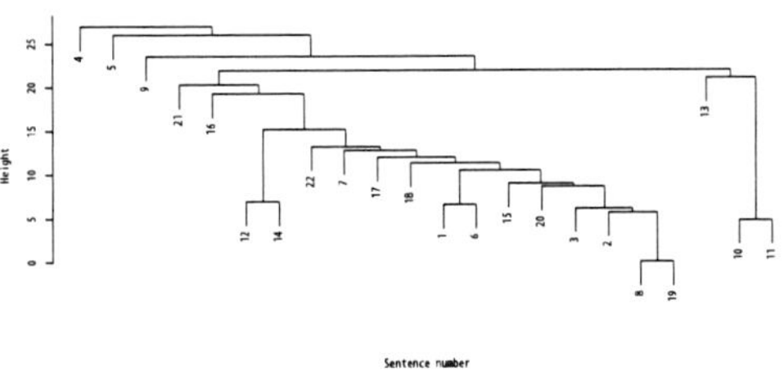

Figure 3: Cluster dendrogram of *Rikken-syugi*

situation is also one of three new conditions by which "use of force" as measures for self-defense is strictly limited[8]. This definition was mentioned two times in Prime Minister Abe's utterances (the 189th session on 26th May and 27th July, 2015). However, it was also mentioned several times that to determine whether a situation is a *Sonritsu-kiki-jitai* requires a **comprehensive analysis** by the government (18th May, 26th May, 29th May, 27th July, 2015; 27th Jan, 2016). Concisely, the concept of *Sonritsu-kiki-jitai* is a 'clear danger' that requires a 'comprehensive analysis' to determine whether it is a clear danger or not. This conceptual inconsistency turns one of the limitations on "use of force" into a mere scrap of paper.

5 Discussion

Political discourse is always vague and ambiguous. Nonetheless, we can still recognize in what manner it is vague and ambiguous. Even though the mission of fact-checking is 'not to measure which candidate "lies most" but rather to provide the public with information about the accuracy of statements' (Amazeen, 2015), in respect of accuracy, the information about how political figures performed their language is as important as the information about what really occurred.

This ongoing work opens a novel perspective on WSD for political discourse as well as fact-checking, by pointing out that a confirmation of concepts of terms which formed discourse is a prerequisite for analyzing formal utterances by political figures.

Our framework makes it possible for the public and/or journalists to recognize the most important terms as well as their stipulative concepts in an objective way. Moreover, we revealed the possibility that conceptual inconsistency can also exist in a single term as exemplified by revealed concept of *Sonritsu-kiki-jitai*. This indicated that there is a possibility that a term could be meaningless due to an inherent self-contradiction in its concept.

Due to inadequate explicit information in Prime Minister Abe's utterances, few concepts were revealed. This identified a weakness of our approach, i.e., it relies on how explicitly a speaker stipulated a term. Nonetheless, from another perspective, by focusing on the lack of explicit definitions and explanations of important terms in

---

[8]http://www.mofa.go.jp

discourse, The vagueness and ambiguity of utterances could be evaluated.

Our work is an ongoing research aims at establishing a practical standard for terminological analysis of political discourse. To start with, we provided this framework for revealing concepts of terms in political discourse. It could be technically improved in the following ways: 1) by analyzing the structure of documents' terminology sets and applying suitable term weighting models, we may generate a more applicable term ranking; 2) by discovering patterns of stipulative definition and explanation, we may assemble a more adequate concordance of a term from discourse; and 3) by applying suitable clustering and summarization methods, we may create a better balance between precision and concision.

Acknowledgments

We would like to thank National Diet Library of Japan for allowing free use of retrieval system of the Diet Record of Japan.

References

Michelle A. Amazeen. 2015. Revisiting the epistemology of fact-checking. *Critical Review* 27(1):1–22.

Tolga Bolukbasi, Kai-Wei Chang, James Y Zou, Venkatesh Saligrama, and Adam T Kalai. 2016. Man is to computer programmer as woman is to homemaker? debiasing word embeddings. In D. D. Lee, M. Sugiyama, U. V. Luxburg, I. Guyon, and R. Garnett, editors, *Advances in Neural Information Processing Systems 29*, Curran Associates, Inc., pages 4349–4357.

Michael Denkowski. 2009. A survey of techniques for unsupervised word sense induction. *Language & Statistics II Literature Review* pages 1–18.

Roberto Navigli. 2009. Word sense disambiguation: A survey. *ACM Computing Surveys* 4(2):10.

Joseph E. Uscinski. 2015. The epistemology of fact checking (is still naive): Rejoinder to amazeen. *Critical Review* 27(2):243–252.

Joseph E. Uscinski and Ryden W. Butler. 2013. The epistemology of fact checking. *Critical Review* 25(2):162–180.

A News Chain Evaluation Methodology along with a Lattice-based Approach for News Chain Construction

Mustafa Toprak
mustafatoprak@iyte.edu.tr
Izmir Institute of Technology,
35430, Urla, Izmir, Turkey

Özer Özkahraman
ozerozkahraman@outlook.com
KTH Royal Institute of Technology,
Stockholm 100-44, Sweden

Selma Tekir
selmatekir@iyte.edu.tr
Izmir Institute of Technology,
35430, Urla, Izmir, Turkey

Abstract

Chain construction is an important requirement for understanding news and establishing the context. A news chain can be defined as a coherent set of articles that explains an event or a story. There's a lack of well-established methods in this area.

In this work, we propose a methodology to evaluate the "goodness" of a given news chain and implement a concept lattice-based news chain construction method by Hossain et al.. The methodology part is vital as it directly affects the growth of research in this area. Our proposed methodology consists of collected news chains from different studies and two "goodness" metrics, *minedge* and *dispersion coefficient* respectively. We assess the utility of the lattice-based news chain construction method by our proposed methodology.

1 Introduction

A news story is a compelling organization of news to give an overall idea about an event or a set of related events. Generally this organization follows a time order and has topical coherence. The most common approach to construct a news chain is called "connecting the dots" (Shahaf and Guestrin, 2010). In this approach, there are predetermined start and end points and the task is to find a coherent sequence of articles between them.

In today's substantial news flow, tracking all news to understand an event or establish connections between related events is a challenge. Thus, automated mechanisms are needed to construct news chains and to support users in making news stories.

Our intended contribution is thus twofold: First, there's a need for a methodology in order to assess the quality of given news chains. Second, we implemented a state-of-the-art method that is based on the concept lattice representation of the news articles and evaluated its effectiveness in a more extensive way than the provided and additionally using our methodology.

In order to establish a news chain assessment methodology, we refer to two independent "goodness" metrics that are proposed, and experimentally validate and compare them in the same experimental setup. As far as we know, there is no such unifying experimental design that has a set of news chains and run of these metrics under the same conditions. Thus, we provide an evaluation regarding the utility of the proposed metrics in the quality assessment of news chains. Our finding is that **minedge** metric proposed by (Shahaf and Guestrin, 2010) behaves in a consistent way, but **dispersion coefficient** metric suggested by (Hossain et al., 2011) does not serve the purpose as expected.

As for the task of news chain construction, utilizing concept lattice-based representation of news articles (Hossain et al., 2011) is in accordance with our intuition. When we considered order relations, the sequence of articles that form a chain has a linear order. This linearity is provided by a total order relation. As partial order relations are more generic than their total order counterparts, our idea was to define a partial order relation over the set of articles and obtain a pool of news chain candidates out of the generated hierarchy. Thus, we create partially ordered news articles using their content. In this sense, we use a proposed pruning and heuristic (Hossain et al., 2011) to extract useful news chains out of the candidate pool. We evaluate the "goodness" of the constructed chains by the use of established methodology.

95

Proceedings of the 2017 EMNLP Workshop on Natural Language Processing meets Journalism, pages 95–99
Copenhagen, Denmark, September 7, 2017. ©2017 Association for Computational Linguistics

2   Related Work

News chain construction aims to discover hidden links between news articles in large news corpora. There are two main works that utilize the connecting the dots approach as the basis.

Connecting the dots approach proposed by Shahaf et al. (Shahaf and Guestrin, 2010) tries to ensure a coherent news chain. A coherent news chain is characterized with smooth transitions between all articles through the whole chain besides strong pairwise connection between consecutive articles. The problem is formalized as a linear program to put constraints for ensuring strong pairwise association and smooth transitions all along the chain.

An alternative method for connecting the dots between news articles is suggested by Hossain et al. (Hossain et al., 2011), which is implemented within the scope of this study. The method is based on Swanson's complimentary but disjoint hypothesis (Swanson, 1991). Swanson characterizes an ideal chain as one that satisfies a distance threshold between consecutive article pairs while does not oversatisfy the threshold between non-consecutive news articles. The method constructs the chain out of a concept lattice. Concepts represent closed termsets. An article's successors are selected from the concept with the largest termset that contains this article. The next article in the chain is determined with respect to two criteria: clique size (k), and distance threshold. k neighbors are determined with respect to Soergel distance at each step and A* search algorithm is run to find out the chain with the given endpoint.

3   Method

3.1   Methodology on the Evaluation of News Chains

In literature, there is no well-established methodology to measure the goodness of a given news chain. Two works propose different, independent mechanisms to evaluate news chains but they are not experimentally validated or compared with each other as part of a methodology. Moreover, there is a lack of ground-truth datasets in this area.

In an effort to establish such a methodology, we were in search of some ground-truth thus we collected already produced news chains by different works. Referring to the example chain provided by (Shahaf and Guestrin, 2010), we constructed that chain by searching the given article titles in the New York Times Portal. We named this chain as **Shahaf et. al. news chain**. As a control condition, we constructed another chain out of this by putting three copies of the fourth document (41070964.xml) in its place. We call this news chain **Shahaf et. al. control 1**.

As another published news chain, we referred to Alderwood story (ah Kang et al., 2009) provided as part of the VAST 2006 challenge (Whiting et al., 2009). The dataset (composed of 1182 documents) provides a ground-truth chain of length 19 (**VAST 2006 Challenge news chain**).

In addition to these news chains, three random news chains of equal length are produced from the New York Times Annotated Corpus (Sandhaus, 2008).

A news chain evaluation methodology needs methods to calculate some "goodness metrics". One such method quantifies a news chain with respect to its coherence by using a linear program (Shahaf and Guestrin, 2010). The linear program uses $kTrans$ and $kTotal$ as constraints to compute the $minedge$ objective value. Thus, our first goodness metric is $minedge$.

3.1.1   Minedge - Linear Programming Approach

The proposed linear program calculates two kinds of scores for every word in the chain. The first one is the activation score (act), which is the frequency difference of a word in two consecutive documents. As for the second; the initiation score (init), the difference between the activation scores of a word in consecutive document pairs is calculated:

$$act = freq(i + 1) - freq(i) \qquad (1)$$

$$\text{init} = \text{act}(i + 1)\text{-act}(i) = \text{freq}(i + 2)\text{-2freq}(i + 1) \text{ - freq}(i) \qquad (2)$$

The linear program makes word selection with respect to these activation and initiation scores. In other words, the linear constraints are defined in terms of activation and initiation variables. The first constraint variable $kTotal$ constrains the sum of initiation scores in the whole chain. The other constraint variable, $kTrans$ limits the sum of activation scores on individual document transitions.

In order to calculate the $minedge$ objective value, the activation score of a word in a document pair is weighted by the influence of that word in connecting those two documents and the weighted activation scores are summed. The objective is to maximize this sum.

The influence of a word in connecting the document pairs is calculated based on the document-word bipartite graph. In this graph, documents and words are nodes and normalized word frequencies are the edge weights. The influence of a word w in connecting the document d_1 to the document d_2 is calculated by the use of the path that connects d_1 to d_2 over w:

$$influence(d_i, d_{i+1}|w) = p(w|d_i).p(d_{i+1}|w) \tag{3}$$

In the original implementation of the *minedge* metric value, (Shahaf and Guestrin, 2010) state that they use random walk on the document-word bipartite graph to calculate the influence of words. On the other hand, we apply the formula in equation 3 for simplicity.

One of the key issues in this linear program is tuning parameters $kTotal$ and $kTrans$ to maximize the *minedge* value. In order to determine the best parameter values, we plotted $kTotal$, $kTrans$, and *minedge* values in 3D (Figure 1). As can be seen from the plot, the dark red areas represent the maximized values of *minedge*, thus, we selected $kTotal$ and $kTrans$ values belonging to those areas.

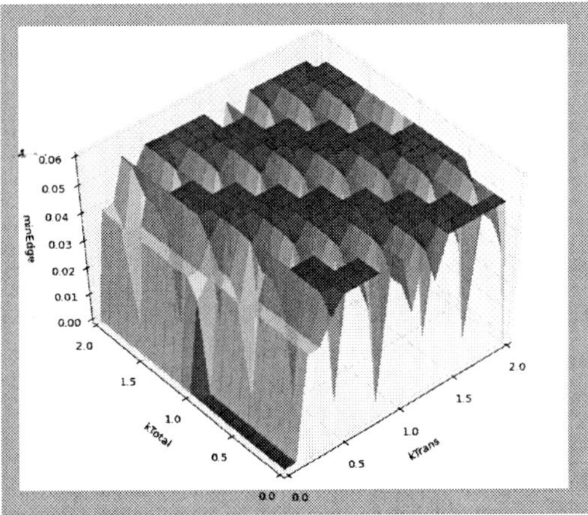

Figure 1: *minedge* values with respect to $kTotal$ and $kTrans$.

We use the maximum *minedge* value to quantify the coherence of a given news chain. Thus, in the given example the coherence score determined by the *minedge* value is 0.053625.

3.1.2 Dispersion coefficient

Another proposed metric to measure the quality of news chains is *dispersion coefficient* that is calculated based on Soergel distances (Hossain et al., 2012b).

Soergel distance between two documents is calculated considering all the words in the set of documents. The difference between the weights in the first and second document is summed for every word and this sum is normalized by the sum of the max. of those two weights for each word:

$$D(d_1, d_2) = \frac{\sum_t |w_{t,d_1} - w_{t,d_2}|}{\sum_t \max(w_{t,d_1}, w_{t,d_2})} \tag{4}$$

The weight of a word for a document is calculated using a variant of TF-IDF cosine normalization (Hossain et al., 2012a).

Soergel distance returns 0 for two identical documents and 1 for documents that do not overlap.

The dispersion coefficient metric-based quality evaluation is premised on Swanson's CBD (complimentary but disjoint) hypothesis (Swanson, 1991). The method computes a coherence score on the basis of Soergel distances between consecutive and non-consecutive pairs along the chain.

Dispersion coefficient is computed using the following formula:

$$V = 1 - \frac{1}{n-2}\sum_{i=0}^{n-3} \sum_{j=i+2}^{n-1} disp(d_i, d_j) \tag{5}$$

In the formula, $disp$ dispersion value inside the nested sums becomes positive when the angle between document pairs is above a specified threshold (or the distance between document pairs is below a specified threshold), otherwise it's 0. In the cases where it's positive, if the position difference of documents of pair is high, it affects by taking a higher value in other words it reduces the value of dispersion coefficient in a larger extent:

$$disp(d_i, d_j) = \begin{cases} \frac{1}{n+i-j}, & \text{if } D(d_i, d_j) > \Theta \\ 0, & \text{otherwise} \end{cases}$$

3.2 News Chain Construction

In this paper, we implemented the chain construction method suggested by Hossain et al.. The work constructs a concept lattice from the inverted index of documents and represents each closed termset

	Chain length	Minedge value
Shahaf et. al.	8	0.02
Shahaf et. al. control	10	0.018
VAST 2006 Challenge	19	0.0064
Random news chain 1	8	0.0055
Random news chain 2	8	0.0036
Random news chain 3	8	0.0023

Table 1: Minedge metric values.

	Chain length	Threshold 0.22	Threshold 0.25
Shahaf et. al.	8	0.836111	0.483333
Shahaf et. al. control 1	10	0.984375	0.615625
Shahaf et. al. control 2	10	0.829167	0.600893
VAST 2006 Challenge	19	0.862132	0.571804
VAST lattice all avg.	7.5	0.873	0.401
Random news chain 1	8	1.0	0.394444
Random news chain 2	8	0.883333	0.316666
Random news chain 3	8	1.0	0.711111

Table 2: Dispersion coefficient values.

by a unique concept. Each concept has terms as extents and documents as intents. We used CHARM-L algorithm (Zaki and Hsiao, 2005) to generate this concept lattice structure.

In order to generate promising candidate chains out of this lattice, an initial document has to be determined. The algorithm then proceeds by looking for the largest extent size concept that includes this initial document in its intent set. After that; inside this concept, candidate chains are sought using local neighborhood-based search. The search heuristic is defined by two criteria. Clique size determines the maximum number of neighbors to evaluate at each stage whereas distance threshold criterion makes a selection out of them.

As we worked with the VAST 2006 Challenge dataset, we selected the start document as the initial document of the VAST 2006 Challenge ground-truth chain. Then, we worked with 3 clique-size and 10 clique candidates (a total of 10 3 cliques) in order to find a good set of successors. As a result, we created all candidate chains from the VAST dataset.

3.3 Experimental Results

We calculated our goodness metrics for the news chains in our experimental design. In Table 2, *minedge* metric values are shown. When we look at the obtained values, we observe that ground-truth chains have higher values than the randomly generated ones. Additionally, **Shahaf et. al. control 1** gets a lower value compared to its original chain. Thus, the results support the claim that *minedge* metric value behaves in a correct and consistent way in measuring the coherence of given news chains.

As a second part of our experiment, we computed the dispersion coefficient values for all the chains by fixing the Soergel distance threshold value as 0.22 and 0.25 respectively.

The obtained dispersion coefficient values do not seem to work well in the quality assessment of news chains. First of all, **Shahaf et. al. control 1** has a higher score than **Shahaf et. al.. Shahaf et. al. control 1** has three copies of the fourth document and it is desired to have a lower dispersion value since repeating exactly the same news will not contribute to chain coherence. However, the dispersion coefficient approach does not consider the repetition of documents as a semantic parameter, it simply penalizes nonconsecutive documents which over-satisfies the distance threshold as a document pair. However, for a given chain we cannot know how close the nonconsecutive documents are beforehand. In order to verify this idea, we added a second control condition (**Shahaf et. al. control 2**) in which we repeated the fourth document at the beginning, middle, and end points, which resulted in lower dispersion coefficient values since non-consecutive identical document pairs have the distance value 0 and penalty is higher due to higher index differences. Moreover, random chains (Random news chain 3) can get comparable higher scores for this measure.

As for the lattice-based news construction algorithm, the average score for all the constructed chains does not make an important difference when compared with the VAST 2006 Challenge ground-truth chain.

4 Conclusion

The first goodness metric, *minedge* gives correct and consistent results. However, the dispersion coefficient values fail to evaluate the "goodness" of given news chains. The reason can be attributed to disregarding the consecutive document pairs in the calculation of the coefficient value. Because penalizing with respect to far away documents in the chain is necessary but not sufficient condition for a chain definition. At the same time, strong pairwise association must be guaranteed.

When it comes to the lattice-based news chain construction algorithm, extensive experimental validation is needed. Moreover, alternative path traversal heuristics can be adapted to the constructed lattice to produce coherent news chains.

Acknowledgments

This paper is based on work supported by the Scientific and Technological Research Council of Turkey (TÜBİTAK) under contract number 114E784.

References

Youn ah Kang, Carsten Görg, and John T. Stasko. 2009. Evaluating visual analytics systems for investigative analysis: Deriving design principles from a case study. In *Proceedings of the IEEE Symposium on Visual Analytics Science and Technology, IEEE VAST 2009, Atlantic City, New Jersey, USA, 11-16 October 2009, part of VisWeek 2009*. pages 139–146. https://doi.org/10.1109/VAST.2009.5333878.

M. S. Hossain, J. Gresock, Y. Edmonds, R. Helm, M. Potts, and N. Ramakrishnan. 2012a. Connecting the dots between PubMed abstracts. *PLoS ONE* 7(1):e29509.

M Shahriar Hossain, Christopher Andrews, Naren Ramakrishnan, and Chris North. 2011. Helping intelligence analysts make connections. *Scalable Integration of Analytics and Visualization* 11:17.

M. Shahriar Hossain, Patrick Butler, Arnold P. Boedihardjo, and Naren Ramakrishnan. 2012b. Storytelling in entity networks to support intelligence analysts. In *Proceedings of the 18th ACM SIGKDD International Conference on Knowledge Discovery and Data Mining*. ACM, New York, NY, USA, KDD '12, pages 1375–1383. https://doi.org/10.1145/2339530.2339742.

E. Sandhaus. 2008. The New York Times Annotated Corpus. *Linguistic Data Consortium, Philadelphia* 6(12).

Dafna Shahaf and Carlos Guestrin. 2010. Connecting the dots between news articles. In *Proceedings of the 16th ACM SIGKDD International Conference on Knowledge Discovery and Data Mining, Washington, DC, USA, July 25-28, 2010*. pages 623–632. https://doi.org/10.1145/1835804.1835884.

Don R. Swanson. 1991. Complementary structures in disjoint science literatures. In *Proceedings of the 14th Annual International ACM SIGIR Conference on Research and Development in Information Retrieval*. ACM, New York, NY, USA, SIGIR '91, pages 280–289. https://doi.org/10.1145/122860.122889.

M.A. Whiting, Chris North, Alex Endert, J. Scholtz, J. Haack, C. Varley, and J. Thomas. 2009. Vast contest dataset use in education. In *Visual Analytics Science and Technology, 2009. IEEE VAST 2009.*. pages 115 –122. https://doi.org/10.1109/VAST.2009.5333245.

Mohammed J. Zaki and Ching-Jui Hsiao. 2005. Efficient algorithms for mining closed itemsets and their lattice structure. *IEEE Trans. on Knowl. and Data Eng.* 17(4):462–478. https://doi.org/10.1109/TKDE.2005.60.

Using New York Times Picks to Identify Constructive Comments

Varada Kolhatkar
Discourse Processing Lab
Simon Fraser University
Burnaby, Canada
vkolhatk@sfu.ca

Maite Taboada
Discourse Processing Lab
Simon Fraser University
Burnaby, Canada
mtaboada@sfu.ca

Abstract

We examine the extent to which we are able to automatically identify constructive online comments. We build several classifiers using New York Times Picks as positive examples and non-constructive thread comments from the Yahoo News Annotated Comments Corpus as negative examples of constructive online comments. We evaluate these classifiers on a crowd-annotated corpus containing 1,121 comments. Our best classifier achieves a top F1 score of 0.84.

1   Introduction

Online commenting allows for direct communication among people and organizations from various socioeconomic classes on important issues. Popular news articles receive thousands of comments, but not all of them are constructive. Below we show examples of a constructive and a non-constructive comment on an article about Hillary Clinton's loss in the presidential election in 2016.[1]

(1) There is something inherently sexist about the assumption that women are incorruptible and naturally groomed to be better leaders than their male counterparts by virtue of being female. It is troubling to see intelligent sexist women relay the disturbingly substandard notion that despite Hillary Clinton's deeply flawed and frankly troubling history, this one here must be revered at all cost. Women are equal under the law, and as such should be held to the same legal, ethical, and job performance standards - regardless of their gender or power.

(2) If you think she lost because she was a women then you are really out to lunch. Gender has nothing to do with it.

---

[1] https://www.theglobeandmail.com/opinion/thank-you-hillary-women-now-know-retreat-is-not-an-option/article32803341/

The first one, which was labelled as constructive by our annotators (see Section 3), presents an argument (that women should be equal in all aspects), a challenge to an assumption (that women are incorruptible), and a protest against overlooking Ms. Clinton's flaws because of her gender. The second comment, labelled as non-constructive, exhibits a dismissive tone (*you are really out to lunch*), and provides no supporting evidence for the claim that gender was not a factor in the election.

There is growing interest in automatically organizing reader comments in a sensible way (Napoles et al., 2017; Llewellyn et al., 2014). One useful way to organize comments is based on their *constructiveness*, i.e., by identifying which comments provide insight and encourage a healthy discussion. For instance, The New York Times manually selects and highlights comments representing a range of diverse views, referred to as *NYT Picks*.

In this paper, we focus on this problem of identifying constructive comments. We define constructive comments as those that contribute to the dialogue, which provide insights relevant to the article, perhaps supported by evidence, and develop computational methods for identifying constructive comments.

The primary challenge in developing a computational system for constructiveness is the lack of annotated data. There is no systematically-annotated training data available for constructiveness of individual comments. So we explore the available resources: a set of NYT Picks as positive examples and non-constructive thread comments from the Yahoo News Annotated Comments Corpus (YNACC) (Napoles et al., 2017) as negative examples for constructiveness. We train support vector machine classifiers and bidirectional long short-term memory networks on this combination dataset and achieve a top F1 score of 0.84 on an

Proceedings of the 2017 EMNLP Workshop on Natural Language Processing meets Journalism, pages 100–105
Copenhagen, Denmark, September 7, 2017. ©2017 Association for Computational Linguistics

unseen test dataset containing 1,121 constructive and non-constructive reader comments from the website of a different newspaper, The Globe and Mail.[2]

2 Related work

Napoles et al. (2017) define constructiveness of comment threads in terms of ERICs—Engaging, Respectful, and/or Informative Conversations. They train four machine learning models on $2.1k$ annotated Yahoo News threads and report an F1 score of 0.73 as their highest when identifying constructive news threads. We deal with a similar problem, but in our case we examine individual comments, rather than threads, as there is value in identifying constructive comments as they come in rather than waiting for a thread to degenerate (Wulczyn et al., 2016). Work closer to ours is that of Park et al. (2016), who explore New York Times comments extracted using the New York Times API to distinguish between NYT Picks and non-picks. They train an SVM classifier on a skewed dataset containing 94 NYT Picks and 5,174 non-picks and achieve a cross-validation precision of 0.13 and recall of 0.60. NYT Picks have also been used to study editorial criteria in comment selection. For instance, Diakopoulos (2015) analyzed 5,174 NYT Picks and found that they show high levels of argument quality, criticality, internal coherence, personal experience, readability, and thoughtfulness.

The data used by Napoles et al. (2017) does not contain constructiveness annotations for individual comments, but only for comment threads. The NYT Picks used by Diakopoulos (2015) and Park et al. (2016) are good representatives of constructive comments, but non-picks are not necessarily non-constructive, as only a few comments among thousands of comments are selected as NYT Picks. We create our training data by combining these two resources: NYT Picks for positive examples and non-constructive comment threads from the YNACC[3] for negative examples.

3 Datasets

Training and validation data We propose to use NYT Picks as representative training data for constructiveness. The New York Times, like many newspaper sites, provides a platform for readers to comment on stories posted on the site. The comments are manually moderated, by a team of only 13 moderators.[4] As a result, only about 10% of the stories published are open for commenting.[5] Comments are classified into three categories: all comments, readers' picks, and NYT Picks. NYT Picks are curated by the team of human moderators, and are chosen because they are interesting and helpful, but also based on the region or the reader.[6] Below we show an example of a NYT pick on an article about a young girl's suicide due to cyber-bullying.[7] The comment urges readers to take an action against cyberbulling, and does so by encouraging others to discuss the hurtful nature of attacks online.

(3) All of us — moms, dads, sisters, brothers, and friends need to talk about how words hurt. We need to take a stronger stance against damaging attacks — Just say no to texting or saying such hurtful comments, racial epithets, etc. We often lament how electronic communication enables uncivil speech, but we need to address the root of the problem here — why 12 year olds (indeed people of any age) are urging another person to kill herself.

Our positive training examples have 15,079 NYT Picks extracted using the NYT API.[8] Our negative training examples consist of 15,950 comments occurring in negative threads in the YNACC (Napoles et al., 2017), which contains thread-level constructiveness annotations for Yahoo News comment threads. Because we are interested in individual comments, rather than threads, we consider all comments from a non-constructive thread to be non-constructive. An example of a comment from a non-constructive thread is shown in (4).

(4) What makes you think that he's not sleeping with the robots already ;).

The training data is split into training set (90%) and validation set (10%).

[2] https://www.theglobeandmail.com
[3] https://webscope.sandbox.yahoo.com
[4] https://www.nytimes.com/times-insider/2014/04/17/a-comments-path-to-publication/?_r=0
[5] https://www.nytimes.com/interactive/2016/09/20/insider/approve-or-reject-moderation-quiz.html
[6] https://www.nytimes.com/content/help/site/usercontent/usercontent.html/#usercontent-nytpicks
[7] http://www.nytimes.com/2013/09/14/us/suicide-of-girl-after-bullying-raises-worries-on-web-sites.html
[8] https://developer.nytimes.com/

Feature	Description
Length features (4)	Number of tokens in the comment, number of sentences, average word length, average number of words per sentence
Argumentation features (5)	Presence of discourse connectives (*therefore, due to*) Reasoning verbs (*cause, lead*), modals (*may, should*) Abstract nouns (*problem, issue, decision, reason*) Stance adverbials (*undoubtedly, paradoxically*)
Named-entity features (1)	Number of named entities in the comment
Text quality features (2)	Readability score & personal experience description score

Table 1: Constructiveness features.

Test data Our test data consists of 1,121 comments downloaded from the site of The Globe and Mail, a Canadian daily. We conducted an annotation experiment using CrowdFlower,[9] asking annotators to read the article each comment refers to (a total of 10 articles), and to label the comment as constructive or not. For quality control, 100 units were marked as gold: annotators were allowed to continue with the annotation task only when their answers agreed with our answers to the gold questions. As we were interested in the verdict of native speakers of English, we limited the allowed demographic region to English-speaking countries. We asked for three judgments per instance and paid 5 cents per annotation unit. Percentage agreement for the constructiveness question on a random sample of 100 annotations was 87.88%, suggesting that constructiveness can be reliably annotated. Other measures of agreement, such as kappa, are not easily computed with CrowdFlower data, because many different annotators are involved. Constructiveness seemed to be equally distributed in our dataset: Out of the 1,121 comments, 603 comments (53.79%) were classified as constructive, 517 (46.12%) as non-constructive, and the annotators were not sure in only one case.[10] We have made the corpus and annotation guidelines publicly available.[11]

4 Experiments

We present results of three sets of experiments: 1) identifying constructive comments using support vector machine classifiers (SVMs) and constructiveness features, 2) predicting constructive comments using bi-directional long-short term memory neural networks (biLSTMs) and word embeddings, and 3) examining the effectiveness of using NYT picks as representative positive examples for constructiveness.

Measure	Training		Testing	
	C	NC	C	NC
Mean	132.06	46.53	100.19	24.06
SD	71.36	87.52	81.34	19.08

Table 2: The mean length in words and standard deviation (SD) for constructive and non-constructive comments. C = Constructive and NC = Non-constructive.

4.1 SVMs with constructiveness features

We train several SVM classifiers with a number of constructiveness features, shown in Table 1.

Word features We wanted to examine whether certain words or phrases are more common in constructive or non-constructive comments. For that we extracted features representing 1- to 4-gram counts and TF-IDF features.

Length features Constructive comments tend to contain long sentences and long content words. We include four length features, as shown in Table 1. Note that this feature class can also serve as a baseline—if the length alone is sufficient to identify constructiveness, we may not need to explore more sophisticated features for constructiveness. Table 2 shows the mean length in words and standard deviation for constructive and non-constructive comments in our training and test data. In general, constructive texts tend to be longer and in all cases there is great variation in length.

Argumentation features We postulate a positive correlation between features of argumentative text and news comments. An argumentative text is one that contains argumentation, i.e., a claim supported by evidence, and presented as a coherent whole. The extensive literature on argumentation has identified linguistics aspects that pinpoint to argumentative texts (Biber, 1988; van Eemeren et al., 2007; Moens et al., 2007; Tseronis, 2011; Habernal and Gurevych, 2017). Based on this research, we include argumentation lexical cues, such as discourse connectives and stance adverbials, in our set of features.

Named-entity features Our hypothesis is that comments providing evidence and personal experiences (i.e., constructive comments) tend to contain named entities (e.g., *Hillary Clinton, the Government,* names of public institutions).

Text-quality features We include two features from Park et al. (2016), readability score and personal experience score. Park et al. (2016) also propose a method to identify high quality comments, in their case modelling on NYT Picks and non-picks. Some of their criteria are external to the comment (relevance to the article, whether it was recommended by other readers), but, since we want to rely exclusively on the comment content, we chose the two criteria that do so, both calculated using their tool.

We trained linear SVM classifiers with several feature combinations from the above set of features using sklearn.[12] These models predict constructive comments in our test data. Some of the best validation and prediction results of these classifiers are shown in Table 3.

4.2 biLSTMs with word embeddings

We wanted to examine to what extent a neural network model is able to learn relevant patterns of constructiveness from NYT Picks. We trained bidirectional long short-term memory networks (biLSTMs) with word embeddings on our training data. We initialized the embedding layer weights with GloVe vectors (Pennington et al., 2014). The biLSTM models are usually used for sequential predictions. Although our task is *not* a sequential prediction task, the primary reason for us-

[12]http://scikit-learn.org/stable/
modules/generated/sklearn.linear_
model.SGDClassifier.html

Model	Validation			Test		
	P	R	F1	P	R	F1
Random	.51	.50	.50	.49	.50	.49
wf	.84	.83	.83	.81	.80	.80
lf	.80	.80	.80	.79	.79	.79
af	.75	.74	.75	.73	.73	.73
tqf	.81	.81	.81	.83	.77	.76
nef	.74	.73	.74	.72	.69	.68
af+tqf+nef	.80	.78	.79	.84	.84	**.84**
biLSTM	.86	.86	.86	.82	.81	.81

Table 3: Constructiveness prediction results. P=average precision (for constructive and non-constructive classes), R=average recall, F1=average F1 score, wf=word (features), lf=length, af=argumentative, tqf=text quality, nef=named entity.

ing biLSTMs is that these models can utilize the expanded paragraph-level context and learn paragraph representations directly. They have recently been used in diverse text classification tasks, such as stance detection (Augenstein et al., 2016), sentiment analysis (Teng et al., 2016), and medical event detection (Jagannatha and Yu, 2016).

We use bidirectional LSTMs as implemented in TensorFlow.[13] We trained with the ADAM stochastic gradient descent for 10 epochs. The important parameter settings are: batch size=512, embedding size=200, drop out=0.5, and learning rate=0.001. Results for the biLSTM classifier are also shown in Table 3. Note that the point of these results is to demonstrate the feasibility of automatically identifying constructive comments and the parameter setting may not be the optimal one.

4.3 Effectiveness of NYT Picks

To examine the effectiveness of using NYT Picks as representative positive training examples for constructiveness, we carried out experiments with training data containing a homogeneous sample from YNACC, in particular, by considering comments from constructive YNACC threads as constructive examples and comments from non-constructive threads as negative examples. When trained on this homogeneous YNACC training data, we observed P, R, and F1 of 0.72, 0.71, and 0.71, respectively. These numbers are markedly lower compared to the numbers we obtained when we used NYT Picks for training (F1 = 0.81), suggesting that using NYT Picks as positive examples for constructiveness does help. NYT Picks

[13]https://www.tensorflow.org/

are chosen by human experts and are better representatives of constructiveness. Although the performance numbers with homogeneous YNACC look similar to the numbers reported in Napoles et al. (2017), recall that Napoles et al. (2017) focus on a different problem of identifying constructive conversation threads. A constructive thread may have a non-constructive comment and vice-versa. Moreover, they report cross-validation results, whereas we are reporting results on our test data containing reader comments from a different news paper.

5 Discussion and conclusion

We have explored several approaches to the problem of detecting constructiveness in online comments, focusing specifically on news comments. Constructiveness is a desirable feature in online discussion, and a constructiveness classifier can be useful for moderation tasks, typically performed by humans. Our methods achieve a top F1 score of 0.84, which is probably sufficient to assist news comments moderators.

We used two sets of available data as positive and negative examples for the classifiers: New York Times Picks as positive examples of constructiveness, and comments belonging to non-constructive threads from the Yahoo News Annotated Comments Corpus. Our test data consisted of 1,121 examples annotated for constructiveness through CrowdFlower.

Our methods can be grouped under two main categories: SVMs with various features and bidirectional LSTMs. For SVMs, we considered five classes of features: word, length, argumentation, named entity, and text quality features. Our best F1 score is 0.84 on the test set with the combination of argumentation, text quality, and named entity features. The length features alone give a high F1 score of 0.79. But when we combine them with other features the performance does not increase. On the other hand, argumentation, text quality, and named entity features seem to be complementary and give the best results when combined together.

Our biLSMT model requires only a vector representation of the text. We use an embedding layer initialized with GloVe vectors, and achieved an F1 score of 0.81 with this model. Note the similar performance of SVMs with word features and biLSTMs. We do not conclude from these experiments that either method is superior, since these are preliminary results and many other parameter combinations are possible. The point of these results is just to demonstrate the feasibility of automating the task of identifying constructiveness in news comments. A more rigourous investigation needs to be carried out in order to compare and understand the differences between SVMs and biLSTMs for this problem.

We achieved superior results when we used NYT Picks as positive training examples for constructiveness, suggesting that human-selected NYT Picks are better representatives of constructiveness.

A number of research avenues are planned for this project. First, we are interested in exploring other relevant features for constructiveness, such as the use of emoticons and fine-grained named-entity features (e.g., occurrences of a journalist's name). Second, we are interested in exploring the relation between constructiveness and toxicity. Finally, we are working towards making our computational system for identifying constructive comments robust and easily accessible.

Acknowledgments

We are grateful to Nicholas Diakopoulos for promptly providing us 5,232 NYT Picks, which are part of our training data. Thank you to the reviewers for constructive feedback.

References

Isabelle Augenstein, Tim Rocktäschel, Andreas Vlachos, and Kalina Bontcheva. 2016. Stance detection with bidirectional conditional encoding. In *Proceedings of the 2016 Conference on Empirical Methods in Natural Language Processing*, pages 876–885, Austin, TX.

Douglas Biber. 1988. *Variation across Speech and Writing*. Cambridge University Press, Cambridge.

Nicholas Diakopoulos. 2015. Picking the NYT Picks: Editorial criteria and automation in the curation of online news comments. *ISOJ Journal*, 6(1):147–166.

Frans H. van Eemeren, Peter Houtlosser, and A. Francisca Snoeck Henkemans. 2007. *Argumentative Indicators in Discourse: A pragma-dialectical study*. Springer, Berlin.

Ivan Habernal and Iryna Gurevych. 2017. Argumentation mining in user-generated web discourse. *Computational Linguistics*, 43(1):125–179.

Abhyuday N. Jagannatha and Hong Yu. 2016. Bidirectional RNN for medical event detection in electronic health records. In *Proceedings of the 2016 Conference of the North American Chapter of the Association for Computational Linguistics: Human Language Technologies*, pages 473–482, San Diego, CA.

Clare Llewellyn, Claire Grover, and Jon Oberlander. 2014. Summarizing Newspaper Comments. In *Proceedings of ICWSM*, Ann Arbor, MI.

Marie-Francine Moens, Erik Boiy, Raquel Mochales Palau, and Chris Reed. 2007. Automatic detection of arguments in legal texts. In *Proceedings of the 11th International Conference on Artificial Intelligence and Law*, pages 225–230, Stanford, California. ACM.

Courtney Napoles, Joel Tetreault, Aasish Pappu, Enrica Rosato, and Brian Provenzale. 2017. Finding good conversations online: The Yahoo News Annotated Comments Corpus. In *Proceedings of the 11th Linguistic Annotation Workshop, EACL*, pages 13–23, Valencia.

Deokgun Park, Simranjit Sachar, Nicholas Diakopoulos, and Niklas Elmqvist. 2016. Supporting comment moderators in identifying high quality online news comments. In *Proceedings of the 2016 CHI Conference on Human Factors in Computing Systems*, pages 1114–1125. ACM.

Jeffrey Pennington, Richard Socher, and Christopher D. Manning. 2014. GloVe: Global vectors for word representation. In *Proceedings of the Conference on Empirical Methods in Natural Language Processing*, pages 1532–1543, Doha, Qatar.

Zhiyang Teng, Duy Tin Vo, and Yue Zhang. 2016. Context-sensitive lexicon features for neural sentiment analysis. In *Proceedings of the 2016 Conference on Empirical Methods in Natural Language Processing*, pages 1629–1638, Austin, Texas.

Assimakis Tseronis. 2011. From connectives to argumentative markers: A quest for markers of argumentative moves and of related aspects of argumentative discourse. *Argumentation*, 25(4):427–447.

Ellery Wulczyn, Nithum Thain, and Lucas Dixon. 2016. Ex machina: Personal attacks seen at scale. *arXiv:1702.08138v1*.

An NLP Analysis of Exaggerated Claims in Science News

Yingya Li
School of Information Studies
Syracuse University
yli48@syr.edu

Jieke Zhang
School of Information Studies
Syracuse University
jzhan150@syr.edu

Bei Yu
School of Information Studies
Syracuse University
byu@syr.edu

Abstract

The discrepancy between science and media has been affecting the effectiveness of science communication. Original findings from science publications may be distorted with altered claim strength when reported to the public, causing misinformation spread. This study conducts an NLP analysis of exaggerated claims in science news, and then constructed prediction models for identifying claim strength levels in science reporting. The results demonstrate different writing styles journal articles and news/press releases use for reporting scientific findings. Preliminary prediction models reached promising result with room for further improvement.

1 Introduction

On April 18, 2017 many science news agencies reported a new study on peer effects in health behavior (Aral and Nicolaides, 2017). Here are a few examples of the headlines:

AAAS: "Exercise is contagious, especially if you are a men"
MIT Sloan press release: "Turns out exercise is contagious"
Medscape: "Exercise may be contagious"
Gulfnews: "Exercise can be contagious, new social network analysis finds".

Regardless of the original finding, these news headlines interpreted and thus reported the finding with different levels of strength (using different verbs such as "is", "may", and "can").

This example illustrates a prominent problem in science communication that original scientific findings might be altered or distorted during the information spread process. Different infor-

mation subsidies such as the university press and news releases have been widely used to deliver research findings. However, possibly caused by different writing purposes of scientists and journalists, those paraphrased versions of the original findings in the reporting may not be as accurate. For example, the university press release has been found to be a major source of misinformation (Sumner et al., 2014).

The ways in which information is framed along with how the audiences decode it has powerful impacts on public behaviors. Hence the aforementioned misinformation diffusion can cause misunderstanding of science findings. A possible approach for curbing such misinformation diffusion in science communication is to compare relevant findings reported in science news and the original journal articles, identifying the strength levels of their claims, and thus to warn writers and readers of potential exaggerations in the science reporting.

Such approach requires two steps: "claims pairing" and "claim strength identification". In this paper we focus on the second task, and leave the first task to future work. We explored the statement of causality in health-related science communication covered by academic journals, university press releases and news stories. We analyzed how causal triggers (i.e., verbs or verb phrases that express causal relations in claims) are associated with different levels of casual relations, using the open-dataset released by Sumner et al. (2014). Also, we developed text classification models to predict the strength levels of claims in academic papers and news articles.

This study seeks answers to the following research questions: (1) What are the linguistic factors distinguishing different reporting styles of journal articles and news/press releases? (2) What are the causal triggers for different levels of claim strength? (3) Is it feasible to automatically identify

Proceedings of the 2017 EMNLP Workshop on Natural Language Processing meets Journalism, pages 106–111
Copenhagen, Denmark, September 7, 2017. ©2017 Association for Computational Linguistics

the strength of claims in science reporting and news? If so, what are the current achievement and challenges?

2 Related Work

In the NLP field scholars have tried to identify misinformation from different perspectives, including credibility prediction (Castillo et al., 2013), rumor detection (Qazvinian et al., 2011; Zubiaga et al., 2016) etc. Although satisfactory accuracy for automatic misinformation detection could be made, the effectiveness of discrediting misinformation on people's belief and perception remains unknown. Prior studies found that false information with exaggerated claims is designed to meet emotional needs and often emerges in situations of uncertainty (Silverman, 2015). For people with strong fixed views, encountering contradicting claims and arguments can cause them to strengthen their original belief. One possible way to reduce the continuing of misinformation is to explain why the information or myth is wrong by showing the rhetorical techniques such as the specific exaggeration that was used (Cook and Lewandowsky, 2012).

A relevant task of analyzing such rhetorical manipulation in science communication is to identify the strength of claims. Light et al. (2004) built a classifier to predict the levels of speculative language in sentences from biomedical abstracts. Vlachos and Craven (2010) also developed a classifier to detect the information certainty in biomedical text, using syntactic dependencies and logistic regression. Blake (2010) proposed a claim framework that tries to capture the ways an author communicates a scientific claim. The framework is built on the certainty of causal relations that were presented, which is closely related to strength identification.

The problem of identifying claim strength is also closely linked to several other science communication and science news reporting problems, especially on casual relation and exaggeration detection. Though many efforts have been made to analyze causal relations in claims (e.g., Mihaila et al., 2013; Sumner et al., 2014; Khoo et al., 2000), massive diffusion of unverified rumors fosters confusions about causation that could adversatively impact the public beliefs and decisions. Under this circumstance, readers' knowledge and personal judgment for claims of different issues will be challenged greatly.

Unlike previous studies mainly focusing on single domain, in the current work we studied claim strength across multiple domains/genres of both academic publication and news/press releases. We tried to automatically identify claim strength in science reporting with special focus on the different types of causal relationship. It is also the first step towards automatic identification of exaggeration and emotion manipulation in science news.

3 Experiment

3.1 Data

In this study, we use an open data set (*http://dx.doi.org/10.6084/m9.figshare.903704*) developed by Sumner et al. (2014). This corpus includes a sample of health-related journal articles and their corresponding press releases and news articles. After manually coding the strength levels of the main claims from the three sources, they found that the press release is a major source of exaggeration in science news reporting.

This open data set includes 462 health-related press releases and their corresponding claims in 668 associated journal articles and news stories. The primary causal claims in the journal articles, press releases and news reports are coded into seven categories with increasing strength of relationship: no mentioned relationship (Category "0"); statement of no relationship (Category "1"), statement of correlation (Category "2"), ambiguous statement of relationship (Category "3"), conditional statement of causation (Category "4"), statement of "can" (Category "5"), and statement of causation (Category "6"). Table 1 lists the category definitions and an example for each category.

3.2 Data Preprocessing

Adjusting category granularity: The original data set contains 1727 claims in 7 categories ("0"–"6"), with Category 6 (statement of causation) and Category 2 (statement of correlation) as the largest groups, accounting for 49% and 21% respectively. The other categories are relatively smaller.

To create a more balanced data set, we adjusted the category granularity, reducing the number of categories from 7 to 4. Category 0 was removed because it contains only 2 examples. Category 1 ("no relationship") remains the same. Category 3 is semantically close to Category 2, and thus was

Category	Statement	Category
No relationship mentioned – No relationship is mentioned	...we report the discovery and characterization of a unique core genome-encoded superantigen, providing new insights into the evolution of pathogenic S. aureus...	0
Statement of no relationship – Explicitly stating there is no relationship	...caesarean section by clinical officers does not result in a significant increase in maternal or perinatal mortality significant increase.	1
Statements of correlation – The IV and DV are associated, but causation cannot be explicitly stated	We found a strong graded relationship between increasing levels of psychological distress and the likelihood of being awarded a new disability pension.	2
Ambiguous statement of relationship – It is unclear what the strength of relationship of these statement is. The statement could mean that IV causes DV, or that the two variables are associated – either would be applicable.	...high levels of a protein called SGK1 are linked with infertility, while low levels of it make a woman more likely to have a miscarriage...	3
Conditional statement of causation – Causal statements show that the IV directly changes the DV. Conditional causal statements carry an element of doubt in them.	Genetic-screening trial could reduce drug side-effects.	4
Statement of "can" - The word "can" is unique as a statement of relationship in that it implies that the IV always has the potential to directly change the DV. it is a stronger statement than any conditional statement of causation.	Chocolate every day can reduce risk of heart disease.	5
Statements of causation – The strongest statements are statements of causation. This statement says that the IV directly alters the DV.	...three antiviral agents we studied significantly reduced the levels of Ab and P-tau...	6

IV: independent variable, DV: dependent variable

Table 1: Examples of different type of causal claims based on their strength.

merged into Category 2 ("correlation"). Categories 4 and 5 were merged into new Category 4 ("conditional causation") because both are weaker levels of causal relationships. Liberman (2011) found that although biomedical scientists clearly distinguished "may cause" (Category 4) and "can cause" (Category 5) types of relationships, science journalists seem not to distinguish them anyway. Category 6 ("causation") remains unchanged as the definitive statement of causation.

After adjusting the claim strength granularity, the original data was converted to four main categories: "no relationship" (Category 1), "correlation" (Category 2), "conditional causation" (Category 4), and "causation" (Category 6). Table 2 shows the distribution of each category before and after merging in the open dataset.

Separating training and testing data: The original data set contains 462 spreadsheets, one for each press release. Each spreadsheet documented the science claims reported in the original journal articles, and their paraphrased versions in the press releases and various news articles. Since all claims in the same spreadsheet involve the same science topic, we kept all statements from the same spreadsheet altogether either in training or in testing set to ensure the generalizability of the trained classifier. Specifically, statements from the first 300 spreadsheets were used for training and the rest 162 for testing.

Separating statements from journals and news/press: An important feature in academic writing is cautions language, often called "hedging" or "vague language", which may differ from the writing style in journalism. To test the homogeneity in writing style, we examined the hedging words in the training data using the Bioscope corpus (Szarvas et al., 2008). The Bioscope corpus marked a number of hedging cues in the abstracts of research articles, such as "may", "suggest", "indicate that", "whether", "appears". It is the most comprehensive hedging cues collection for biomedical writings we can find so far.

We calculated the document percentage of the statements with hedging words in the training data and consistently higher occurrences in journals than in news/press articles among all categories. See Table 3 for the distribution. The difference is the highest in Category 1 ("no relationship"), where hedges occurred in 81.5% journal claims but only in 58.6% press/news claims.

Due to the difference in writing style, we further separated statements in journal articles from those in press/news reports, and prepared training and testing data sets for each genre. Table 4 shows the distribution of statements after training/testing and journal/press separation.

Even though researchers claimed publication and reporting bias against negative findings (Dwan et al, 2008), our data consist of paired statements from different reporting sources; the percentage of the biased reporting should be comparable in journal articles and press releases. However, the category distribution in Table 4 shows that in journal articles a lot more correlations are reported, while in news/press releases more causation relations are reported. This observation along with the hedging words distribution supports our argument for the genre difference be between journal articles and news/press releases, justifying our decision to separate the statements according to their sources.

We did not further separate press release and news article to avoid overly small data sets, assuming no significant style difference in these two genres.

Claim Strength	Original	Merged
1 (no relationship)	82	82
2 (correlation)	366	519
3 (ambiguous relation)	153	
4 (conditional causation)	163	278
5 (statements of "can")	115	
6 (causation)	846	846
Total	1725	1725

Table 2: Claim strength distribution in the open dataset before and after category adjusting.

Claim Strength	Journal Count (Percentage)	News/press Count (Percentage)
1 (no relationship)	.815	.586
2 (correlation)	.756	.698
4 (conditional causation)	1.00	.984
6 (causation)	.706	.582
Total	.759	.690

Table 3: Hedging words distribution in journal and news/press.

Claim Strength	Journal Train	Journal Test	News/ Press Train	News/ Press Test
1	27 (.050)	11 (.039)	29 (.048)	15 (.050)
2	213 (.397)	115 (.405)	126 (.208)	65 (.218)
4	51 (.095)	24 (.085)	127 (.209)	76 (.255)
6	245 (.457)	134 (.472)	325 (.535)	142 (.477)
Total	536	284	607	298

Notes: numbers in the brackets are the percentages.

Table 4: Statement distribution after source and training/testing separation.

3.3 Feature Extraction

We constructed four feature vectors using different representations: 1) BOW: simple bag-of-words; 2) B-BOW: bag-of-words with the bolded linguistic cues that are manually-highlighted in the open data set; 3) N-BOW: bag-of-words with doubled negation words in the statements; 4) E-BOW: bag-of-words enriched with enhanced dependency parsing. We did not do stemming in order to keep word inflections. We did not remove stopwords because function words are likely style markers, for example "*that*" could indicate a subordinate clause.

For 2), the bolded linguistic cues (e.g., "*associated*", "*increased risk*", "*appears to offer*") were words/phrases labeled by annotators for identifying the claim strength. For 3), we searched for all the negation words (e.g., "*no*", "*not*") marked in the Bioscope corpus, and then doubled their occurrences in the statements by appending these words to the end of that statement (e.g. "*Water softeners provided no additional benefit to usual care.*" becomes "*Water softeners provided no additional benefit to usual care. no*"). For 4), we used the Stanford dependency parsing to extract all enhanced dependency relations in the statement. Dependency labels like *nsubj* and dependency words are tokenized separately and used as word features alone or combined with BOW to train our model).

For example,

Original statement from the open data set:
"A quick and cheap test could save the lives of babies born with congenital heart defects. (Category 4)"
Dependency words:
"test- A- test- quick- quick- and- quick- cheap- save-test- save- could- ROOT- save- lives- the- save- lives-

Claim Strength	MNB (tf)		SVM (boolean)		SVM (tf)	
	Journal	Press	Journal	Press	Journal	Press
1 (no relationship)	.632	.000	.696	.261	.667	.190
2 (correlation)	.649	.512	.629	.537	.639	.512
4 (conditional causation)	.400	.759	.766	.847	.783	.833
6 (causation)	.670	.748	.709	.784	.716	.768
Macro-average F1 score	.587	.505	.700	**.607**	**.716**	.576

Table 5: Classification accuracy of BOW unigram approach.

Claim Strength	Journal (SVM-tf)	Press (SVM-boolean)
1 (no relationship)	.667	.273
2 (correlation)	.648	.508
4 (conditional causation)	.826	.825
6 (causation)	.730	.780
Macro-average F1 score	**.718**	.596

Table 6: Classification accuracy of BOW unigram+bigram approach (using the best unigram model).

Claim Strength	B-BOW		N-BOW		E-BOW	
	Journal	Press	Journal	Press	Journal	Press
1 (no relationship)	.522	.182	.526	.105	.696	.250
2 (correlation)	.642	.542	.636	.512	.626	.545
4 (conditional causation)	.727	.821	.766	.836	.766	.831
6 (causation)	.702	.780	.716	.761	.704	.770
Macro-average F1 score	.648	.581	.661	.554	.698	.599

Table 7: Classification accuracy of B-BOW, N-BOW, and E-BOW approach.

lives- of- of- babies- babies- born- born- with- defects-congenital- defects- heart- with- defects"
Dependency tags:
"det amod cc conj nsubj aux root det dobj prep pobj vmod prep amod nn pobj"

The final vector is a combination of the three parts above.

3.4 Classification Results

Unigram features: We built two unigram models using Multinomial Naïve Bayes (MNB) and SVMs (Liblinear) with default settings in the Sci-kit Learn toolkit. Macro F1 scores are reported for evaluating the model performance in Table 5. For journal articles, SVM (with term frequency) has the best performance (F1 score = .716). For press/news articles SVM (with Boolean vectors) performed the best (F1 score = .607). Both models performed significantly better than the random guess baseline .25. Overall the model for the Journal genre performs better than the model for the press/news genre. Category wise the "no relationship" category has the lowest F1 scores, especially for statements in news/press releases. The "conditional causation" category has the highest F1 score among all claim strengths.

Enriched features: We continued to use SVM to build more models with enrich features. Adding bigrams resulted in slightly higher F1 score (.718) for journal and lower F1 score (.596) for press (as shown in Table 6). Therefore, we kept using the unigram features in later experiments. Table 7 reports the best classification results for the rest of each representation method mentioned in Section 3.3. As for B-BOW, we trained our model with bolded words only (with term frequency), bolded words only (with Boolean), and bolded words combined with the original statements (with term frequency).

4 Error Analysis

Error analysis shows that the classifier has a lot more to learn, such as variations in negation and distracting relationships mentioned in subordinate clauses. Analysis on the error cases in both journal articles and press releases shows that the most common disagreement is between categories 2 and 6, even though the two categories are not semantically close in the open dataset. This is largely caused by the location of the causal triggers for claim strength.

To further test the difficulty of identifying these two types of claim strength, we extracted about 50 statements in categories 2 and 6 from our misclassified cases and then invited two graduate students to judge their strength. The F1 scores compared to the ground truth (labeled score) were .440 and .630, with many Category 6 misjudged into Category 2 and vice versa, which is consistent to the machine performance. This low human performance also suggests the challenge of correctly identifying the claim strength even for well-educated readers.

5   Conclusion

In this study, we conducted an NLP analysis of claim strength and constructed prediction models for identifying claim strength levels in science reporting. Our best models reached .718 F1 score for distinguishing claim strengths in journal articles, and .607 F1 score in news/press releases, with very high performance for identifying conditional causations. Our analysis shows even though scientific writing follows a well-defined style, scientists' and journalists' creative use of language still poses significant challenge to our task. The major challenges are the variations in negation and distracting relationships mentioned in subordinate clauses for correlation and causation statements. We will conduct deeper syntactic analysis to improve the model performance in our future work.

References

Sinan Aral and Christos Nicolaides. 2017. Exercise contagion in a global social network. *Nature Communications* 8.

Catherine Blake. 2010. Beyond genes, proteins, and abstracts: Identifying scientific claims from full-text biomedical articles. *Journal of biomedical informatics* 43(2):173–189

Kerry Dwan, Douglas G Altman, Juan A Arnaiz, Jill Bloom, An-Wen Chan, Eugenia Cronin, Evelyne Decullier, Philippa J Easterbrook, Erik Von Elm, Carrol Gamble, et al. 2008. Systematic review of the empirical evidence of study publication bias and outcome reporting bias. *PloS one* 3(8): e3081.

John Cook and Stephan Lewandowsky. 2011. *The debunking handbook*. Sevloid Art.

Panagiotis Takis Metaxas Eni Mustafaraj Markus Strohmaier Harald Schoen Gayo-Avello, Daniel Peter Gloor, Carlos Castillo, Marcelo Mendoza, and Barbara Poblete. 2013. Predicting information credibility in time-sensitive social media. *Internet Research* 23(5):560–588.

Christopher SG Khoo, Syin Chan, and Yun Niu. 2000. Extracting causal knowledge from a medical data-base using graphical patterns. In *Proceedings of the 38th Annual Meeting on Association for Computational Linguistics*. Association for Computational Linguistics, pages 336–343.

Marc Light, Xin Ying Qiu, and Padmini Srinivasan. 2004. The language of bioscience: Facts, speculations, and statements in between. In *Proceedings of BioLink 2004 workshop on linking biological literature, ontologies and databases: tools for users*. Association for Computational Linguistics, pages 17– 24.

Claudiu Mihaílâ, Tomoko Ohta, Sampo Pyysalo, and Sophia Ananiadou. 2013. Biocause: Annotating and analysing causality in the biomedical domain. *BMC bioinformatics* 14(1):2.

Vahed Qazvinian, Emily Rosengren, Dragomir R Radev, and Qiaozhu Mei. 2011. Rumor has it: Identifying misinformation in microblogs. In *Proceedings of the Conference on Empirical Methods in Natural Language Processing*. Association for Compu- tational Linguistics, pages 1589–1599.

Craig Silverman. 2015. Lies, damn lies, and viral content. how news websites spread (and debunk) online rumors, unverified claims, and misinformation. *Tow Center for Digital Journalism.*

Petroc Sumner, Solveiga Vivian-Griffiths, Jacky Boivin, Andy Williams, Christos A Venetis, Aime ́e Davies, Jack Ogden, Leanne Whelan, Bethan Hughes, Bethan Dalton, et al. 2014. The association between exaggeration in health related science news and academic press releases: retrospective ob servational study. *Bmj* 349:g7015.

György Szarvas, Veronika Vincze, Richárd Farkas, and János Csirik. 2008. The bioscope corpus: annotation for negation, uncertainty and their scope in biomedical texts. In *Proceedings of the Workshop on Current Trends in Biomedical Natural Language Processing*. Association for Computational Linguistics, pages 38–45.

Andreas Vlachos and Mark Craven. 2010. Detecting speculative language using syntactic dependencies and logistic regression. In *Proceedings of the Fourteenth Conference on Computational Natural Language Learning – Shared Task*. Association for Computational Linguistics, pages 18– 25.

Arkaitz Zubiaga, Maria Liakata, Rob Procter, Geraldine Wong Sak Hoi, and Peter Tolmie. 2016. Analysing how people orient to and spread rumours in social media by looking at conversational threads. *PloS one* 11(3): c0150989.

Author Index